An Essay on Stress

Current Studies in Linguistics Series
Samuel Jay Keyser, general editor

An Essay on Stress

Morris Halle and Jean-Roger Vergnaud

The MIT Press
Cambridge, Massachusetts
London, England

First MIT Press paperback edition, 1990

This book was set in Times New Roman by Asco Trade Typesetting Ltd., Hong Kong, and printed and bound by Halliday Lithograph in the United States of America.

Library of Congress Cataloging-in-Publication Data

Halle, Morris.
  An essay on stress.

  (Current studies in linguistics series; 15)
  Bibliography: p.
  Includes index.
  1. Accents and accentuation.   I. Vergnaud, Jean-Roger.   II. Title.   III. Series.
  P231.H35   1987   414   87-3613
  ISBN 0-262-08168-7 (hardcover)
          0-262-58105-1 (paperback)

Contents

Preface

This study, which is appearing after a period of gestation lasting well over a decade, started out as an attempt to deal with the issue of locality in rules of a phonology within the framework of *The Sound Pattern of English* (Chomsky and Halle 1968; henceforth *SPE*). It seemed to many in the early 1970s that an understanding of the role of locality held the key to further progress in phonology. In particular, it was felt that phonological processes are essentially local and that all cases of apparent nonlocality should derive from universal properties of rule application. There are basically two kinds of phenomena that present a challenge to any theory that claims phonological processes to be local. The first kind includes processes of "action at a distance," like vowel harmony or the placement of stress in such languages as Sanskrit, Russian, and Lithuanian. The second includes processes that involve repetition of a motif, like the alternating stress patterns of English.

Two main approaches to the problem emerged. On the one hand, there were what we might call the "iterativist" theories. According to them, all phonological processes were in fact represented in terms of local rules. Action at a distance and periodicity of pattern were obtained by applying the relevant local rules in an iterative fashion. To illustrate, a rule for the left-to-right spreading of a harmonic feature like [+back] would be represented as in (1) in an iterativist theory.

$$(1) \quad V \rightarrow [+back] / C_0 \begin{bmatrix} V \\ +back \end{bmatrix} \underline{\quad\quad}$$

Similarly, a rule generating an alternating stress pattern would be represented as in (2).

$$(2) \quad V \rightarrow [+stress] / \left\{ \begin{matrix} \#C_0V \\ \begin{bmatrix} V \\ +stress \end{bmatrix} C_0V \end{matrix} \right\} C_0 \underline{\quad}$$

The iterative algorithm for applying the rules accounted for the long-distance effect of the harmony rule in (1), as well as for the periodicity of the pattern associated with (2).

Within the iterativist approach there were two variants, one advocated by S. Anderson (1969, 1974) and the other by C. D. Johnson (1972). According to Anderson, rules were not linearly ordered and, in particular, they could reapply to their own immediate output, subject to various principles. It was this capacity that accounted for the iterativity of the rule application. Johnson's theory differed in important ways from Anderson's. Johnson maintained the constraint of linear ordering on all rules of the grammar. Within his theory, iterativity was directly encoded as a universal property of the algorithm for applying individual rules.

As an alternative to the iterativist approach an attempt was made to deal with the locality theme by constructing a theory for interpreting variables that would significantly restrict their notational power. Our earliest efforts were directed along these lines in unpublished research conducted jointly with A. Prince (some references to which are to be found in Halle 1975). The linear character of the representations assumed in *SPE*, which we did not think to question at the time, imposed fundamental limits to this line of research. This stumbling block was soon removed by the introduction of the autosegmental model, due to E. Williams (1971/6) and J. Goldsmith (1976), and of the metrical model, due to M. Liberman (1975), Prince (1976), and Liberman and Prince (1977). These new frameworks seemed quite promising to us, and we attempted to utilize them in seeking further answers to our circle of questions. The fundamental ideas underlying this piece of work were first presented publicly in a lecture at MIT in November 1976. They were further elaborated and explored in a manuscript entitled "Metrical Structures in Phonology," written in the summer of 1978 and revised in 1979. This paper dealt with harmony as well as with stress.

Since then metrical theory has developed in a number of directions. What might be called the standard version of the theory was elaborated in the Doctoral dissertation of B. Hayes (1980), where a large variety of languages, both well-studied (e.g., English) and relatively unknown (e.g., Aklan), were subjected to a consistent and detailed analysis. Further elaborations of this variant are to be found in Halle and Clements (1983) and in Hammond (1984b).

A critical appraisal of the tree formalism of the standard version was offered by F. Dell (1984), who proposed to extend the role of the metrical grid introduced by Liberman (1975) and Liberman and Prince (1977). This approach was adopted independently by Prince, who has pursued it to its ultimate reductionist conclusions, namely, to a theory that no longer makes use of trees (see Prince 1983). The treeless model has been further illustrated and defended, largely on the basis of English material, by E. O. Selkirk (1984).

In this essay we develop a third position, intermediate between the standard version of metrical theory and the treeless grid theory proposed by Prince and others. We recognize the import of the evidence adduced by Prince and Selkirk against the nested and labeled constituent trees of the standard version and in support of the grid representation. At the same time we show that constituents are necessary in any adequate account of stress phenomena. Our theory shares with the standard version the view that strings are hierarchically organized into metrical constituents. It departs from the standard version in narrowly restricting the type of constituents that are admitted and adheres to the treeless theories in assigning a central role to the metrical grid. It also adapts Johnson's (1972) and Anderson's (1969, 1974) treatment of repetitive motifs by means of iterative rules.

The scope of this essay is much narrower than that of our original 1978 paper, but we hope to have progressed modestly toward the goal of providing a local account of all action at a distance.

Note for the paperback edition:
The decision of the MIT Press to issue a paperback edition of the book has made it possible for us to correct the unfortunately large number of typographical errors that we failed to catch in reading proof for the first edition. We are grateful to Professor S. Haraguchi of Tsukuba University for sharing with us the results of his careful reading of the text, in the course of which many of the typographical errors were discovered.

Acknowledgments

For comments, criticism, and advice on matters of substance and form we are grateful to D. Archangeli, E. Barton, R. Berwick, G. Bohas, S. Bromberger, G. N. Clements, S. Chung, J. Cole, S. Davis, F. Dell, M. Hammond, B. Hayes, J. Kaye, J. Levin, P. Martin, D. Osherson, D. Pulleyblank, I. Roca, B. Schein, D. Steriade, and L. Trigo. We have incorporated much of their advice into the pages that follow, and we have little doubt that our monograph would have been further improved had we but seen our way clear to incorporating even more of it. Responsibility for shortcomings in the text is ours and ours alone.

We thank Elisabeth Ritter for preparing the index. The arduous task of copyediting our constantly changing manuscript was performed by Anne Mark. We are in her debt for the competence, care, and personal commitment with which she accomplished her work.

This work was supported in part by the Centre Nationale de la Recherche Scientifique, Paris; the Center for Cognitive Science at M.I.T., Cambridge; and the Office of Graduate Studies and Research of the University of Maryland, College Park.

Morris Halle and Jean-Roger Vergnaud
January 1, 1987

PART I

The Metrical Theory of Stress

Chapter 1
On the Representation of Stress

1.1 Metrical Constituents

We begin our investigation by listing a few elementary facts encountered in many languages that an acceptable theory must be capable of handling simply and perspicuously.

(1)

a. Not all phonemes may bear stress; different languages select specific subsets of phonemes to bear stress.

b. In some languages, every word has one and only one stress.

c. In some languages, every word has at least one stress but may have more than one.

d. The location of stress is often governed by fairly transparent principles.

i. In languages with a single stress per word, the location of the stress is determined by the position of the stressable element in the word (final, initial, penultimate, and so on) or by its position and its phonetic context (for example, the stress falls on the penultimate vowel if it is long, otherwise on the antepenultimate).

ii. In the case of words with multiple stresses, there appear to be three major principles of distribution:

• Stressed and unstressed syllables alternate; for example, stress falls on every other syllable or every third syllable in a word.

• Stress falls on phonemes in particular environments—for example, on vowels in heavy syllables, or in lexically marked morphemes.

• A combination of the preceding.

A crucial part of our task is to devise a notation that will allow us to represent these facts and to express various significant generalizations about them. Beginning at the top of our list (1), we must first propose a way to reflect the fact that not every phoneme in a string is capable of bearing stress. In this respect, stress is quite similar to tone, for it is usually the case in tone languages that only certain phonemes are tone-bearing. The work of the last decade on autosegmental phonology, beginning with the pioneering studies of Williams (1971/6), Goldsmith (1976), and others, has made it clear that there are languages where the tones of a word constitute a sequence of segments that is separate and distinct from the sequence of its phonemes. In other words, in tone languages phonological representations must consist of two parallel lines of units: the phonemes and the tones. Thus, the autosegmental representation of the tonal properties of a word will have the form exemplified in (2), where the *T*-line is the tonal line and the *P*-line is the central line of phonemes and where the tone-bearing phonemes are all the elements on the *P*-line, except *P2* and *P6*.

(2)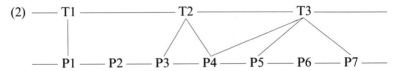

The autosegmental formalization provides a natural representation of the fact that a tone may dominate a discontinuous sequence of phonemes. The correspondence between the tonal line and the central line respects the ordering of the elements in the following sense: given a tone *T* that is associated with some phoneme *P*, a tone *T'* that precedes *T*, and a phoneme *P'* that follows *P*, *P'* cannot be associated with *T'* (see Sagey 1986, chap. 5). If we represent the mapping between the two lines by means of links drawn between associated elements, this condition on the mapping can be expressed as a constraint prohibiting the crossing of links (see Goldsmith 1976). The representation in (2) is well formed from the point of view of this constraint, whereas the representation in (3), where a line connecting T2 and P5 has been added, is ill formed.

(3)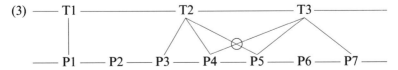

The prohibition on the crossing of lines applies to each autosegmental line.

However, two distinct autosegmental lines will in general behave independently with respect to this prohibition; that is, the domain of some autosegment on one line may in general overlap with the domain of an autosegment on another line, as is illustrated in (4) with the line of the *T*-autosegments above the central line of phonemes and the line of the *S*-autosegments below it.

(4)
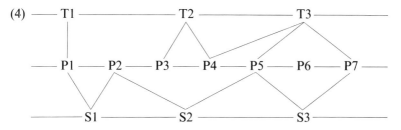

Thus, we are led to consider that each autosegmental line above the central line of phonemes defines with the latter an autonomous *autosegmental plane* (more accurately, a half-plane), which is distinct from the planes defined by the other autosegmental lines but intersects with them in the central line of phonemes.[1]

Following an idea originating with Liberman (1975), we propose to treat stress by means of the same basic formalism as tone: we shall set up a special autosegmental plane on which one line will contain the sequence of phonemes and a second line will consist of a sequence of marks representing the stressed phonemes. This formalization will allow us to account for the fact that stress or the absence thereof is a property that is associated in general with discontinuous subsequences in the string of phonemes. We shall represent the autosegmental line for stress as a sequence of abstract positions or slots associated with the stress-bearing units on the central line. A slot corresponding to a stressed element will be filled by an asterisk. We illustrate this in (5) with English words well known to students of stress.

---

1. It has been shown by McCarthy (1979), Archangeli (1984), Kaye and Lowenstamm (1985), Levin (1985a), and others that the central line of phonemes must be decomposed into a sequence of timing slots whose (phonetic) content is given by a sequence of autosegments. Where nothing in the discussion hinges on this decomposition, we shall not effect it in our representations. Since we are led to this simplification of the notation exclusively by considerations of expository convenience, our procedure is not to be seen as reflecting any doubts on our part about the validity of the central results of the work mentioned above.

(5) * . * . * .   * * . * .   * . *
    Apalachicola   Ticonderoga   Hackensack

It is on the *stress plane* that all our computations will be carried out.

As this study will show, the placement of stress reflects an organization of the sequence of stress-bearing elements that is not directly linked to the phonological or phonetic substance of these elements. From the point of view of stress, the stress-bearing elements are mere positions, identified by their sequential order counted from right to left or from left to right. In that respect, stress crucially differs from tone, which is associated with units identified by their phonetic substance and which partakes of this phonetic substance.

Another characteristic of stress that distinguishes it from tone and is related to the difference just mentioned is that the abstract elements (asterisks) on the stress line that mark the stressed phonemes do not necessarily occupy consecutive slots: two successive asterisks may be separated by one or more stress-bearing slots. By contrast, two successive tonal autosegments will always occupy consecutive tone-bearing slots, by definition. It thus appears that, in the representation of stress, the discontinuous substring of stress-bearing phonemes is not merely a derivative object but must be defined as an independent entity with an autonomous status in the representation of the string. This is in fact the notion of *projection* in the sense of Halle and Vergnaud (1978). Accordingly, we shall set up a special line in the stress plane on which each stress-bearing phoneme will be represented by an asterisk. This line, which we shall designate as *line 0*, will mediate the correspondence between the central line of phonemes and the stress line, *line 1*, postulated above and exemplified in (5). We give in (6) the representations incorporating line 0 that correspond to the forms in (5).

(6) * . * . * .   * * . * .   * . *   line 1
    * * * * * *   * * * * *   * * *   line 0
    Apalachicola   Ticonderoga   Hackensack

We postpone to section 1.2 the discussion of how differences in degree of stress are to be represented and concentrate for the present on how stress is located on particular stress-bearing elements.

An observation fundamental to our entire procedure is that when linguistic elements are concatenated, it is not generally the case that all elements in the sequence are treated on a par like beads on a string. Rather, sequences of linguistic elements are composed of one or more constituents in which one element is specially marked—made the *head*—and the rest are said to constitute the *domain*. This is true both in phonology and in syntax. Thus, a sentence like (7)

(7) many arrows hit the explorers

is composed of the noun phrase *many arrows*, whose head is the noun *arrows*, and of the verb phrase *hit the explorers*, whose head is the verb *hit*.

It is customary to represent syntactic constituent structure by means of tree diagrams such as (8).

(8)

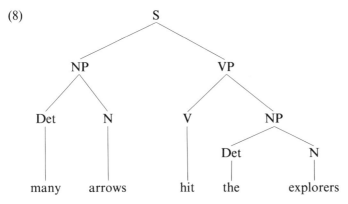

This tree represents a hierarchically organized set of analyses, of which the list in (9) is a subset.

(9) S
    NP VP
    Det N VP
    many N VP
    many arrows VP
    many arrows V NP
    many arrows hit NP
    many arrows hit Det N
    many arrows hit the N
    many arrows hit the explorers

Given such a list, the various constituents are identified in terms of the relation *is a*. A string *is a C*, *C* some category, iff some occurrence of the category C is found in the same context as that string. Thus, in (9) *many arrows* is an NP since it shows up in the same context (_____ VP) as one of the occurrences of NP. Similarly, *hit the explorers* is a VP because it shares with that category the context *many arrows* _____. Each analysis in a list such as (9) is an exhaustive description of the string of formatives as a sequence of nonoverlapping constituents; that is, the parenthesization is complete and well formed.

A fundamental property of syntactic constituents that is relevant to our discussion is that they are projections of lexical *heads*. This property, which is formalized within X-bar theory (Chomsky 1970; Jackendoff 1977), can be characterized as follows.

(10) A string u is a constituent of category x just in case there is an occurrence X of x such that u is analyzed at some level as . . . , X, . . . and at some higher level as the singleton string X. *The formative corresponding to X is the head of the constituent.*

For example, consider the verb phrase *hit the explorers*, which is analyzed as the sequence of categories V Det N. There is a level at which the substring Det N is analyzed as a nominal category (NP), which we represent here by an N on a hierarchically higher line; and there is another level at which the string V NP is analyzed as a verbal category (VP), which we represent here as a V on a still higher line. Thus, the different analyses can be organized into an autosegmental-like diagram, as shown in (11).

(11)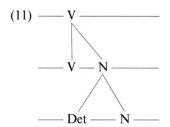

This diagram is equivalent to the standard tree structure in (12).

(12)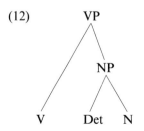

A formalization like (11), which is equivalent to an X-bar formalization, has the advantage of separating the morphological labeling of the constituents (V, N, Det, and so on) from their hierarchical characterization, and it brings to light the exact nature of the notion *projection* that is involved in syntactic phrase markers. Specifically, the occurrence X of some category in a string u is the head of a constituent dominating u just in case there is a line on which the string u is projected as X. On the higher line, which constitutes a distinct mode of representation of the string u, the projection of the head functions as a representative of the constituent from which it is drawn. Thus, the copy (or projection) of the head stands for the constituent. This formalization, like X-bar theory, establishes an intrinsic connection between the notions of head and constituent.[2]

It is a notable result that the formalization of stress assumed here gives rise precisely to the kind of structure exemplified in (11). In particular, each stress domain contains exactly one rhythmic position that is distinguished from all the others as being more prominent. We shall refer to structure of this kind as *metrical constituent structure* to distinguish it from syntactic and morphological constituent structure. To illustrate, in the case of the forms in (6) we assume a representation in which the string of stressable elements is analyzed into a sequence of constituents, whose boundaries are indicated by parentheses and whose heads are designated by an asterisk on line 1.

(13) * . * . * .   * * . * .   * . *   line 1
      (* *)(* *)(* *)   (*)(* *)(* *)   (* *) (*)   line 0
      Apa lachi cola   Ti conde roga   Hacken sack

Assuming this formal organization of the string of positions, each stressed element in the string will be characterized as the head of one of the constituents delimited. The notation we have adopted is thus in harmony with this formal definition: the stressed elements are identified by occurrences on the higher line of the very same mark that is used to identify the stress-bearing elements on line 0.

Since the stress patterns encountered in all languages are to be expressed by means of the metrical constituents sketched above, these constituents might well be expected to be quite numerous and varied. As a matter of fact, their number is small and their variety highly constrained: they are limited to the constituents that can be generated by setting the binary parameters (14) and (15):

(14) whether or not the head of the constituent is adjacent to one of the constituent boundaries, and

---

2. A similar approach to the notion of constituent is sketched in de Cornulier (1982/5).

(15) whether or not the head of the constituent is separated from its constituent boundaries by no more than one intervening element.

The parameter (14), whose settings are represented as $[\pm HT]$, determines whether or not a constituent is *head-terminal*. The parameter (15), whose settings are represented as $[\pm BND]$, determines whether or not a constituent is *bounded*. Since a constituent has two boundaries, one at its beginning and one at its end, there can exist only the four $[\pm HT]$ constituents illustrated in (16).

(16) [−BND]   [+BND]

  a. * . . . .   b. * .

     (* * * * *)   (* *)

  c.   . . . . *   d. . *

    (* * * * *)   (* *)

A third parameter, (17), is set in order to select between the left-headed constituents (16a, b) and the right-headed constituents (16c,d).

(17) $[+HT]$ constituents are $\begin{Bmatrix} \text{left} \\ \text{right} \end{Bmatrix}$-headed.

As illustrated in (18), only two kinds of $[-HT]$ constituent can be generated.

(18) [−BND]   [+BND]

  a.   . . * . . .   b. . * .

    (* * * * * *)   (* * *)

Though there are ternary stress patterns where constituents of the type (18b) must be utilized, no instances have been found where constituents of the type (18a) need to be invoked. This follows from the fact that metrical constituents are subject to the *Recoverability Condition* (19).

(19) *Recoverability Condition*

Given the direction of government of the constituent heads in the grammar, the location of the metrical constituent boundaries must be unambiguously recoverable from the location of the heads, and conversely the location of the heads must be recoverable from that of the boundaries.

Thus, for the $[+HT]$ constituents illustrated in (16), once the direction of government is known, the location of the heads is determined by the location of the boundaries, and conversely.

It is obvious that $[-HT, -BND]$ constituents of the type (18a) cannot in principle satisfy the Recoverability Condition since recoverability depends on there being some relationship between the location of the boundaries and that of the head of a constituent; and in constituents of type (18a) no such relationship exists because the parameters [HT] and [BND], which establish this relationship, both have negative settings. We conclude that in all actual cases at least one of these two parameters must have a positive setting. As for [−HT, +BND] constituents, our examination of Cayuvava will show that the Recoverability Condition is not satisfied in all contexts (see discussion surrounding (48)–(56)).

The [HT], [BND], and headedness parameters thus define the following kinds of constituents: *unbounded left-headed* = [+HT, −BND, left] (16a); *unbounded right-headed* = [+HT, −BND, right] (16c); *ternary* = [−HT, +BND] (18b); *binary left-headed* = [+HT, +BND, left] (16b); *binary right-headed* [+HT, +BND, right] (16d). The setting of the parameters does not assign constituent structure to concrete strings of stress-bearing elements. In order to assign constituent structure, we need rules that construct metrical constituent boundaries and heads in specific positions in the string. As shown in (20), when binary constituents are constructed on a string containing an odd number of elements, different results are produced depending on whether the constituents are constructed— that is, boundaries are introduced—from left to right or from right to left.

(20)
a. (* *)(* *)(*)   b. (*)(* *)(* *)
   1 2 3 4 5   1 2 3 4 5

When boundary construction proceeds from left to right, the constituents (1 2), (3 4), and (5) are formed; when it proceeds from right to left, the constituents formed are (1), (2 3), and (4 5). Similarly, different results will be produced depending on whether ternary constituents are constructed from left to right or from right to left. Unbounded constituents, however, are not affected by direction of construction. The rule for boundary construction will therefore be of the form (21).

(21) Construct constituent boundaries $\left\langle \begin{Bmatrix} \text{left to right} \\ \text{right to left} \end{Bmatrix} \right\rangle$ on line L.

The option enclosed in angled brackets must be specified if the constituent is bounded ([+BND]); it is omitted if the constituent is unbounded ([−BND]).

The rule for locating the heads is of the form (22).

(22)   Locate the heads of the line L metrical constituents on line L + 1.

Consider such simple stress patterns as those of Latvian, where stress is word-initial, and French, where stress is word-final. We shall characterize these stress patterns by postulating that constituents in both languages have the setting [+ HT, − BND]. Moreover, both languages are subject to the short version of rule (21). What differentiates the two languages is (22). In Latvian the constituents are left-headed; in French they are right-headed. We formalize this as follows.

(23)

a.   Line 0 constituents are [+ HT, − BND, left$_{Latv}$/right$_{Fr}$].

b.   Construct constituent boundaries on line 0.

c.   Locate the heads of line 0 constituents on line 1.

In (24) we illustrate the effects of (23) graphically.

(24)

```
a.   *  ..        b.  . . . . . *    line 1
     (*  **)          (* * * * **)   line 0
     Latvija          originalité
```

To illustrate the capabilities of the devices just sketched, we briefly analyze with their help the stress patterns given in (25), all but the last of which have been discussed by Hayes (1980/1).

(25)

a.   Koya: Stress falls on the vowel of closed or long syllables and on the vowel in the first syllable. (Tyler 1969)

b.   Maranungku: Stress falls on all odd-numbered syllables counting from the beginning of the word. (Tryon 1970)

c.   Weri: Stress falls on all odd-numbered syllables counting from the end of the word. (Boxwell and Boxwell 1966)

d.   Warao: Stress falls on even-numbered syllables counting from the end of the word. (Osborn 1966)

e.   Southern Paiute: Stress falls on even-numbered moras, counting from the beginning of the word, except that it never falls on the final mora but always on the penultimate. (Sapir 1930; K. Hale, personal communication)

f.   Garawa: Stress falls on even-numbered syllables counting from the end of the word, and on the first syllable, but never on the second. (Furby 1974)

g. Aklan: Stress falls on all closed syllables, on certain lexically marked syllables, and in a sequence of open syllables on every odd syllable counted from the right if the sequence is word-final and on every even syllable counted from the right if the sequence is not word-final. (Chai 1971; Hayes 1980/1)

h. Yidin^y: Stress falls on even-numbered syllables if the word contains an even-numbered syllable with a long vowel; otherwise, stress falls on odd-numbered syllables. (Hayes 1980/1; Dixon 1977a)

i. Cayuvava: Stress falls on every third mora from the end of the word. In words with $3n + 1$ or $3n + 2$ moras the word-initial syllable is unstressed. (Levin 1985b; Key 1961)

The distribution of stresses in words in these different languages is clearly far from simple. We shall demonstrate that the fairly rudimentary constituent mechanism sketched above, supplemented by one diacritic feature, enables us to provide a straightforward and transparent account not only of the facts in (25) but also of another interesting set of facts.

The first pattern to be examined is that of Koya (25a), where stress falls on the vowel of the initial syllable, as well as on that of every closed or long syllable. The fact that there is no limit to the number of syllables that may intervene between two consecutive stresses—for example, between the initial syllable and the nearest heavy syllable—suggests that unbounded constituents are involved. From that point of view, the stress pattern of a Koya word may be analyzed as the juxtaposition of left-headed constituents of the type encountered in Latvian (see (24)); more formally, in Koya line 0 constituents have the parameter settings [+HT, −BND, left]. Having established this, our next question is how to obtain more than one unbounded constituent per word.

In terms of the theoretical framework developed here, the fact that all long and closed syllables in Koya are invariably stressed means that long and closed syllables are always heads of constituents. Since each head is the head of a constituent, there are as many constituents in a string as there are heads. We therefore need a means for indicating that particular elements in the string are necessarily heads. We shall call such elements *accented elements*. In earlier versions of metrical theory (for instance, Halle and Clements 1983) a special diacritic feature was utilized for this purpose. Given the formalism sketched here, however, there is no need for such an arbitrary feature: as observed by Prince (1983) (see also Pulleyblank 1983), all necessary results are obtained if the accented elements are identified by being provided with an asterisk on line 1—in other words, as being inherently stressed. We therefore postulate that Koya is subject to the rule (26), and we illustrate the effects of this rule with the schematic example (27), where consecutive line 0 elements are indicated by Arabic numerals and elements 3 and 7 are assumed to be in a long or a closed syllable.

(26) Assign a line 1 asterisk to a vowel in a closed or long syllable.

```
(27) . . * . . . * . .   line 1
     1 2 3 4 5 6 7 8 9   line 0
```

Since constituents in Koya are left-headed and unbounded, application of the rule of Constituent Construction (21) will result in the bracketing shown in (28).

```
(28) . . * . . . * . .     line 1
     (1 2)(3 4 5 6)(7 8 9)  line 0
```

The manner in which (28) was generated deserves comment. We have constructed the bracketing (1 2), which differs from the others in the string in not having a head marked on line 1. We distinguish such *constructed* constituents that result from the application of Constituent Construction (21) from *obligatory* constituents that are associated with accented elements in the string. Constructed constituents are not supplied with heads in underlying representation; instead, their heads are generated by an application of rule (22), as shown in (29), which correctly represents the actually observed stress pattern of the Koya word.

```
(29) * . * . . . * . .     line 1
     (1 2)(3 4 5 6)(7 8 9)  line 0
```

Since every constituent must have its own head, (28), unlike (29), is not well formed. If rule (21) had not applied, the constructed constituent (1 2) in (28) would not have been present in the output string. On the other hand, the metrical constituents (3 4 5 6) and (7 8 9) would be present in the output form even in the absence of a rule constructing metrical boundaries, for, as we shall demonstrate below and in chapter 4, accented elements induce metrical boundaries in accordance with the setting of the parameter [left-/right-headed]. This fact has consequences of considerable interest. There are languages with stress patterns such as that in (27), which we shall characterize by means of grammars that do not include a rule constructing metrical boundaries. In such languages only obligatory constituents will surface.

In (30) we state formally the rules involved in generating the stress patterns of Koya.

(30)

a. Assign a line 1 asterisk to a vowel in a closed or long syllable.

b. Line 0 parameter settings are [+HT, −BND, left].

c. Construct constituent boundaries on line 0.

d. Locate the heads of line 0 constituents on line 1.

The rule constructing constituent boundaries, (30c) (or more generally (21)), is subject to a number of conditions. First, such rules must obey the *Exhaustivity Condition* (31).

(31) *Exhaustivity Condition*
    The rules of constituent boundary construction (21) apply exhaustively subject to the Recoverability Condition (19).

In particular, when head-terminal constituents are constructed, the structure resulting from the application of Constituent Construction (21) will cover the string of positions exhaustively in such a way that every position is included in some constituent. Moreover, the rule of Head Location (22) will ensure that in every substring enclosed between consecutive constituent boundaries one element is marked as head. In the case of some ternary constituents (which are [−HT]), however, certain positions in the string remain outside the metrical constituent structure because head marking would generate structures that violate the Recoverability Condition.

   Since the Exhaustivity Condition could be met trivially in every case by constructing constituents consisting solely of a head, constituent construction is subject to the *Maximality Condition*.

(32) *Maximality Condition*
    Each constituent constructed by a rule of boundary construction must incorporate the maximal substring, provided that other requirements on constituent structure are satisfied.

In a case where metrical constituents are left-headed, Head Location (22) will assign a line 1 asterisk to the word-initial syllable. By the same token, in a case where constituents are right-headed, rule (22) will assign stress to the word-final syllable.

   The notion of accented element gives rise to the *Faithfulness Condition* on the output metrical structure.

(33) *Faithfulness Condition*
    The output metrical structure respects the distribution of heads (accented elements), in the sense that each head is associated with

constituent boundaries in the output structure and that these are located at the appropriate positions in the sequence. Constituent boundaries are erased in the output when none of the elements enclosed by the boundaries is marked as head.

Strictly speaking, the Faithfulness Condition does not have to be invoked as an independent principle in the case of unbounded constituents because its effects follow automatically from the existence of obligatory constituents. However, as we shall illustrate below, the Faithfulness Condition also applies in the case of bounded constituents, although accented elements do not give rise to obligatory constituents in that case. We must then postulate this condition as an autonomous principle.

According to the Faithfulness Condition, constituent boundaries must be "located at the appropriate positions in the sequence." In constructing the boundaries of head-terminal [+HT] constituents, we adopt the convention of always locating the boundaries of left-headed constituents immediately before the head and those of right-headed constituents immediately after the head. The significance of this direct link between the constituent boundary on a given grid line and the asterisk on the line above it will become especially apparent when we examine the effects of elision and epenthesis and the formalism required to express stress retraction.

Given the Recoverability Condition (19), the representation (29) is somewhat redundant; in particular, we may omit either the parentheses, as in (34a), or the marking of the heads, as in (34b), for each can be readily reconstructed from the other once it is stipulated that metrical constituents in Koya are left-headed.

(34)

a. $*$. $*$ . . . $*$ . .

  1 2 3 4 5 6 7 8 9

b. (1 2)(3 4 5 6)(7 8 9)

We shall say that the pure representation of the heads exemplified in (34a) and the pure representation of the domains exemplified in (34b) are *conjugate representations*. The relation of government is equivalent to the conjunction of the two conjugate structures: to have government is to have a head (that is, an element that is projected upward) *and* a domain for that head. Conversely, the property of being a head is the same as that of being a governing element in a constituent, and the property of being in some domain is the same as that of being governed by some head.

We have shown that there are two distinct means for ensuring that a given element in the string will be the head of its constituent: on the one hand, the rules (21) and (22) and, on the other hand, as is the case in Koya, accent rules that mark headship directly by assigning a line 1 asterisk to particular elements before the rules of metrical construction apply. In Koya both head-marking mechanisms must be invoked. We shall examine a number of instances where all heads are generated by rules (21) and (22); we shall also discuss a case where only accented elements receive stress.

Returning to the stress patterns illustrated in (25), we examine next the patterns of Maranungku (25b) and Weri (25c). Since both languages have alternating stresses, we must assume that in these languages metrical constituents are binary. Maranungku requires the structures in (35a) and Weri, those in (35b).

(35)

a. *   . * . *   * . * .   * .   line 1
    (1   2)(3 4)(5)   (1 2) (3 4) (5   6)   line 0
    lángka ráte tí   wéle péne mánta

b. . * .   *   * . * . *   line 1
    (4 3)(2   1)   (5) (4 3)(2 1)   line 0
    ulú amít   á kuné tepál

In Maranungku the constituents are left-headed and in Weri the constituents are right-headed. Of particular interest here are the sequences containing an odd number of elements. Since we are using binary constituents, each odd-numbered sequence will contain a "defective" constituent consisting of a single element. Since our theory requires that each constituent contain a head, it predicts that such "defective" constituents should be stressed. This prediction is borne out by the facts of both Maranungku and Weri.[3]

Examination of (35a,b) reveals that the binary constituents were constructed in a definite order: those of Maranungku were constructed from left to right, whereas those of Weri were constructed from right to left.[4] We give in (36) a formal statement of the stress rules of Maranungku and Weri.

---

3. Cayuvava presents an instance where the principles of constituent construction prevent us from constructing particular "defective" constituents (see discussion following (48)); in such cases we expect to find no stress associated with the substring in question.

4. If the constituents in Maranungku (35a) had been constructed from right to left rather than from left to right, we should have obtained the stress distribution *lángkáratéti* instead of *lángkaráteti*.

(36)

a. Line 0 parameter settings are [+HT, +BND, left$_{Mar}$/right$_{Weri}$, left to right$_{Mar}$/right to left$_{Weri}$].

b. Construct constituent boundaries on line 0.

c. Locate the heads of line 0 constituents on line 1.

We turn now to the stress pattern of Warao (25d), where stress falls on even-numbered syllables counting from the end of the word. The stress pattern of Warao is identical with that of Weri, except that it is "shifted" one syllable to the left. We therefore need a device that will allow us to begin our syllable count, not at the very end of the word, but one syllable in. As it happens, the theoretical machinery of metrical phonology already includes the diacritic feature of *extrametricality*, which possesses the required properties (Hayes 1982; Harris 1983; Archangeli 1984, 1986). Units marked with this feature are rendered invisible to rules of metrical constituent construction. However, it has a further property that limits its effectiveness in an interesting way: it does not render invisible just any unit in the sequence, but only one that is *terminal*—initial or final—at the point in the derivation where Constituent Construction applies. As illustrated in (37), in Warao the last syllable is marked extrametrical; that is, it is enclosed in angled brackets, indicating that it is invisible to the rules of metrical constituent construction. The construction therefore begins with the penultimate syllable. Going from right to left, the positions are then assembled into binary right-headed constituents.

(37)

a. . * . * .   b. * . * . * .

   (5 4)(3 2)⟨1⟩   (6)(5 4)(3 2)⟨1⟩

The three cases with binary constituents that we have examined up to this point might give the impression that there is a connection between the position of the head within the constituent and the direction of constituent construction. The facts of Southern Paiute (see (25e)) show that this inference must be incorrect, for in this language the stress distribution is as follows.

(38) . * . * * .   line 1

     (1 2)(3 4)(5)⟨6⟩   line 0

To obtain this distribution of stresses, binary right-headed constituents must be constructed from left to right. As noted by Sapir (1930), Southern Paiute is a mora-counting language, which means that stress can be assigned to any timing slot dominated by a vowel, not just to a vowel that is also the head of its syllable. To obtain the stress distribution in (25e), we mark the last mora of the word extrametrical; this will account for the fact that it is never stressed. We then construct over the vowels of the word right-headed binary constituents from left to right. This will give stress on the penultimate mora whether it is even- or odd-numbered, yielding a distribution of stresses such as the one shown in (38).

In Garawa (see (25f)) stress falls on even-numbered syllables counting from the end of the word, with the important exception that stress never falls on the second syllable. As illustrated in (39), the essentials of this type of pattern are readily captured with the help of left-headed binary constituents constructed from right to left, except for the fact that, in the case of words with an odd number of syllables, this construction will invariably assign stress to the second syllable.

(39) $*$ $*$. $*$. $*$. $*$.   line 1
      (9)(8 7)(6 5)(4 3)(2 1)   line 0

Our problem, then, is to eliminate the stress on the second syllable of such words. We can obtain this result by postulating a special stress deletion rule that destresses a syllable (deletes the associated line 1 asterisk) if it is preceded directly by a stressed syllable (that is, by another line 1 asterisk).[5] It should be noted that the deletion of the line 1 asterisk in (39) has as a concomitant the deletion of the constituent boundaries enclosing the elements 8 7. This is required by the Faithfulness Condition (33), since neither of the elements enclosed by these boundaries is marked as head.

The alternating stress patterns examined to this point were all generated by rules of binary constituent construction and did not involve accented

---

5. In Garawa the stress deletion rule is the only means available to obtain this result. In particular, we cannot have recourse to the diacritic feature of extrametricality in order to prevent stress from being assigned to the second syllable. This observation is relevant here since it points up an essential difference between the stress patterns of Garawa and Warao, in both of which stress falls on even-numbered syllables counting from the end of the word. As suggested by Hayes (1980/1), it is possible to capture the Warao pattern (where only even-numbered syllables counting from the right are stressed) by constructing left-headed constituents from right to left. Since this would invariably result in stress on the first syllable of the word, a rule of stress deletion like the one just proposed for Garawa would have to be postulated for Warao. The solution proposed here for Warao, which has recourse to extrametricality, is to be preferred since it does not involve reference to a phonetically defined context such as "stressed syllable." In Garawa this alternative is not available.

elements. We found accented elements in addition to constructed heads in Koya, where the constituents, however, were unbounded rather than binary. The stress pattern of Aklan (see (25g)) parallels that of Koya in that it involves accented elements as well as constructed heads. It differs from that of Koya in that its constituents are binary rather than unbounded. In Aklan all closed syllables as well as certain lexically marked morphemes are stressed. Moreover, sequences of open syllables exhibit an alternating stress pattern: when the sequence is word-final, stress falls on every odd-numbered syllable counting from the right, whereas when the sequence is nonfinal, stress falls on every even-numbered syllable counting from the right. To account for the fact that closed syllables are stressed, the grammar of Aklan obviously must include a rule such as (26) that assigns closed syllables an asterisk on line 1. In addition, certain morphemes will be assigned an asterisk in their lexical representation. To account for the alternating stresses in word-final sequences of open syllables, right-headed binary constituents must be constructed from right to left. The stress pattern of nonfinal sequences of open syllables will follow automatically from this procedure if we assume that the construction of the binary constituents respects the heads previously marked (by rule or otherwise). We illustrate this in (40), where (40a) indicates the location of the accented elements and (40b) shows the sequence of binary constituents constructed so as to respect this initial distribution of heads.[6]

(40)

a. * * . . . * . . .   b. * * . . . * . . .   line 1

  9 8 7 6 5 4 3 2 1 $\rightarrow$ (9)(8)(7 6)(5 4)(3)(2 1)   line 0

The manner in which we have chosen to respect previously established metrical structure is not the only one logically possible. Instead of proceeding as just suggested, we might assume that the rule constructing constituent boundaries first constructs the constituents of the previously marked heads and then only constructs the constituents over the elements that

---

6. The stress pattern of Aklan is essentially identical to that of Tübatulabal, where, as noted by Prince,

a. Final syllables are always stressed.
b. Long vowels are always stressed.
c. Some stresses are fixed in certain morphemes.
d. In a stretch of short-voweled syllables not stressed by (a) or (c), stress alternates right to left. (Prince 1983, 63)

See also Anderson (1969, 1974).

remain outside any constituent. To see how the two proposals for respecting previously assigned structure differ, consider how they would affect the construction of binary left-headed constituents from right to left on the string (41), where element 3 has been previously marked as a head.

(41) . . * . .   line 1
   5 4 3 2 1   line 0

The procedure utilized in (40b) will generate the constituent structure (42a), whereas the procedure described in the preceding paragraph will generate the structure (42b).

(42)

a. * . * * .   line 1
  (5 4)(3)(2 1)   line 0

b. * . * . *   line 1
  (5 4)(3 2)(1)   line 0

The choice between these alternatives is clearly an empirical matter. We shall conclude in the discussion of Odawa stress in chapter 6 that the correct procedure is the one adopted in (40b) and (42a).

Our analysis of Aklan stress differs in an important respect from that of Hayes (1980/1). Like almost all metrical phonologists of the early 1980s, Hayes represented constituents by trees in which head nodes were labeled S(trong) and nonhead nodes, W(eak). Metrical structures such as those illustrated in (42a,b) would be represented in his system as shown in (43a) and (43b), respectively.[7]

(43)

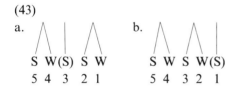

a.
S W(S) S W
5 4 3 2 1

b.
S W S W(S)
5 4 3 2 1

An important further aspect of the tree notation utilized by Hayes and others, most notably Hammond (1986), is that it imposes restrictions on the kinds of elements a given terminal node may dominate. As formulated most clearly by Hammond (1986), these restrictions are based on the two binary choices in (44).

---

7. Hayes does not label nodes of nonbranching trees, since they are invariably S. It seems to us more perspicuous if these nodes are also labeled; accordingly, we have parenthesized the Ss that Hayes systematically omits.

(44)

a. Must nonheads dominate nonbranching rimes?

b. Must heads dominate branching rimes?

Of the four logically possible constituent types defined by (44), Hayes's system uses only three. In *quantity-insensitive* constituents there are no restrictions on either heads or nonheads. In *quantity-sensitive* constituents nonheads must dominate nonbranching rimes, but there is no restriction on head elements. Finally, in *obligatory branching* constituents heads must dominate branching rimes and nonheads must dominate nonbranching rimes. In Hayes's framework no role is assigned to the fourth constituent type, the one in which heads must dominate branching rimes but nonheads are unrestricted, called *revised obligatory branching* by Hammond. A major point made by Hammond (1986) is that the latter should be utilized in place of obligatory branching constituents. We show in section 2.3 that all relevant cases can be dealt with more adequately in a framework that has no recourse to the parameter (44b).

Hayes uses the contrast between quantity-sensitive and quantity-insensitive constituents to distinguish between cases like Maranungku or Weri, where stress is assigned to alternating syllables regardless of their rime structure, and cases like Aklan, where all heavy syllables must be stressed. Hayes postulates that in Maranungku and Weri the constituents constructed are quantity-insensitive, whereas in Aklan they are quantity-sensitive. There is no direct analogue to this in our grid theory. Instead, in order to capture distinctions like those between Maranungku and Weri, on the one hand, and Aklan, on the other, we make use of rules like (26) that mark certain elements as heads (assign them a line 1 asterisk). As illustrated earlier, in our grid theory the difference between these two language types is captured by the fact that Aklan includes a rule assigning a line 1 asterisk to syllables with branching rimes, whereas there is no such rule in either Weri or Maranungku. Thus, both theories capture this distinction equally well. This, however, is not true of the following facts.

In Aklan obligatory stress falls not only on closed syllables but also on the prefixes *ka* and *ga*. Hayes's system can readily ensure stress on closed syllables by postulating that in Aklan constituents are quantity-sensitive. W nodes will then dominate only nonbranching rimes, and every closed syllable will necessarily have to be dominated by an S node. However, this does not account for the fact that the prefixes *ka* and *ga* are invariably stressed. Hayes writes,

Recall that two prefixes in Aklan, *ka-* and *ga-*, behave in the same way as closed syllables for purposes of stress. We can account for this behavior by marking them with the diacritic [+H] mentioned above, which causes them to be treated as honorarily heavy. More specifically, I propose the following:

(21) Rules of foot construction must treat rimes marked [+H] as dominant nodes.

It should be clear that in a language like Aklan . . . the principle (21) will insure that any rime marked [+H] will receive stress. However, the diacritic [+H] should not be equated with the feature [+stress]. (Hayes 1980/1, 59)

In sum, in order to deal with these two suffixes Hayes's system requires a diacritic that marks particular elements as heads. If specific morphemes may be marked with the diacritic, there is no reason why syllables with branching rimes should not also be marked with the same diacritic. But if that is the case, one can dispense with the distinction between quantity-sensitive and quantity-insensitive feet altogether, thus reducing the expressive power of the theory. This is the procedure we adopt.

By eliminating the distinction between quantity-sensitive and quantity-insensitive constituents, we also eliminate the first of the two parameters in (44). We show in section 2.3 that the facts that motivate the postulation of obligatory branching constituents can be readily accounted for without recourse to this constituent type, thereby eliminating the need for the other parameter in (44) as well.

We now turn to another difference between the Hayes/Hammond framework and our own, namely, that the former expresses stress distinctions by node labeling, whereas the latter, like that of Prince (1983), expresses them by means of columns of asterisks in the metrical grid.[8]

---

8. Hammond's framework differs from Hayes's mainly in the following two respects. Unbounded constituents, which in Hayes's framework are represented by multiply embedded binary trees of the kind illustrated in (i), are represented in Hammond's framework by means of multiply branching n-ary trees of the kind illustrated in (ii). Moreover, whereas in Hayes's framework the nodes of the trees are labeled s(trong) and w(eak), in Hammond's framework s nodes are marked with a circle and w nodes are unmarked. We illustrate the difference with the respective representations of the Khalkha Mongolian word xotElbErE 'leadership' (Hayes 1980/1, 64; Hammond 1986, 197).

(i) xötElbErE   (ii) xötElbErE

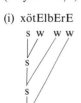

The stress pattern of Yidinʸ (see (25h)) bears directly on this issue. The basic facts were characterized by Hayes (1980/1, 126) as follows.

(45) Stress falls on even-numbered syllables if the word contains an even-numbered syllable with a long vowel; otherwise, stress falls on odd-numbered syllables.

An essential aspect of our framework has been the separation of the setting of the parameters that determine the metrical constituents of a given line from the rules that construct the boundaries and place the heads on the next higher line in the grid. This separation permits us to account for the Yidinʸ facts somewhat more simply than Hayes. The rules needed to account for the facts in (45) are given in (46).

(46)

a. Line 0 parameter settings are [+HT, +BND, left to right] and [right] (that is, right-headed) if the word contains an even-numbered syllable with a long vowel; otherwise, [left] (that is, left-headed).

b. Construct constituent boundaries on line 0.

c. Locate the heads of line 0 constituents on line 1.

d. Delete a line 1 asterisk if it is directly preceded by a stress-bearing element with a line 1 asterisk.

What differentiates this language from those examined above is that the setting of the parameter that determines whether constituents are left- or right-headed requires information about the position of long vowels relative to constituent boundaries—in other words, information that is not available until rule (46b) has applied. There is no contradiction here. We shall assume that (46a) is formally implemented by constructing metrical constituents on two planes simultaneously and deleting the inappropriate one by a subsequent rule.[9] As we shall see below, construction of metrical constituents on two planes simultaneously is required in a number of other languages, such as Tiberian Hebrew (section 2.3.3) and Pirahã (section 6.6).

To account for these facts formally, Hayes (1980/1, 131) proposes the rule (47).

(47) Going from left to right, form quantity-insensitive binary feet with right nodes dominant.

---

9. For additional discussion of Yidinʸ stress, see section 6.5.

This rule is supplemented (p. 132) with a special tree adjustment rule, which ensures that final syllables in words with an odd number of syllables are not stressed.

Hayes accompanies rule (47) with the following comment:

> The labeling of the feet as w s is obviously preliminary, and is often revised later in the derivation. *It isn't absolutely necessary for the feet to be labeled at this stage.* [Emphasis added.] However, under my schema for stress rules, an unmarked rule of tree construction MUST specify either right or left nodes as dominant. . . . (Hayes 1980/1, 131)

The account presented above is thus the functional equivalent of Hayes's node relabeling. We believe that the account above is superior to that of Hayes in that node relabeling introduces new principles into the theory, whereas our account makes do with the independently motivated theoretical machinery. Moreover, node relabeling allows for the characterization of a number of stress phenomena that are never encountered in actual languages. For example, by recourse to node relabeling it is possible to describe a stress pattern in which right-headed binary constituents alternate with binary constituents that are left-headed.[10]

Hayes mentions the stress pattern of the Bolivian language Cayuvava (see (25i)) as presenting a challenge to his attempt to restrict bounded constituents to those having no more than two elements. More recent work by Levin (1985b) has shown a way in which the theoretical framework might be extended to incorporate these facts, and in essence we follow her suggestions here.

As illustrated in (48), stress in Cayuvava falls on every third mora counting from the end of the word.

(48)
a. cáadiróboBurúruce   'ninety-nine'
   ráibirínapu   'dampened manioc flour'

b. maráhahaéiki   'their blankets'
   kihíBere   'I ran'

c. ikitáparerépeha   'the-water-is-clean'
   Bariékimi   'seed of squash'

---

10. In chapter 2 we discuss further examples showing that the node labeling aspect of the tree framework leads to descriptions of the facts that are inferior to alternative descriptions available in the metrical framework advocated here.

Especially interesting is the fact that in words where the number of moras is $3n + 1$ or $3n + 2$, as in (48b) and (48c), the first mora in the word is not stressed.

In order to account for the above facts, we shall assume with Levin (1985b) that Cayuvava constituents are ternary—that is, generated with the parameter settings $[-HT, +BND]$. As shown in (49), we can readily account for the stress patterns of words with $3n$ moras (48a) and $3n + 1$ moras (48b) if we postulate that the last mora is extrametrical and that the (ternary) constituent boundaries are constructed from right to left.

(49) * . . * . . * . .   . * . . * . .   line 1
      (9 8) (7 6 5) (4 3 2)⟨1⟩   (7 6 5) (4 3 2)⟨1⟩ line 0
      ca a diroboBururu ce   maraha ha e i ki

Like all other cases of metrical constituent construction, that of ternary constituents is subject to the Recoverability Condition (19). Constituents that fail this constraint cannot be constructed. This requirement accounts for the surprising fact that there is no stress on the initial syllable in words with $3n + 2$ moras, as illustrated in (48c). To see this, consider a word of five moras. We mark the last syllable extrametrical and construct ternary constituents right to left, producing the structure (50).

(50) (5) (4 3 2)⟨1⟩   line 0
      Ba ri eki mi

We complete the derivation by marking the heads of the constituents, in this case the elements numbered 3 and 5. This placement of line 1 asterisks results in the conjugate structure (51).

(51)   * . * . .   line 1
       5 4 3 2 1   line 0
       Bari ekimi

Given (51), however, it is not possible to reconstruct (50) unambiguously because the structure (52) is also compatible with (51).

(52) (5 4) (3 2)⟨1⟩   line 0
      Bari eki mi

Since marking element 5 as a head of a constituent thus results in a violation of the Recoverability Condition (19), element 5 is not so marked. Pursuant to the Faithfulness Condition (33), such a headless constituent cannot surface, with the consequence that the rules generate the structure in (53), where the word-initial mora belongs to no constituent.

(53)   .   .   *   .   .   line 1
    5(4 3 2)⟨1⟩   line 0
    Bari eki mi

It is important to keep in mind here that the Recoverability Condition (19) relates three variables: direction of government, location of the heads, and location of the constituent boundaries. Given any setting of any two of these three variables, the Recoverability Condition requires that the setting of the third be uniquely determined. This condition is violated in the example under discussion and consequently no constituent is generated on the word-initial syllable. We emphasize here that recoverability has to be understood in the restricted technical sense of definition (19). In a more general sense of recoverability it is obvious that a complete constituent structure can be recovered from the representation in (51), taking into account the direction of construction and the Maximality Condition.

In the case of a word with $3n$ moras such as those illustrated in (48b), stress is placed on the initial mora although the initial constituent contains two rather than three moras. This is because the asterisk distribution in (54)

(54)   *   .   .   *   .   .
    6 5 43 2⟨1⟩
    ra ibirinapu

is unambiguously associated with the constituent boundaries in (55) and the Recoverability Condition is thus satisfied.

(55)   (6 5)(43 2)⟨1⟩
    ra i birina pu

It may perhaps be somewhat surprising that the only ternary constituent admitted by the theory has the form of an *amphibrach* and that *dactyls* and *anapests* are ruled out. We shall therefore briefly compare the proposed solution with one in which the theory is modified so as to admit ternary constituents where heads are located at one of the two ends. Unlike the theory in which constituents are generated by setting the two independently motivated parameters [HT] and [BND], a theory admitting dactyls and anapests will require additional parameters for which there appears to be no independent motivation. This complication in the theory would not seem to be outweighed by possible simplifications in the description of the facts. For example, if dactylic constituents are admitted, then the stress pattern of Cayuvava will be formally accounted for by constructing left-headed dactyls from right to left, as illustrated in (56).

(56) * . . * . . * . .   * . * . . * . .   * * . . * . .
      (9 8 7)(6 5 4)(3 2 1)   (8 7)(6 5 4)(3 2 1)   (7)(6 5 4)(3 2 1)
      ca adi roboBu ruruce   iki tapare repeha   ma rahaha e iki

No moras are marked extrametrical in this solution, and this must clearly be counted in its favor. On the other hand, it will require deleting the stresses assigned to the initial mora in the last two words in (56). The required rule of asterisk deletion will be quite complicated, for it will have to state that asterisks are deleted when they appear in constituents consisting of one or two elements (that is, fewer than three). It is not clear how such a rule should be stated formally, or even whether such a rule should be allowed by the principles of rule well-formedness. None of these problems arises in the solution presented here, where the absence of initial stress in the two words under discussion is accounted for without recourse to a special rule.

1.2 The Effects of Syncope and Epenthesis on Stress

Having described the main features of the formal framework we shall use for the treatment of stress patterns, our next step is to investigate some of its less obvious ramifications and to confront them with facts from actual languages. The first phenomenon to be examined is the effect of deletion on the stress patterns of words. Consider once again the stress pattern of Koya, where words have the metrical constituent structure given in (29) (repeated here as (57)) and where constituents are left-headed.

(57) * . * . . . * . .   line 1
      (1 2)(3 4 5 6)(7 8 9)   line 0

The question that interests us is how the constituent structure will be affected if a stressed element (a constituent head) is deleted by some rule.[11] Since in Koya the head of the constituent is its leftmost element, it would be a plausible guess given the formalism developed above that the deletion of, say, element 7 in (57) will result in element 8 becoming head of the third constituent of the word. Symmetrically, if 7 were the head of a right-headed constituent, deletion would transfer headship to the left element 6. In other words, since the bracketing is not affected by the deletion of an asterisk, the

---

11. It is a widely held belief that stressed vowels are immune—or at least peculiarly resistant—to deletion. Our examination of a fair number and variety of languages convinces us that the empirical support for this belief is slight, not to say nonexistent.

formalism predicts that, when a stressed element is deleted, the number of stresses in the word will be preserved. The stress of the deleted element will not be lost but will be transferred to the nearest stressable element on the right if the constituents are left-headed, or to the nearest stressable element on the left if the constituents are right-headed.[12] In light of the preceding, we expect to find languages where the deletion of a stressed vowel results in stress being shifted to the left, as well as languages where deletion results in stress being shifted to the right. In (58) and (59) we present an example of each type of stress shift, drawn respectively from Russian and Sanskrit.

In (58) we give the singular forms of the Russian noun *zajom* 'loan'.

(58) zajóm   nom., acc.
     zájma   gen.
     zájmu   dat.
     (o) zájme   prep.

The *o* in the stem *zajom* is deleted if the following syllable contains a full vowel. Since all endings except for the nom.sg. contain a full vowel, deletion takes place in all but the nom.sg. What is noteworthy from our point of view is that the deletion causes the stress to be transferred to the adjacent syllable on the left, which suggests that line 0 constituents in Russian must be right-headed.

The different case forms of the Sanskrit noun *devī* 'goddess' in (59a) and (59b) show stress shift to the right.

(59)
a. devī́
    devī́bhis
    devī́ṣu

b. devyā́
    devyā́s

The cause of the stress shift in Sanskrit is not the deletion of a vowel, as in Russian, but the rule of *kṣaipra sandhi*, which turns high vowels into glides in prevocalic position. Since in Sanskrit glides are not stress-bearing, the effects of glide formation on the stress contour of a word are identical with those of deletion, for in both cases a stress-bearing element is eliminated

---

12. The deletion of an element in the string (that is, of a line 0 asterisk) is to be distinguished from the destressing of an element (that is, from the deletion of a line 1 asterisk). In the latter case the constituent is not preserved but instead is eliminated by the Faithfulness Condition (33).

from line 0. The effect of glide formation is to transfer the stress to the next vowel on the right, which suggests that, unlike Russian, Sanskrit has left-headed metrical constituents.[13]

These facts provide support for the assumption that has been fundamental to the approach outlined here, that stress patterns are a by-product of metrical constituent structure. The data in (58) and (59) show that, as postulated by our theory, there is a definite link between a head and the immediately adjacent nonhead element on one of its sides. This result constitutes a direct challenge to alternative theories like that of Prince (1983) in which the existence of metrical constituents is explicitly denied.

Like the effects of deletion, the effects that vowel epenthesis (insertion) has on the stress contour of words provide further insight into the nature of metrical constituent structure. Vowel epenthesis adds stress-bearing elements to the string, and in the absence of additional empirical data it might be hypothesized that all effects of interest are adequately captured by the relative order of epenthesis and the rule of constituent construction. On this hypothesis it would be expected that when epenthesis precedes constituent construction, epenthetic vowels will be stressed provided that they occupy an appropriate position in the string, whereas when epenthesis follows constituent construction, no epenthetic vowel will ever be stressed. The facts of Winnebago stress show that the second expectation is empirically incorrect, for in this language epenthesis causes concomitant displacement of stress only in certain contexts, which like those encountered in deletion crucially involve metrical constituent structure.

Hale and White Eagle (1980), on whose study we base our discussion, note that in Winnebago stress is assigned to every odd-numbered mora in a word, except for the first, as illustrated in (60a). Moreover, they observe that in bimoraic words stress falls on the final mora (see (60b)) and that in all other words with an even number of moras the last mora remains unstressed (see (60c)). (We omit any indication of vowel nasalization.)

(60)
a. haakítujìk   'I pull it taut' (plain)
   haakítujìkshanà 'I pull it taut' (decl.)
b. wajé   'dress'
   wijúk   'cat'

---

13. The literature includes additional instances of stress shift triggered by deletion or desyllabification; see, for example, Kenstowicz (1983), Al-Mozainy, Bley-Vroman, and McCarthy (1985), Rappaport (1984), and section 2.2.3.

c. hochichínik   'boy'
    naaná?a   'you weigh'
    hakirújikshàna   'he pulls it taut'

It is easy to account for the stress distribution in (60a) and (60b) by stipulating that the initial mora is marked extrametrical and that right-headed binary constituents are constructed from left to right. The examples in (60c) are less straightforward, however, for as shown in (61), in words with an even number of moras this procedure will yield stress on the last two moras.

(61)

a. . . * *
    ⟨1⟩ (2 3)(4)
    hochichin ik

b. . . * *
    ⟨1⟩(2 3)(4)
    na   ana? a

c. . . * .   * *
    ⟨1⟩(2 3)(4   5)(6)
    hak iruj ikshan a

We shall eliminate the incorrect stress on the last mora by a special rule that destresses a mora directly preceded by a stressed mora (compare the very similar rule postulated for the Garawa example (39)).

Winnebago is subject to an epenthesis rule, known as Dorsey's Law, which in a sequence obstruent-sonorant-vowel inserts a copy of the vowel between the obstruent and the sonorant. Hale and White Eagle express this rule in the transformational format given in (62) and exemplify it by the forms in (63), in which the epenthetic vowels are marked with arrowheads.

(62)
$$[-\text{sonorant}] \begin{bmatrix} -\text{syllabic} \\ +\text{sonorant} \end{bmatrix} V$$
$$1 \qquad\quad 2 \qquad 3 \;\rightarrow\; 1\ 3\ 2\ 3$$

(63)

a. hoshạwazhá   'you are ill'
    harakíshụrujìkshạnà   'you pull taut'

b. maashárach   'you promise'
    wakịripáras   'flat bug'
    hirakọrohò   'you dress, prepare'
    hirakọrohòni   'you don't dress'

hirakǫ́rohònirà   'the fact that you do not dress'

wakį̆ripǫ́ropǫ̀ro   'spherical bug'

As illustrated in (64), there is a fundamental difference between the examples in (63a) and those in (63b). In the forms in (63a) none of the epenthetic vowels is stressed and the vowels stressed by the regular rule of Constituent Construction remain unaffected by epenthesis (see (64a)). By contrast, in the forms in (63b) stress is shifted away from certain vowels to which it was assigned by the rule of Constituent Construction for Winnebago onto an adjacent epenthetic vowel (see (64b)).

(64)

a. hoshwazhá   → hoshawazhá

$\langle 1 \rangle$ (2 3) → $\langle 1 \rangle$ x (2   3)

ha rakíshrujìkshnà   → ha rakíshurujìkshanà

$\langle 1 \rangle$(2 3) (4 5)   (6) → $\langle 1 \rangle$(2 3) x(4 5)   y (6)

b. ma ashrách → ma ashárach

$\langle 1 \rangle$(2   3)   → $\langle 1 \rangle$(2   x 3)

wakriprás → wakiripáras

$\langle 1 \rangle$(2 3) → $\langle 1 \rangle$x(2 y 3)

hi rakróhò → hi rakórohò

$\langle 1 \rangle$(2   3)(4) → $\langle 1 \rangle$(2   x 3)(4)

hi rakróhonì rà → hi rakórohòni rà

$\langle 1 \rangle$(2   3)(4 5)(6) → $\langle 1 \rangle$(2   x 3)(4 5)(6)

wakripróprò → waki ripóropòro

$\langle 1 \rangle$(2   3) (4) → $\langle 1 \rangle$x(2 y 3) z(4)

As Hale and White Eagle observe, the difference between the examples in (64a) and those in (64b) is that in the former the vowel is inserted *between* metrical constituents, whereas in the latter Dorsey's Law inserts a vowel *inside* a constituent already present. Hale and White Eagle propose that in the latter situation the insertion triggers a restructuring of the metrical constituents that results in the reassignment of some of the stresses, and we adopt their proposal.[14]

To express the alternating stress pattern of Winnebago words, it is necessary to construct binary constituents. As illustrated in (64b), the insertion of vowels by Dorsey's Law may result in constituents that contain more

---

14. Hale and White Eagle employ the nested and labeled constituent structure that was generally accepted before the appearance of Prince (1983). We have reformulated their proposal in our notation.

than two elements. Since the only constituents allowed in Winnebago are binary, the effect of epenthesis in such cases is to destroy the constituents. The destruction of one constituent automatically triggers destruction of the next constituent on its right and so on down the line, a true *domino effect*. The destruction of the constituents in turn triggers a reapplication of the Winnebago Constituent Construction rule that begins with the leftmost element of the destroyed structure. To motivate this procedure, we stipulate that metrical constituent structure is subject to the *Domino Condition*.

(65) *Domino Condition*
      The introduction of an additional position inside a bounded constituent destroys that constituent and all constituents to its right if the Constituent Construction rule applied from left to right, and all constituents to its left if the Constituent Construction rule applied from right to left. Constituent structure is reimposed on the affected substring by a subsequent reapplication of the Constituent Construction rule.

We illustrate the effects of the Domino Condition in (66), where above the central line of phonemes we have copied the line 0 constituents after the application of Dorsey's Law, and where below the central line we have given the constituent structure resulting from the repair action of the Domino Condition.

(66)   ⟨1⟩(2   x   3)   ⟨1⟩ x(2 y 3)
       ⟨ma⟩ ashar ach   ⟨wa⟩ki ripa ras
         ⟨1⟩(2   x)(3)   ⟨1⟩ x(2 y)(3)

       ⟨1⟩(2 x   3)(4)   ⟨1⟩ x(2 y 3) z (4)
       ⟨hi⟩r akor oho   ⟨wa⟩ki ripor opor o
         ⟨1⟩(2 x)(3 4)   ⟨1⟩ x(2 y)(3 z)(4)

       ⟨1⟩(2 x   3)(4 5)   ⟨1⟩(2 x   3)(4 5)(6)
       ⟨hi⟩r akor ohoni   ⟨hi⟩r akor ohonir a
         ⟨1⟩(2 x)(3 4)(5)   ⟨1⟩(2 x)(3 4)(5 6)

All the forms with an even number of syllables are subject to the rule of stress deletion, which destresses a mora to the right of a stressed mora. The application of this rule yields the attested distribution of stresses.

   It is important to note that, unless constituent structure is postulated, it is impossible to express the difference between the cases where epenthesis triggers reconstruction and those where it does not. Thus, for example, in an account based on the theoretical framework of Prince (1983), where the existence of metrical constituent structure is explicitly denied, the forms *maasharach* and *hoshawazha* would have the stress grids of (67a) before the application of Dorsey's Law and those of (67b) after the application of Dorsey's Law.

(67)

a. . .   *   .   . *
    ⟨*⟩*   *   ⟨*⟩   * *
    ma ashrach   hoshwazha

b. . . . *   . . .   *
    ⟨*⟩* * *   ⟨*⟩ * * *
    ma asharach   hoshawazha

Since no principle in Prince's theory distinguishes between the two grids in (67a) in terms of well-formedness, it is impossible to construct a natural account of the Winnebago stress pattern within this framework.[15]

---

15. An alternative procedure for obtaining the stress pattern in words such as *maasharách* or *wakiripóropòro* without reference to constituent structure was suggested to us by R. Hogg at the Linguistic Association of Great Britain meeting in April 1985. The procedure requires complicating Dorsey's Law: namely, in copying the right-hand vowel, Dorsey's Law also copies its asterisk, if any has been assigned to it. The rule of asterisk deletion must also be complicated, in that it must apply iteratively from left to right.

We illustrate this proposal with the derivation of the surface stress patterns of *harakishrujikshna* and *wakripropro*. In the first case the proposed procedure will derive the output form *harakishurujikshana* without difficulty. Since the stress rule will not assign an asterisk to the underlying /u/ in *shru*, no asterisk will be copied by the modified Dorsey's Law when it generates the surface string *shuru*. Dorsey's Law will copy an asterisk when it applies to the word-final sequence *shna* and converts it to *shana*. However, the word-final asterisk will be deleted by the asterisk deletion rule operating iteratively on the subsequence *jikshana*. The application of the modified Dorsey's Law to the second example will yield *wakiriporoporo*. Here again the even-numbered asterisks are correctly deleted by the asterisk deletion rule, which applies iteratively from left to right. But the procedure fails to derive the correct stress pattern from the underlying representation *hirakrohonira*. Here the stress rule and the modified Dorsey's Law will generate the form *hirakorohonira*, with asterisks on the third, fourth, sixth, and seventh syllables. Asterisk deletion will then remove the asterisks on the fourth and seventh syllables, leaving in stresses on the third and sixth. However, the correct surface stress contour, is *hirakórohònirà*, with stresses on the third, fifth, and seventh syllables. It is not obvious how the proposed alternative might plausibly be modified so as to generate the correct output in this case. Thus, it cannot be regarded as a viable competitor to our account, since as we have shown in (66) our proposed set of rules handles this word correctly.

Note also that the modifications required by the alternative proposal are

1.3 Grids

We have shown that capturing the distributions of stresses in words encountered in a variety of languages requires a notation that organizes
sequences of elements into constituents each of which is headed by a
designated element. Following an old tradition, we have assumed that
languages have a certain amount of discretion in selecting the elements in
the sequence that are capable of bearing stress, and we have notated them
by associating an asterisk with each such element in the sequence. These
asterisks representing the stressable elements constitute the bottom line on
a separate plane of representation, and it is on this bottom line (line 0) that
the metrical constituents are constructed. In this framework a constituent
is a maximal string of positions that is copied as a single position onto the
line of positions above line 0. This position functions as the representative
of the constituent and is said to dominate it. This parallels the situation in
syntax, where a category like NP or VP represents the string of elements
that it dominates. The parallel with syntax goes even further. In syntax a
given constituent is the categorial projection of a specific element within it,
which by definition is the head of the constituent. A metrical constituent is
also the projection of a specific position within it, which by definition is the
head of the constituent.

It was assumed above that the distinction between stressed and unstressed elements in a string was the surface manifestation of the contrast
between heads and domain elements. The notation thus reflects differences
in degrees of stress by the height of the associated asterisk columns. We
would like at this point to give additional justification for this aspect of the
notation. Among the properties that a stress notation must be capable of
dealing with are these:

(68)

a. In languages where words have multiple stresses it is usually the case
   that the stress of one syllable is greater than that of all others. Degrees
   of stress must therefore be distinguishable in the notation.

---

major from the point of view of the theoretical framework we have developed. In
particular, we have suggested that the only iterative rules allowed in a phonology
are those generating metrical structure. Thus, in our framework there can be no
iterative rule of asterisk deletion, and the alternative proposal would be ruled out
on the basis of this fact alone. The fact that even with this weakening of the theory a viable account of the empirical data cannot be produced provides what
Calvinist divines would call "comfortable assurance" that the theory we have
illustrated and defended is not completely off the mark.

b. In many languages the main stresses of the words in a syntactic constituent are not all of the same degree of prominence. Rather, in such collocations the main stress of some word is enhanced above those of others in a manner determined at least in part by the syntactic structure of the collocation. Moreover, it is difficult to place an upper bound on the number of degrees of stress to be distinguished.

c. There exist rules of stress displacement (such as the Rhythm Rule of English) that shift stress from one syllable to another.

An adequate notation of stress must be able to express all these facts in a perspicuous manner. Our task, therefore, is to examine different stress notations in order to eliminate those that fail to do so.

Noncompound words of English have both stressed and stressless syllables, the latter being reduced in certain contexts to schwa. As illustrated in (69), among stressed syllables in noncompound words at most three degrees of stress are distinguished.

$$
\begin{array}{lll}
\overset{1\ \ \ 3\ \ 0\ 2}{\text{(69) formaldehyde}} & \overset{2\ \ 1\ \ 3\ \ 0}{\text{expectation}} & \overset{2\ \ 0\ \ 3}{\text{Japanese}} \\[4pt]
\overset{3\ \ \ 2}{\text{torment}} & \overset{3\ \ 0}{\text{poison}} & \overset{3}{\text{book}}
\end{array}
$$

Since degrees of stress are entities that can be ordered on a scale like degrees of temperature, it is natural and convenient to notate them by Arabic numerals.[16]

---

16. The notation of stress in noncompound words is a fairly direct translation of that used by Kenyon and Knott (1944). These authors distinguish main stress from secondary stress by special diacritics. They distinguish—somewhat irregularly—vowels with weak stress (our degree 1) from stressless vowels by indicating reduction in the latter case. They remark, for example: "In ʌn'dʌn the first syllable is not quite without accent, but has sufficient accent (though not marked) to make it audibly more prominent than the *un-* of *unless* (spoken colloquially) ..." (p. xx). Thus, in Kenyon and Knott (1944) a schwa without a stress mark represents a vowel with stress of degree 0, and the majority of unreduced vowels without stress mark correspond to vowels with stress of degree 1. Moreover, Kenyon and Knott represent the final syllable of bisyllabic nouns like *torment* without accent mark but with a full vowel, whereas in trisyllabic words like *intercept* they represent the final syllable with an accent mark, thus indicating a distinction between [2 stress] in trisyllabic words and [1 stress] in bisyllabic words. We assume here that this is a purely notational convention without basis in actual pronunciation, and we mark the final syllable in both types of English words uniformly as [2 stress].

The notation of stress by means of Arabic numerals will turn out to be inadequate and will be replaced by another notation in a later part of this section. The use of numerals to indicate stress distinctions must, of course, be kept separate from the use of numerals to identify consecutive positions in the string.

We assume that in noncompound words pronounced in isolation the main stresses are of the same degree, namely, 3. Hence, main stress in *formaldehyde* and in *book* is notated with 3 even though the latter word contains no other syllables and hence no contrasting stresses.

As noted in (68b), the main stresses of the different words in a syntactic collocation are not all the same. Rather, they are subject to rules that enhance the stress of one word in the collocation above the rest. A simple example is provided by the effects of the Nuclear Stress Rule of English illustrated in (70).

(70)

a. $\overset{\text{1}}{\text{for}}\overset{\text{3 0 2}}{\text{maldehyde}}\overset{\text{0 0}}{\text{ is a}}\overset{\text{4 0}}{\text{poison}}$

b. $\overset{\text{0 3 0}}{\text{the poison}}\overset{\text{0 1}}{\text{ was}}\overset{\text{4 0 2}}{\text{formaldehyde}}$

c. $\overset{\text{1 4 0 2}}{\text{formaldehyde}}\overset{\text{0 0}}{\text{ is a}}\overset{\text{3 0 0}}{\text{powerful}}\overset{\text{5 0}}{\text{poison}}$

The Nuclear Stress Rule enhances the main stress of the rightmost constituent in the phrase above that of the rest.[17] Hence, in (70a) the main stress of *poison* is greater than that of *formaldehyde*. Since the main stress of *formaldehyde* is of degree 3, the main stress of *poison* in (70a) must be of degree 4. In (70b) the prominence relations are reversed; here the main stress of *poison* is less than that of *formaldehyde*. Moreover, the main stress of *poison* is greater than the nonmain stresses of *formaldehyde*. Thus, *poison* is given the stress contour 3 0, whereas *formaldehyde* has the contour 1 4 0 2.

It is well known that stress enhancement by the Nuclear Stress Rule operates cyclically. This fact is reflected in (70c), where the main stress of *formaldehyde* is less than that of *poison*, yet greater than that of *powerful*. Since main stresses are of degree 3 in isolation, the main stress on *formaldehyde* must be of degree 4 and that of *poison* of degree 5. In sum, six degrees of stress—0, 1, 2, 3, 4, 5—are distinguished in this phrase, and as syntactic nesting increases, the number of potential stress distinctions increases as well.

The difficulty of placing an upper bound on the number of degrees of stress that need to be distinguished derives from the fact that there is no upper bound on the depth of syntactic embedding of a phrase. (71) is an example of a reasonably elegant phrase with a depth of embedding of six.

---

17. For more discussion of this rule, see section 7.9.1.

(71) a vote for the rejection of the proposal to place a limit on the length of lectures

Readily understandable phrases with considerably greater embedding can easily be composed. Because of this, it is generally assumed that the theory of syntax may not impose an upper limit on the depth of embedding of phrases. However, if there can be no upper limit on the depth of embedding, then there can be no upper bound either on the number of degrees of stress that may need to be distinguished. This conclusion is, of course, not affected by the fact that no speaker has ever successfully distinguished more than ten or twelve or twenty-seven different degrees of stress.

From the fact that there is no upper bound on the degrees of stress, it follows directly that stress cannot be represented by means of diacritic marks of the sort recommended in *The Principles of the International Phonetic Association* (pp. 17–18), of which different versions are in wide use among writers on phonetic topics. Since each diacritic mark must be defined in a separate statement, no treatise can include more than a fixed number of such statements. Hence, the use of diacritics implies that there must be an upper bound on the number of stresses to be distinguished. But, as we have just seen, the facts do not permit us to limit the degrees of stress to be distinguished to any fixed number. Hence, the diacritic notation must be rejected as being inadequate in principle.

The notation of stress by means of integers, which is an adaptation of a notation first used by P. Passy at the end of the last century, does not suffer from this inadequacy, since the integers are defined not by a list but by a recursive procedure. There are various ways of representing integers, and the Arabic numeral representation adopted for convenience here is only one of them. In fact, this mode of representation is not entirely appropriate for our purposes, since it cannot handle naturally the phenomenon of stress displacement cited in (68c). Thus, consider the effects of the English Rhythm Rule illustrated in (72).

(72) a.   b.

  2 0 3   3 0 2   4 0
Tennessee   Tennessee Williams

  2 0 3   3 0 2   4 0
Japanese   Japanese beetle

  2 0 3 0   3 0 2 0 4 0
Mississippi   Mississippi River

<pre>
 1   3   3   2   4 0
New York   New York City
 3   4   0   4   3   0   5 0
cold blooded   cold blooded malice
 3   4   4   3   5
John Paul   John Paul Jones
</pre>

In the examples in (72a) the main stress is on the last stressed syllable of the (last) word. In the examples in (72b) the main stress has been shifted to the left, specifically, onto the preceding stressed syllable. Two features of this displacement deserve mention. First, the site of the original main stress does not become stressless as a result of stress shift; instead, it retains a certain degree of stress, a vestige of its former prominence, as it were. Second, the new stress peak has the same degree of stress as the old stress peak; in particular, the degree of stress of the new peak is independent of the stress that the syllable had at the outset. Thus, after stress shift both *New York* and *Japanese* in (72) have 3 stress on the initial syllable, even though in isolation the initial syllable of *New York* has less stress than that of *Japanese*. Consider now how the Rhythm Rule must be stated if stress is marked with Arabic numerals.

(73) Assign the highest stress number N in the lefthand constituent to the syllable with the highest stress number M on its left, simultaneously reducing the original N by one degree.

This is hardly a perspicuous manner of stating the facts, but given a numerical notation there does not seem to be any alternative. There is, however, an alternative to the numerical notation itself. Integers may be represented by sequences of marks of the sort often used in counting: 1 = *, 2 = **, 3 = ***, 4 = ****, and so on. Such a notation was introduced into phonology for purposes of stress representation by Liberman (1975) and was further developed by Liberman and Prince (1977) and by Prince (1983). In Liberman's notation the integers are represented by columns of marks (by convention, asterisks) placed above the individual stress-bearing phonemes in the sequence. It was suggested by Prince (1983, 33) that, given this notation of stress, the Rhythm Rule could be formulated as an operation that moves a stress mark (hereafter an *asterisk*) laterally from one position to another. Implicit in this procedure is the assumption that the asterisk columns are not just columns of marks associated with particular elements in the string but in fact columns set in a two-dimensional array of points in which lateral movement on a given line is possible, as illustrated in (74).

(74) . . *   . *
      * . *   . *
      * . *   * *
      * . *   * *
      Japanese   New York

Following Liberman and Prince (1977), we refer to this two-dimensional array of points as the *metrical grid*. We discuss the mechanism producing lateral movement following example (84).

Columns of asterisks are generated by imposing metrical constituent structure on a string of elements. In locating stress, we first mark each stress-bearing element in the string and thus obtain the line called line 0. We then impose a constituent structure on this line and mark on a line above it each element that is a head of a constituent. This produces a rudimentary grid where the heads of constituents have two marks, whereas other stress-bearing phonemes in the string have only a single mark. To obtain additional rows of asterisks, we need to postulate additional layers of constituent structure. Thus, for example, in Maranungku (see (25b)) main stress falls on the initial syllable, whereas in Warao (see (25d)) it falls on the penult. We reproduce representative stress patterns from these two languages in (75).

(75)
a. Maranungku   b. Warao

     * . * . *   line 1   * . * . * .   line 1
    (1 2)(3 4)(5) line 0   (6)(5 4)(3 2)⟨1⟩ line 0

To place an extra asterisk above the elements numbered 1 in the two examples, we erect a left-headed unbounded constituent over the line 1 asterisks in (75a) and a right-headed unbounded constituent over the line 1 asterisks in (75b). Such structures are standardly subject to rule (76).

(76) Locate the heads of line 1 constituents on line 2.

This rule will produce the representations in (77).

(77)
a. * . . . .   line 2   b. . . . . * .   line 2
   (* . * . *)   line 1   (* . * . *) .   line 1
   (1 2)(3 4)(5) line 0   (6)(5 4)(3 2)⟨1⟩ line 0

In (77) the parentheses that correspond to the upper constituent have been drawn around the string of line 1 asterisks. This notation deviates from the standard way of representing nested constituent structure, which draws all the parentheses on the line of terminals. Thus, for the cases under discussion, the standard notation would be the one shown in (78).

(78)
a. (corresponding to (77a))   b. (corresponding to (77b))

*	.	.	.	.	line 2
*	.	*	.	*	line 1
((1 2)(3 4)(5))					line 0

.	.	.	.	*	.	line 2
*	.	*	.	*	.	line 1
((6)(5 4)(3 2))⟨1⟩						line 0

The notation in (77) is clearly equivalent to the standard notation displayed in (78). For reasons of perspicuity, we shall use the notation illustrated in (77) instead of the standard notation. The configurations illustrated with Maranungku and Warao are quite common in the languages of the world. The metrical rules will in general generate a composite constituent structure in the metrical plane. In the most common case this composite structure is made up of two layers of metrical constituents, of which the lower layer consists of a sequence of bounded or unbounded constituents and the upper layer of a single unbounded constituent constructed on line 1.

To illustrate further the procedure advocated here, we again consider Koya, in which the constituents on line 0 are unbounded and left-headed. Consider the sequence of positions in (79), in which 3 and 7 are closed syllables and hence supplied with an asterisk by rule (30a).

(79) . . * . . . * . .   line 1
     1 2 3 4 5 6 7 8 9   line 0

Applying the rest of the Koya stress rules (see (30)) yields the structure in (80).

(80) * . * . . . * . .   line 1
     (1 2)(3 4 5 6)(7 8 9)   line 0

Suppose now that Koya has a rule that erects a left-headed unbounded constituent above the first layer of metrical structure just described. This rule will yield the structure in (81), in conformity with rule (76).

(81) * . . . .   line 2
     (* . * . . . * . .)   line 1
     (1 2)(3 4 5 6)(7 8 9)   line 0

(81) illustrates the stress pattern of an actual word in Koya, described verbally in (25).

The direction of constituent construction on the lower layer of constituents, commonly called the *foot layer*, does not determine the position of the head in the upper layer.[18] Thus, although Garawa shares with Warao and Weri the fact that feet are constructed from right to left, main stress in

---

18. Such a connection was suggested by Hammond (1984a). According to Hammond, the headedness of an unbounded constituent on a given line is determined by the direction of constituent construction on the line immediately below. However, the arguments adduced in support of this suggestion are not especially compelling. Consider, for example, Hammond's treatment of the "tonal accent" of Creek, discussed in section 2.3.1. This "accent" is placed on the penultimate or on the final syllable of certain words, depending on which is an even number of syllables from the beginning of the word. Hammond proposes to account for these facts as follows. Right-headed binary constituents are constructed on line 0 from left to right; the last constituent so constructed is marked extrametrical if it is nonbranching, and subsequently a right-headed unbounded constituent is constructed on line 1. Since the line 0 constituents are constructed from left to right, the line 1 constituent would have to be left-headed, if Hammond's proposed principle holds. Hammond explains away this apparent counterexample by referring to the fact that the last constituent on line 0 ("last foot") is marked extrametrical and in such a situation the principle is overridden. In section 2.3.1 we advance two solutions for the Creek facts, neither of which needs recourse to extrametricality of a final nonbranching constituent on line 1. Both solutions are thus simpler than Hammond's. Creek therefore constitutes a counterexample to Hammond's proposal, for the added complexity of his solution is imposed not by the facts but by the theoretical framework used to express them.

But our main objection to Hammond's proposal is more than just technical: the proposal is ad hoc in that it lacks organic connection with the rest of the theory. Hammond accepts the standard view that directionality and head location are independent parameters that must be set in constructing (bounded) metrical constituents on a given line (see his text on page 5, for example). If these two parameters are independent with respect to constituents on a given line, it is totally unclear why they should not also be independent with respect to constituents constructed on separate lines. Moreover, directionality of construction is a parameter only in the case of bounded constituents: for unbounded constituents, the direction of construction is meaningless. Hence, it is impossible for Hammond to explain the headedness in two of the four logically possible situations. He does not discuss the third logically possible case, where the constituents on two consecutive lines in the grid are bounded. Finally, in the one case where he does investigate the predictions of the proposal, the evidence is far from overwhelming. It has been our experience that true theoretical principles are based on firmer foundations; we persist therefore in the belief that *pace* Hammond there is no connection between the headedness of constituents on a given line in the grid and the direction of constituent construction on the next lower line.

Garawa falls on the initial syllable, not on the final or penultimate syllable, as in Weri or Warao, respectively. To capture the Garawa facts, we construct a left-headed unbounded constituent over the asterisks of line 1, as illustrated in (82).

```
(82)  *  .  .  .  .  .  .      line 2
      (* * . * . * .)          line 1
      (7)(6 5)(4 3)(2 1)       line 0
```

As noted above, rule that deletes the asterisk in a position directly following an asterisk will subsequently apply and destress the element in position 6.

In Garawa the stress on the penultimate syllable is weaker than that on the first syllable yet stronger than that on all other syllables. In this language, as in English and certain other languages, noncompound words have three degrees of stress in addition to total stresslessness.[19] To express this fact, it is necessary to add a line between the two lines of asterisks in (82), as illustrated in (83).[20]

```
(83)  *  .  .  .  .  .  .      line 2
      (* . . . . * .)          line 1a
      (* * . * .)(* .)         line 1
      (7)(6 5)(4 3)(2 1)       line 0
```

As indicated by the numbering of the lines in (83), the inserted line is regarded as being split off from line 1 in (82) and as therefore having the same parameter settings as line 1. There are two aspects to the operation of a stress enhancement rule. On the one hand, the rule adds an asterisk above some designated position, and on the other hand, it introduces the conjugate bracketing that is required by the extra asterisk. Note that as a consequence of this bracketing another asterisk will be introduced on this new line in the position of the main stress of the word.

As detailed in chapter 7, stress enhancement is also involved in the generation of the stress contours of English words. Main stress and secondary stresses are assigned by means of a two-layered constituent structure, as illustrated in (84).

---

19. To the best of our knowledge, languages distinguish at most four degrees of stress in noncompound words. If further research confirms this restriction, it will be necessary to reflect it formally in the theory. Since the matter is peripheral to the issues under discussion, no attempt has been made to do so here.

20. The line 1 asterisk associated with position 6 will be deleted by the rule mentioned in the discussion of (82).

```
(84)  .  . *   . . *     .  . . *     line 2
     (* . *) (* . *)   (* * . *)    line 1
     (* *)(*) (* *)(*)  (*) (* *)(*)  line 0
     Tennessee  Japa nese  formalde hyde
```

The English enhancement rule applies to the representations in (84) and yields the structures in (85).

```
(85)  .  . *   . . *     .  . . *     line 2
     (* . *) (* . *)   (.  * . *)    line 1a
     (*) (. *) (*)(. *)  (* *)(. *)   line 1
     (* *)(*) (* *)(*)  (*) (* *)(*)  line 0
     Tennessee  Ja pa nese  formalde hyde
```

This formalization sets the stage for the application of the Rhythm Rule discussed with respect to the examples in (72). Since stress is represented by columns of asterisks, stress retraction such as that exemplified in (72) must be formally characterized as the leftward displacement of an asterisk marking the head of a constituent. We propose to implement this by a rule moving the constituent boundary to the left over the element representing its (former) head. In view of the convention of locating a constituent boundary adjacent to the element that is its head (see the discussion of the Faithfulness Condition (33)), the application of the proposed rule will have the effects shown in (86).

```
(86)  *  . .   * . .     .  * . .     line 2
     (*) . *  (*) . *   (.  *) . *    line 1a
     (*) (. *) (*)(. *)  (* *)(. *)   line 1
     (* *)(*) (* *)(*)  (*) (* *)(*)  line 0
     Tennessee  Ja pa nese  formalde hyde
```

The Rhythm Rule will apply to *Tennessee* and *Japanese* only in specific syntactic contexts; it applies to *formaldehyde* independently of its syntactic environment. (See rules (21) and (90) of chapter 7 for further details.)

Finally, since only a line 1a boundary is moved, the asterisks on lines 1a and lower will not be affected, implying correctly that the former head syllable will retain some degree of stress. Moreover, since boundary movement takes place on a given line, the degree of stress on the landing site will always be identical with that of the syllable from which the asterisk was removed. This latter implication is also supported by the facts, as already noted.

Asterisk movement is crucially involved in the assignment of main stress in Aklan. As stated in (25g), in Aklan stress falls on all closed syllables, on certain lexically marked syllables, and, in a sequence of open unmarked syllables, on every odd-numbered syllable counted from the end if the sequence is word-final, and on every even-numbered syllable if the sequence is not word-final. We argued that in Aklan the basic stress location rules are (87a–d).

(87)

a. Assign a line 1 asterisk to all closed syllables and certain lexically identified syllables.

b. Line 0 parameter settings are [+ HT, + BND, right, right to left].

c. Construct constituent boundaries on line 0.

d. Locate the heads of line 0 constituents on line 1.

The string in (88a) exemplifies a closed penultimate syllable that has been affected by rule (87a); (88b) exemplifies a word without syllables subject to (87a).

(88)

```
a. . . . * .     b. . . . . .   line 1
   5 4 3 2 1        5 4 3 2 1   line 0
```

Applying the rules (87b–d) to (88a) and (88b) produces (89a) and (89b).

(89)

```
a. . * . * *     b. * . * . *   line 1
  (5  4)(3  2)(1)   (5)(4  3)(2  1)  line 0
```

Main stress in Aklan falls either on the final or on the penultimate syllable (Hayes 1980/1). The latter pattern is found in all words with a penultimate syllable that is closed, as well as in certain specially marked words. In all other cases main stress falls on the final syllable. There is no problem about assigning main stress to the final syllable. This result will be produced by a rule that constructs a right-headed unbounded constituent on line 1. This rule will yield (90a) and (90b) when applied to (89a) and (89b).

(90)

```
a. . . . . *     b. . . . . *   line 2
  (. * . * *)       (* . * . *)   line 1
  (5  4)(3  2)(1)   (5)(4  3)(2  1)  line 0
```

Since words with a closed penultimate syllable have stress on the penult, the output is correct in (90b) but not in (90a). We could obtain the stress shift in (90a) if we deleted the line 1 asterisk on the final syllable by means of a rule such as (91).

(91) $* \rightarrow \emptyset / *$ _____ line 1 word-finally

$ * \quad *$ line 0

What makes rule (91) especially attractive is that nothing needs to be said about the landing site of the shifted main asterisk. Since rule (91) deletes a line 1 asterisk but leaves intact the line 1 constituent, the effect of the rule is to shift the line 2 asterisk—the head of the line 1 constituent—to the left so that it is positioned over the rightmost line 1 asterisk. It therefore accounts for the important fact that when a stress is shifted, it generally lands on the nearest stress peak—that is, on the syllable that is the head of the adjacent constituent.

Rule (91), however, fails to account for the fact that after stress shift in Aklan the final syllable is not stressless but instead bears secondary stress (see Hayes 1980/1, 22). In fact, our discussion of the English examples (84)–(86) has shown that stress shift can take place without rendering the affected syllable stressless. The device available for this shift is movement of a constituent bracket. The difference between the English and the Aklan cases is primarily that in Aklan the affected syllable must be word-final as well as directly preceded by a stressed syllable, whereas in English the preceding stressed syllable need not be adjacent to the head being retracted. What is needed, therefore, is a rule metathesizing an asterisk and its boundary, as shown in (92).

(92) $*) \rightarrow) * / *$ _____ line 1 word-finally

$ * \quad *$ line 0

In (93) we illustrate the effects of (92) on (90a).

(93) . . . . *   . . . * .   line 2
  (. * . * *) → (. * . *) *   line 1
  (5 4)(3 2)(1)   (5 4)(3 2)(1) line 0

Aklan also has a set of words that consistently take penultimate main stress yet whose penultimate syllable is not closed and hence will not be supplied with a line 1 asterisk by our rule. We assume that such words are entered in the lexicon with a line 1 asterisk on the penultimate syllable. The words so marked in the lexicon will then be subject to stress retraction by rule (92).

In previous studies (for example, Liberman and Prince 1977, Halle and Vergnaud 1978, Hayes 1980/1) different degrees of stress were indicated by

node labeling in binary branching structures such as those illustrated in
(94) with words from Maranungku (Hayes 1980/1, 51).

(94) lángkaràtetì   wélepènemànta

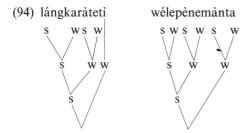

Prince (1983) has shown that neither the labeling of nodes nor the multiple
embedding of the trees is functional in the treatment. Hayes's trees thus
reduce to a bracketing of the sort illustrated in (95).

(95) lángka ràte tì   wéle pène mànta
      [(*   *)(* *)(*)]   [(* *)(* *) (* *)]

In order to interpret this bracketed sequence of elements in stress terms, it
is necessary to add to the phonology interpretive statements such as (96).

(96) The designated element (head) of a constituent has greater stress than
      all other elements in the constituent.

With respect to the internal bracketing in (95) the interpretive convention
(96) correctly indicates that odd-numbered elements have greater stress
than even-numbered elements. Since the initial syllable has main stress, we
know that the external bracketing of (95) must be interpreted by (96) to
indicate that the designated element of the designated (leftmost) constituent has greater stress than the designated elements of the remaining
constituents. Without an interpretive statement such as (96) there is no way
to read off these stress relations among the stress-bearing elements in (95).
As Prince (1983) notes, it is clearly a weakness of such formalizations that
they fail to establish a direct relation between the constituent structure
representation and the degrees of stress.

Chapter 2
Elaborations and Refinements

2.1 More on Extrametricality

An element that is marked extrametrical is invisible to the rules of constituent construction provided that at the point in the derivation at which these rules apply the extrametrical element terminates—begins or ends—the string under consideration (see Archangeli 1984). Archangeli (1986) has proposed that extrametricality of a terminal element —for instance, a word-final phoneme—percolates up to the rime node, but not to the syllable node, that dominates the terminal element. The percolation renders the rime, but not the entire syllable, extrametrical.

As Archangeli points out, a good example of this special property of extrametricality is provided by the stress pattern of Western Aranda, an Australian language discussed by Davis (1984). In trisyllabic and longer words in this language, primary stress falls on the second syllable if the word begins with a vowel; if the word begins with a consonant or has fewer than three syllables, primary stress falls on the first syllable. In Davis's words, "... the Western Aranda stress rule for trisyllabic words or longer is that primary stress falls on the first syllable containing an onset. Secondary stress is usually on every other syllable after the one with main stress. Final syllables never receive any stress; they are extrametrical." He cites the examples in (1).

(1)
a. Consonant-initial words of three or more syllables

    túkura   'ulcer'
    kútunùla   'ceremonial assistant'
    wóratàra   (place name)

b. Vowel-initial words of three or more syllables

ergúma	'to seize'
artjánama	'to run'
utnádawàra	(place name)

c. Bisyllabic words

káma	'to cut'
ílba	'ear'
wúma	'to hear'

To account for these facts, we shall assume, following Archangeli (1986), that Western Aranda is subject to the rules of extrametricality in (2).

(2)

a. Mark the last segment of the word extrametrical.

b. Mark the first segment of the word extrametrical.

In addition, we assume the following rules of metrical constituent construction.

(3)

a. Stress-bearing elements are vowels (that is, the heads of rimes).

b. Line 0 parameter settings are [+HT, +BND, left, left to right].

c. Construct constituent boundaries on line 0.

d. Locate the heads of line 0 constituents on line 1.

e. Line 1 parameter settings are [+HT, −BND, left].

f. Construct constituent boundaries on line 1.

g. Locate the heads of line 1 constituents on line 2.

We illustrate the operation of these rules in (4).

```
(4)  * . . .      * . .    . * . . .   * .    line 2
     (* . *) .    (* .) .  . (* . *) . (*) .  line 1
     (1 2)(3) .   (1 2) .  . (1 2)(3) . (1) . line 0
     kát u nù⟨la⟩ túku⟨ra⟩ ⟨u⟩tnádawà⟨ra⟩ íl⟨ba⟩
```

As Archangeli (1986) observes, the effect of rule (2a) will be to render extrametrical the last rime of every word. Since, unlike the syllable structure of many Arabic languages (see section 2.3.2), the syllable structure of Western Aranda does not include word-final syllables where consonants follow the rime, the extrametricality marked on the word-final consonant will percolate upward and mark the word-final rime extrametrical. By contrast, extrametricality will not percolate up from a word-initial consonant to the first rime node in the word since the consonant is part of the onset—and not of the rime—of the word-initial syllable. In consonant-initial words, then, the first rime is not extrametrical and remains visible to the stress rules. In vowel-initial words, on the other hand, extrametricality percolates up to the rime node, which is thereby excluded from stress assignment. Thus, primary stress falls on the first syllable in the first two words in (4), but not in *utnádawàra*, which begins with a vowel and whose first rime is therefore extrametrical.

It would seem that by the same token the first syllable in *ílba* should also be invisible to the rules in (3). Since the word has stress on its first vowel, we know that this is incorrect. The reason that extrametricality does not render this vowel invisible to the rules of constituent construction is that extrametricality may never render an entire phonological string invisible to these rules. Thus, for example, in languages like English or Latin, where the last rime of a word is extrametrical, monosyllabic words are generally stressed rather than stressless. We summarize these observations in (5), where we list the conditions under which an element marked extrametrical becomes invisible to rules of constituent construction.[1]

(5) An element marked extrametrical is invisible to the rules constructing metrical constituents only if at the point in the derivation at which these rules apply (a) the element begins or ends the phonological string and (b) does not constitute the entire string.

2.2 Line Conflation and Some of Its Consequences

2.2.1 Line Conflation and the Stress Patterns of Eastern Cheremis and Turkish

Almost all examples discussed to this point have involved instances where words have both primary and subsidiary stresses. There are, of course, numerous languages with but a single stressed syllable in each word. A few such languages were briefly discussed in section 1.1, where their stress patterns were captured by constructing unbounded constituents over the positions on line 0. It might be thought that this is typical of such languages—

---

1. Davis (1985) argues that the Western Aranda stress facts provide an example where properties of the syllable onset affect the location of stress. Archangeli's analysis summarized in the text supports Davis's contention only to the extent that stress distribution is affected by the presence or absence of an onset in the word-initial syllable, which in turn is a consequence of condition (5) governing the visibility of extrametrical elements. For another example of onsets affecting the placement of stress, see section 6.6.

that is, that they invariably have only one layer of metrical constituents and hence only one line of asterisks above line 0. Given the framework that has been developed to this point, only unbounded constituents can be constructed in these cases, for bounded constituents would generate more than one stress in longer words. But if in these languages bounded constituents cannot be employed and stress must be assigned by means of unbounded constituents, then it should also be the case that stress in such languages will fall on one of four syllables in the word. It can fall either on the first syllable or on the last syllable, or, if these are marked extrametrical, on the second or on the penultimate syllable. No machinery exists for capturing a fact such as that in Macedonian stress systematically falls on the antepenultimate syllable (Lunt 1952) or the even more interesting stress pattern (6) first brought to our attention by Kiparsky (1973) with examples from Eastern Cheremis and subsequently documented by Hayes (1980/1) with languages as diverse as Classical Arabic, Chuvash, Hindi, Huasteco, and Dongolese Nubian.

(6) Stress falls on the last syllable that has a full vowel, but in words where all syllables have only reduced vowels, stress falls on the first syllable.

Given the machinery presented here, it would be a straightforward matter to account for the stress distribution in (6) if it characterized the location of main stress and there were also subsidiary stresses on all full vowels. We could then postulate the rules in (7) and produce the stress patterns illustrated in (8).

(7)
a. Stressable elements are vowels.

b. Assign line 1 asterisks to full vowels.

c. Line 0 parameter settings are [+HT, −BND, left].

d. Construct constituent boundaries on line 0.

e. Locate the heads of line 0 constituents on line 1.

f. Line 1 parameter settings are [+HT, −BND, right].

g. Construct constituent boundaries on line 1.

h. Locate the heads of line 1 constituents on line 2.

(8)
a. . . . . . . * . .   b. * . . . .   line 2
    (* . * . . *) . .   (*) . . . .   line 1
    (1 2)(3 4 5 6)(7 8 9)   (1 2 3 4 5 6 7 8)   line 0

In (8a) the syllables 3 and 7 are marked with an arrowhead to indicate that they have a full vowel. Rule (7b) then assigns line 1 asterisks to these syllables. Next, rules (7c–e) construct unbounded left-headed constituents on line 0 and assign an asterisk to the initial syllable. Finally, rules (7f–h) construct an unbounded right-headed constituent on line 1 and assign a line 2 asterisk above the rightmost line 1 asterisk. The rules in (7) thus place main stress correctly, but they also incorrectly generate subsidiary stresses.[2]

Once the problem has been put in these terms, the solution is all but self-evident: having constructed the representations in (8), we need only suppress the asterisks on line 1 in order to obtain the correct output. We achieve this by adding to (7) the rule (9).

(9) Conflate lines 1 and 2.

When two lines in a metrical grid are conflated, a constituent on the lower line is preserved only if its head is also the head of a constituent on the higher line. Therefore, the effect of rule (9) is to suppress all but the last constituent in line 0, yielding the required output as shown in (10). It is important to note in this regard that when constituents are destroyed, their heads are automatically eliminated.

(10) . . . . * . .   line 2
      (. . . . . . *) . .   line 1
       1 2 3̭ 4 5 6 (7̭ 8 9)   line 0

Kiparsky (1973) also drew attention to the stress pattern of Komi, which is the mirror image of that in (6).

(11) Stress falls on the first syllable that has a full vowel, but in words where all syllables have only reduced vowels, stress falls on the last syllable.

This stress pattern is readily accounted for by a set of rules identical with those in (7), except that constituents on line 0 must be right-headed and those on line 1 must be left-headed.

---

2. Since few of the languages exhibiting stress pattern (6) have been investigated in depth, it is conceivable that some of them indeed have secondary stresses that were overlooked in the published descriptions. It is highly improbable, however, that these secondary stresses should have been overlooked in every one of the cited languages. It is, of course, essential to our argument that there should exist languages of this type without secondary stresses, because it is the facts of these languages that motivate line conflation (9) as a formal device in the theory.

A pattern essentially identical with that of Komi is found in Turkish, a fact that has unfortunately been overlooked in some recent treatments. As Poser observes,

In Turkish stress generally falls on the last syllable of the word. This is true both of non-derived forms and of derived forms .... Exceptions are of two kinds. First, there are a number of words with inherent stress on some non-final syllable. In this case, stress does not shift when suffixes are added .... (Second,) there are a number of suffixes that never bear stress. (Poser 1984, 128).

In Turkish thus stress falls on the syllable immediately preceding the first or only suffix of this kind in the word. This is illustrated with the examples in (12).

(12)

a. adám   'man'
   adam-lár   'men'
   adam-lar-á   'to the men'

b. mása   'table'
   mása-lar   'tables'
   mása-lar-a   'to the tables'

c. adám-im   'I am a man'
   gít-me-di-m   'I did not go'

d. yorgún-dur-lar 'they are tired'
   but
   yorgun-lár   (same)
   however
   Kenédi-dir-ler 'they are the Kennedys'
   Kenédi-ler   'Kennedys'

The large majority of Turkish words conform to the pattern in (12a); most place names and many Western borrowings conform to the pattern in (12b). Hammond (1986) notes that in this class of words stress is on the penultimate stem syllable except when the penultimate syllable ends with a short vowel and the antepenult with a consonant; in that case stress goes on the antepenult. This is illustrated in (13).

(13)

a. Kenédi
   jubíle
   Adána
   Vasíngton

Ayzinhó:ver
Istánbul

b. ševrole   'Chevrolet'
   samándira   'buoy'
   Ánkara

Among the "unstressable" suffixes exhibiting the stress pattern in (12c) are most forms of the copula, as well as the verbal negative suffix /mE/ and the past tense morpheme /dI/. As the form *gít-me-di-m* 'I did not go' shows, stress surfaces on the syllable preceding the first "unstressable" suffix. Moreover, examples in (12d) show that this holds only in words with native stems. In words with "foreign" stems, "unstressable" suffixes do not place stress on the preceding syllable; in these words the stress remains on the stem syllable as it does before "stressable" suffixes.

To account for these facts, we shall postulate that "unstressable" suffixes are assigned a line 1 asterisk by an early rule. In similar fashion, "foreign" words are assigned a line 1 asterisk on the penultimate syllable. If we now assume that the stress rules postulated for Komi apply also in Turkish, we obtain the correct surface stress assignment in all "native" words with "stressable" suffixes and in all "foreign" words that have penultimate stress. In "native" words with "unstressable" suffixes and in "foreign" words that have antepenultimate stress, the surface stress is placed one syllable to the right of its actual location. We assume that such words are subject to the rule (14).

(14) Delete the line 0 asterisk of the stressed syllable if stress falls on an "unstressable" suffix or on a "foreign" word where the penult ends with a short vowel and the antepenult with a consonant.

By rendering such syllables non-stress-bearing, we correctly shift the word stress one syllable to the left because in Turkish line 0 constituents must be right-headed. We summarize these facts in (15), which should be compared to (7).

(15)

a. Stressable elements are vowels.

b. Assign line 1 asterisks to "unstressable" suffixes and to the penultimate syllable of the stem of "foreign" words.

c. Line 0 parameter settings are [+ HT, − BND, right].

d. Construct constituent boundaries on line 0.

e. Locate the heads of line 0 constituent on line 1.

f. Line 1 parameter settings are [+HT, −BND, left].

g. Construct constituent boundaries on line 1.

h. Locate the heads of line 1 constituents on line 2.

i. Conflate lines 1 and 2.

j. (14)

Some of the facts given here are discussed by Hammond (1986) within the theoretical framework originally developed by Hayes (1980/1) where the rules constructing metrical constituents have direct access to certain aspects of syllable structure. Hammond limits his discussion to words without "unstressable" suffixes. He proposes (pp. 199–200) that the stress patterns in (12c) provide part of the motivation for setting up a novel type of constituent where heads "must dominate a heavy syllable but nonheads are unrestricted" (p. 187). Even with this extension of the theory not all cases are accounted for, and additional conventions are required. We show in section 2.4 that the central set of examples that Hammond adduces to justify direct access to syllable structure by the constituent construction rules can readily be accounted for without this extension. It would seem, therefore, that the Turkish facts just reviewed constitute yet another challenge to the Hayes/Hammond proposal that constituent construction rules must have direct access to certain aspects of syllable structure.

2.2.2 Antepenultimate Stress in Macedonian and Latin

The antepenultimate stress of words in a language like Macedonian (Lunt 1952; Franks 1983) will be expressed by the rules in (16).

(16)

a. Mark the final syllable extrametrical.

b. Line 0 parameter settings are [+HT, +BND, left, right to left].

c. Construct constituent boundaries on line 0.

d. Locate the heads of line 0 constituents on line 1.

e. Line 1 parameter settings are [+HT, −BND, right].

f. Construct constituent boundaries on line 1.

g. Locate the heads of line 1 constituents on line 2.

h. Conflate lines 1 and 2.

It is significant that although there are words with exceptional stress in Macedonian, none of these has stress on a syllable preceding the antepenult. As Franks (1983) observes, since only one syllable can be extrametrical, it is impossible to utilize extrametricality as a means for locating stress on a syllable before the antepenult.[3] By contrast, lexically assigned stresses (inherent line 1 asterisks) can be utilized freely to locate the stress on a syllable to the right of the antepenult, as shown by the examples in (17).

(17) literatúra
komunízam
konzumátor   'consumer'
citát   'quotation'
autobús
restorán

When suffixes are added, the "exceptional" stress remains on its original syllable "if it is not more than three syllables from the end of the word.... Otherwise, the antepenultimate syllable will be stressed" (Franks 1983). For example, in *konzumátor-i* 'consumers' stress falls on the same syllable as in *konzumátor*, but in *konzumatór-i-te* 'the consumers' the stress is shifted forward to the antepenultimate syllable. This behavior is readily explained by the assumption that the "exceptional" stresses are due to lexically supplied (obligatory) line 1 asterisks. If a syllable with a lexically supplied line 1 asterisk becomes pre-antepenultimate as a result of suffixation of one or more syllables, the stress rule of Macedonian will apply regularly and place surface stress on the antepenult. To account for the words in (17) with final stress, we shall assume that extrametricality rules do not apply to a (word-final) syllable with stress (line 1 asterisk).

Languages like Latin, where stress in polysyllabic words falls on the antepenult if followed by a syllable with a nonbranching rime and on the penult otherwise, and where monosyllabic words are normally stressed, also make use of the rules in (16). These languages differ from Macedonian in that they are subject to rule (18).

(18) Assign a line 1 asterisk to any metrical syllable of the word if it has a branching rime.

In conjunction with the rules in (16) this rule will assign stress to the penultimate syllable in words such as *agricolárum*, *delénda*, and *magíster* but to the antepenult elsewhere.

---

3. The fact that monosyllabic words are normally not stressless follows from condition (5b), which restricts extrametricality so that it may not render the entire string invisible to the stress rules.

2.2.3 Penultimate Stress in Polish

The formal devices developed to this point offer two means for deriving stress contours in languages with a single word stress that is located on the penult. In such languages stress may be assigned either by marking the last syllable extrametrical and then constructing a right-headed unbounded constituent over the rest or by applying the rules in (16) minus extrametricality assignment (16a). It may seem at first that the former alternative is much the simpler and should therefore be adopted in every case. However, in a number of languages with penultimate stress other facts indicate that this proposal is not viable and that stress in these languages must be assigned by the rules (16b–h).

A relevant example is modern Polish, where main stress falls on the penult as shown in (19) with different case forms of the noun meaning 'hippopotamus'.[4]

(19) hipopótam   nom.sg.
     hipopotám-a   gen.sg.
     hipopotam-ámi   inst.pl.

This type of stress location can be accounted for by either of the above-mentioned alternatives.

Polish also has a number of exceptions to penultimate stress, all of which take stress on the antepenult. It is these exceptions that show that stress must be assigned by (16b–h) rather than by constructing unbounded right-headed constituents. The exceptions fall into two classes (Franks 1985). In one class, illustrated in (20a) with the word meaning 'grammar', antepenultimate stress is found only before monosyllabic suffixes; in the second class, illustrated in (20b) with the word meaning 'university', antepenultimate stress is found only in suffixless forms.

(20)
a. gramátyk-a
   gramátyk-i
   but
   gramatyk-ámi
   gramátyk

---

4. As discussed by Rubach and Booij (1985), in careful speech Polish words are supplied with secondary stresses on alternating syllables preceding the main stress. This pattern of secondary stresses is thus sensitive to the location of main stress and must be assigned by a rule that applies after the placement of main stress. For further discussion of secondary stress assignment following main stress assignment, see section 3.4.

b. uniwérsytet
   but
   uniwersytét-u
   unwersytét-y
   uniwersytet-ámi

To account for the examples in (20a), we must assume that Polish has a special rule that supplies extrametricality to the syllable following certain marked stems. It is obvious that if more than one syllable follows the stem the extrametricality marking of the poststem syllable will not render it invisible to the rules of metrical constituent construction, since only elements in absolute string-final position become invisible to these rules. It is equally obvious that a suffixless form cannot be subject to the proposed rule of extrametricality and will therefore receive regular penultimate stress.

To account for the examples in (20b), it will be necessary to assume that certain noun stems are represented in the lexicon with a final extrametrical syllable. This will render the last syllable invisible to the rules of stress assignment only if no suffix follows the stem; in cases where a suffix is added to the stem the lexically marked extrametrical syllable loses its invisibility and stress is assigned to the penult.

If stress were regularly assigned by marking the last syllable of a word extrametrical and constructing a right-headed unbounded constituent over the remaining syllables, we would be unable to account for the exceptional antepenultimate stress because in the theoretical framework developed here only a single entity may be marked extrametrical, which specifically prevents us from treating the forms with antepenultimate stress by exceptionally marking their last two syllables extrametrical. Clearly, the proposal to weaken the theory to admit this type of extrametricality marking is purely ad hoc and therefore unacceptable. The exceptional stress facts of Polish thus argue in favor of stress assignment by the rules (16b–h) rather than by means of unbounded constituents.

2.3 Binary Constituents as a Counting Device

The construction of bounded metrical constituents performs two separate functions. On the one hand, it subdivides the string into substrings of two (resp. three) elements each; on the other hand, it marks a particular element in the substring as its head by assigning it an asterisk that is then interpreted as stress. In this section we examine cases where binary constituents are used primarily in the former function, that is, as counting devices of a limited sort.

2.3.1 Tone Assignment in Creek

Perhaps the simplest example of this functioning of bounded constituents is in the placement of the "tonal accent" in the native American language Creek. In this language syllables with "tonal accent" are phonetically implemented with a high tone. According to Haas (1977), in a large class of Creek words composed exclusively of light syllables (syllables with nonbranching rimes) "the tonal accent will be placed on the last even-numbered syllable. . . . If the total number of syllables in the word is odd, the tonal accent is on the penult, but if the total number is even, the tonal accent is on the ultima" (pp. 202ff.). In words of this class that contain one or more heavy syllables—syllables with branching rimes—the tonal accent is again placed on the last even-numbered syllable, except that in this case the count begins after the last heavy syllable rather than at the beginning of the word. We illustrate this with the examples in (21).

(21)
a. itiwanayipíta   'to tie to one another'
   isimahicitá   'one to sight at one'

b. alpatóci   'baby alligator'
   hoktakí   'woman'

In order to place the tonal accent, it is thus necessary to determine the location of the last even-numbered syllable counting from a reference point that may be arbitrarily far away. Binary constituent structure provides the required mechanism. We obtain the correct distribution of stresses by means of the rules in (22), and we illustrate in (23) the results of applying rules (22a–i).

(22)
a. Assign line 0 asterisks to all vowels.

b. Assign line 1 asterisks to vowels that head branching rimes.

c. Line 0 parameter settings are [+ HT, + BND, right, left to right].

d. Construct constituent boundaries on line 0.

e. Locate the heads of line 0 constituents on line 1.

f. Line 1 parameter settings are [+ HT, − BND, right].

g. Construct constituent boundaries on line 1.

h. Locate the head of the line 1 constituent on line 2.

i. Delete line 1 asterisk directly following a line 1 asterisk.

j. Conflate lines 1 and 2.

k. Link H tone to vowel with line 2 asterisk.

```
(23) . . . . . * .   . . . . . *    . . * .    . . *   line 2
     (. * . * . *).  (. * . * . *)  (* . *).   (* . *)  line 1
     (1 2)(3 4)(5 6)7 (1 2)(3 4)(5 6) (1)(2 3) 4 (1)(2 3)  line 0
     iti wana yi pí ta  isi mahi citá  alpatóci  hoktakí
```

This procedure yields the correct output in all cases provided that the metrical grid is interpreted in tonal terms as shown in the examples.

2.3.2 The Stress Pattern of Cairene Arabic

Like many Semitic languages, Cairene Arabic distinguishes three kinds of syllables: *light* (syllables with a nonbranching rime), *heavy* (syllables with a branching rime that dominates either a long vowel or a vowel + consonant sequence), and *superheavy* (syllables where a heavy rime is followed by a consonant). We shall assume—and this assumption is crucial to our account of Cairene stress—that the final consonant in a superheavy syllable is not part of the rime but instead is adjoined to the syllable as a sister of the rime. Thus, superheavy syllables have the structure shown in (24).

(24)

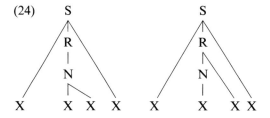

We now summarize the Cairene stress facts as described by McCarthy (1979, 105) and Langendoen (1968, 102).[5]

---

5. Welden (1980) and Harms (1981) among others have suggested that there are secondary stresses in Cairene words. However, in 1984 J. McCarthy (personal communication) noted that his phonetic studies of Cairene speech to that point had revealed no trace of secondary stresses in the word and that the syncope facts cited by Kenstowicz (1980) in support of the existence of secondary stress in Cairene can readily be accounted for without postulating secondary stresses. In view of this we assume (in agreement with most students of Cairene) that Cairene has no secondary stresses.

(25)

a. Stress is on the last syllable, if it is superheavy.

b. Otherwise, stress is on the penult, if it is heavy.

c. Otherwise, stress is on the antepenult or penult, whichever is separated by an even number of syllables from the immediately preceding heavy syllable if there is one, or from the beginning of the word if there is none, where zero is counted as even.

(26)

a. katábt	'I wrote'	sakakíin	'knives'
b. Ṣamálti	'you (fem.sg.) did'	haðáani	'these (fem.du.)'
c. martába	'mattress'	búxala	'misers'
katabítu	'they wrote'	kátaba	'he wrote'
šajarátun	'tree'	šajarátuhu	'his tree'
ʔadwiyatúhu	'his drugs'	ʔadwiyatúhumaa	'their drugs'

Two features make Cairene stress especially interesting. First, as illustrated in (26c), in one class of words the stressed syllable must be separated from some arbitrarily distant reference point by an *even* number of syllables. Second, stress is located on the final syllable only if it is superheavy, but not otherwise.

As noted in our discussion of Creek, in the metrical framework developed here the device for determining whether the number of elements in a sequence is even or odd is the binary constituent. If binary constituents are constructed over a sequence from left to right and the last constituent is "degenerate" (composed of a single element), the number of elements in the sequence is odd; otherwise, it is even.

There are two separate reference points from which the count begins in the case of Cairene stress: the rightmost syllable with a branching rime and, in words without such syllables, the beginning of the word. There is, of course, no problem about locating the beginning of the word. To locate the rightmost syllable with a branching rime, we propose that in Cairene the elements over which constituent structure is constructed and that are therefore represented by line 0 asterisks are neither the head vowels of syllables nor all vowels in the string, as in most languages examined to this point, but rather all rime phonemes—in other words, the head vowels and, in the branching rime of a heavy syllable, also the phoneme immediately following the head. Moreover, we postulate that the head of a branching rime is supplied by rule with a line 1 asterisk. We illustrate in (27) the representations of two of the words cited in (26) at the stage in the derivation before constituent boundary construction rules have applied.

(27)   *. .   .   . .   line 1
         12 3   .   1 2 3 4   .   line 0
         martab⟨a⟩   šajaratuh⟨u⟩

Before constructing the metrical constituents we need to account for the fact that the word-final syllable is stressless unless it is superheavy. We shall do this by capitalizing on the observation that in superheavy syllables the rime is not syllable-final but is followed by another consonant. Specifically, we postulate that word-final segments are marked extrametrical. In conformity with Archangeli's (1986) percolation convention, this will render word-final rimes invisible to the rules of metrical constituent construction and hence stressless except in superheavy syllables, for here the word-final consonant is not part of the rime and hence extrametricality will not percolate upward and extend from it to the rime. We illustrate this in (28), where in *ʔadwiyatúhumaa* the two elements of the last rime are invisible to the constituent construction rules whereas in *sakakiin* the extrametricality of the word-final *n* does not percolate upward to the rime.

(28)   * . . . . *.   line 1
         1 2 3 4 5 6   . .   1 2 34   line 0
         ʔa dwiyatuhum⟨a a⟩   sakaki i⟨n⟩

Finally we need a rule that constructs left-headed binary constituents on line 0 from left to right and a rule that constructs an unbounded right-headed constituent on line 1. We summarize the rules in (29) and illustrate in (30) the application of rules (29a–i) to the forms in (27) and (28).

(29)

a. All phonemes in the rime are stress-bearing.

b. Mark the last segment of the word extrametrical.

c. Assign a line 1 asterisk to the head of each branching rime.

d. Line 0 parameter settings are [+ HT, + BND, left, left to right].

e. Construct constituent boundaries on line 0.

f. Locate the heads of line 0 constituents on line 1.

g. Line 1 parameter settings are [+ HT, − BND, right].

h. Construct constituent boundaries on line 1.

i. Locate the heads of line 1 constituents on line 2.

j. Conflate lines 1 and 2.

(30)   . . * .   . . * .   .   line 2
        (* . *) .   (* . *).   .   line 1
        (1 2)(3) .   (1 2)(3 4) .   line 0
        ma r tab⟨a⟩   šaja ratuh⟨u⟩

        . . . . * . . .   . . * .   line 2
        (* . *. *). . .   (* . *).   line 1
        (1 2)(3 4)(5 6) . .   (1 2)(3 4)   line 0
        ʔa dwiya tuhum⟨a a⟩   saka ki i⟨n⟩

In each form, line conflation due to rule (29j) subsequently eliminates all but the last constituent and its column of asterisks.

2.3.3 The Stress Pattern of Tiberian Hebrew

Tiberian Hebrew, the language in which most of the books of the standard text of the Jewish bible are written, presents one of the most intricate examples we know of the effects of desyllabification on stress. In our discussion we follow the treatment proposed by Rappaport (1984).

As illustrated in (31), primary stress in Tiberian Hebrew falls either on the penultimate or on the last syllable.[6]

(31) qám 'arise'   kaatáb 'write'   3sg.masc.
      qamtém   k'tabtém   2pl.masc.
      qamtén   k'tabtén   2pl.fem.
      qámtii   kàatábtii   1sg.
      qáamuu   kàatbúu   3pl.
      qáamaa   kàatbáa   3sg.fem.

When the word ends with a closed syllable, main stress is always on the final syllable. When the last syllable is open, stress is either on the penultimate or on the last syllable. This alternation is found in the paradigm of verbs with bisyllabic (that is, triliteral) stems such as *katab* but not in the paradigm of verbs with monosyllabic (biliteral) stems such as *qam*. Moreover, in the forms where stress falls on an open final syllable, the second syllable of the stem is elided: *kaatáb* and *kaatáb-tii*, but *kaatb-úu* (from *kaatab-uu*) and *kaatb-áa* (from *kaatab-aa*). These facts suggest that the basic rule of stress assignment places stress on the penultimate syllable in all words ending with an open syllable but that stress is shifted to the last syllable when the

---

6. Vowel quantity and stress on the first syllable are discussed below.

penultimate syllable is elided. The fact that stress moves to the right as a result of vowel elision implies that the rule of stress assignment constructs left-headed constituents. Since stress alternates between the penult and the ultima, we infer that line 0 constituents are binary and that they are constructed from right to left. To obtain final stress for words with closed syllables, we follow Rappaport in postulating a general rule that is ordered before the stress rule and supplies word-final closed syllables with a line 1 asterisk. A right-headed unbounded constituent is then erected over the asterisks on line 1. This has the effect of placing main stress on the head of the rightmost binary constituent constructed over the asterisks of line 0. We thus obtain metrical constituent structures such as those in (32a–c). The rule of vowel reduction—to be stated below—then deletes the penultimate vowel in (32c) (but not in (32a) or (32b)), yielding (32d).

(32)

a. . . *   b. . * .
    (* . *)   (* *) .
    (3 2) (1)   (3)(2 1)
    k' tabtem   kaatabtii

c. . * .   d. . . *
    (* *) .   (* . *)
    (3)(2 1)   (3)(. 1)
    kaatabuu   kaat'buu

Rappaport points out that there is additional support for the proposed analysis, in particular, for a stage in the derivation like that in (32a–c). Tiberian Hebrew includes a rule of Pretonic Lengthening that lengthens an open syllable in position before main stress, as in the following words.

(33) m'laakíim   <   malakíim   'kings'
     kaatábtii   <   katábtii   'I wrote'
     ʕeenáab   <   ʕenáb   'grape'[7]

If Pretonic Lengthening (PTL)[8] is ordered before Vowel Reduction (VR),

---

7. The lengthening of the last vowel is due to a second lengthening rule, which does not apply in verbs; see Rappaport (1984, 93ff.).

8. Rappaport notes (p. 91) that PTL is limited to nonhigh vowels and has a number of idiosyncratic exceptions. Moreover, if the pretonic vowel is rounded, PTL results in gemination of the following consonant rather than in vowel lengthening (thus, ʕagolloot/*ʕagooloot 'round', (fem.pl.)). We consider here only the core examples and disregard these further refinements.

but after stress placement, we can easily account for the long vowel in (32d), as illustrated in (34).

(34) . * .   . * .   . *   line 2
   (* *) .   (* *) .   (*   *)   line 1
   (3)(2 1)   (3)(2 1)   (3)   (1)   line 0
   ka tab-uu $\xrightarrow{\text{PTL}}$ kaatabuu $\xrightarrow{\text{VR}}$ kaat'buu

An explanation is now in order for the rightward shift of the stress as a result of VR. VR erases element 2 on line 0. This leaves the constituent intact but transfers headship to the remaining element, namely, 1. The convention of placing the right boundary of a right-headed constituent immediately to the right of the element that marks its head then automatically relocates the boundary.

We turn now to an examination of VR itself. We note, following Rappaport, that it does not always elide a vowel: in certain cases it produces a reduced vowel that is either ultra short or schwa. In all cases, however, the vowel affected by VR becomes incapable of bearing stress. Consequently, when the rule applies to a stressed vowel, it will result in stress shift. Since the different treatments of the vowel affected by VR are not relevant to the issues under discussion, we shall omit them from consideration here and only retain the fact that the vowel becomes non-stress-bearing. To reflect formally the fact that the rule renders the vowel to which it applies incapable of bearing stress, we postulate that it deletes an asterisk on line 0. We transcribe each vowel affected by VR with an apostrophe (').

The conditions under which VR takes place are fairly complex. In a sequence of short vowels it affects the even-numbered vowels counting from right to left (Prince 1975). Moreover, it does not affect either vowels in closed syllables or long vowels, including those lengthened by PTL. As Prince observes, these conditions resemble those encountered in languages with stress alternations. In fact, the contexts in which VR applies in Tiberian Hebrew are precisely the complement of the contexts where stress is placed in Aklan (see section 1.2). We illustrate this in (35).

(35) kotobeka   → k'tob'ká   'your (masc.sg.) writing'
     yaladehem   → yal'deehém   'their (masc.) children'
     yiktobuu   → yikt'búu   'they (masc) will write'
     wayyadabberuu   → wàyy'dabb'rúu   'and they (masc.) will speak'

These observations almost force on us the conclusion that, since the two situations are so similar, they should be treated with identical formal means. Specifically, since stress in Aklan has been assigned by constructing right-headed binary constituents from right to left, the same device should be used to account for vowel reduction in Tiberian Hebrew. The problem is that stress assignment in Tiberian Hebrew requires us to construct binary *left-headed* constituents from right to left, whereas VR needs right-headed constituents. Thus, if the proposed solution were adopted, it would entail countenancing the possibility of assigning two distinct metrical constituent analyses to the same string of phonemes, and it is this fact—more than any other—that stopped scholars prior to Rappaport from exploring this solution further. It did not stop Rappaport, primarily because the conclusion that there might be several simultaneous constituent analyses of a given sequence of phonemes appeared much less implausible to her since she viewed phonological representations in much the same terms as we do here—that is, as three-dimensional objects consisting of (half-) planes intersecting in a single center line. To postulate two distinct analyses of a string in this type of theoretical framework implies that the string is supplied with two planes on which are constructed distinct metrical constituent structures. The addition of yet another plane to the representation does not appear particularly implausible once it is realized that phonological representations must in any event include quite a number of separate planes. For example, McCarthy (1979) has shown that, in the Semitic languages, vowels and consonants, which constitute separate morphemes in these languages, must be represented on separate planes. Tones have long been represented on a separate plane (see Williams 1971/6), and arguments have also been given for representing syllable structure on a separate plane (Halle and Vergnaud 1980; Levin 1985a).

Once it is assumed that metrical constituent structure for a given word may be represented on two distinct planes, it is not hard to find additional arguments for this step. First VR constituents must be right-headed, whereas stress constituents must be left-headed. Second, VR does not affect long vowels or vowels in closed syllables, whereas stress assignment is not sensitive to syllable structure, except for the special case of word-final closed syllables. Third, VR does not affect vowels lengthened by PTL, but PTL itself is dependent on the prior assignment of stress. Thus, VR must be ordered after PTL, whereas stress assignment must precede PTL (see (34)).

In (36) and (37) we state formally the set of rules required for generating the metrical grids on the two planes. The rules for the stress plane must precede those for the reduction plane.

(36)

a. The stress-bearing elements are vowels that are heads or rimes. (These are the elements marked with asterisks on line 0.)

b. Assign a line 1 asterisk to the last vowel if the word ends with a consonant.

c. Line 0 parameter settings are [+HT, +BND, left, right to left].

d. Construct constituent boundaries on line 0.

e. Locate the heads of line 0 constituents on line 1.

f. Line 1 parameter settings are [+HT, −BND, right].

g. Construct constituent boundaries on line 1.

h. Locate the heads of line 1 constituents on line 2.

Though partially identical with the rules in (36), the rules generating metrical grids on the reduction plane are distinct from them. As already observed, the rules generating the "stress" grid must be ordered before those generating the "reduction" grid (37).

(37)

a. Assign line 0 asterisks to vowels that are rime heads.

b. Assign line 1 asterisks to vowels that are heads of branching rimes.

c. Line 0 parameter settings are [+HT, +BND, right, right to left].

d. Construct constituent boundaries on line 0.

e. Locate the heads of line 0 constituents on line 1.

In stating VR, we follow Rappaport's account, according to which a vowel that undergoes the rule thereby becomes incapable of bearing stress, a fact that must be reflected formally by deleting the vowel's line 0 asterisk in the stress grid. The rule is therefore given as in (38).

(38)   .   line 1
        $* \rightarrow . / \underline{\qquad}$ line 0

where asterisk deletion takes place on the stress plane and the environment refers to asterisk configurations on the reduction plane.

We illustrate the generation of the stress patterns of the words in (35) in (39), where the stress plane is represented above the line of phonemes and the grid of the reduction plane below that line.

(39)

a.
```
      . . . *
line 2  . . *                    . . *              . . *
line 1 (* . *).      does       (* . *).           (. * . *)
line 0 (* *)(* *)    ─PTL→ not   (* *)(* *)          (. *)(. *)
       koto beka         apply   koto beka  ─(37)→  koto beka  ─(38)→  koto beka  ⟶  [k'tob'ká]
                                                                        (* *)(* *)
line 0                                                                  . *
line 1
```

b.
```
          *                      . . *              . . *              . . *
line 2   . . *                   . . *              . . *              . . *
line 1  (* . *).     does       (* . *)            (* . *)(*)          (*)(. *)(*)
line 0  (*)(* *)(*)  ─PTL→ not   (*)(* *)(*)         (*)(* *)(*)        (*)(. *)(*)
        ya lade hem       apply  ya ladeehem ─(37)→ ya ladeehem ─(38)→ ya ladeehem  ⟶  [yàl'deehém]
                                                                        (*)(* *)(*)
line 0                                                                  . * . *
line 1                                                                  . * . *
```

c.
```
        . *                      . *                . *                . *
line 2  . *                      . *                . *                . *
line 1 (* *).       does        (* *).             (* . *)            (* . *)
line 0 (*)(* *)     ─PTL→ not    (*)(* *)           (*)(. *)           (*)(. *)
       yiktobuu          apply   yiktobuu  ─(37)→  yiktobuu  ─(38)→   yiktobuu  ⟶  [yikt'búu]
                                                                       (*)(* *)
line 0                                                                 . *
line 1
```

d.
```
        . *                      . * .              . *                . *
line 2  . *                      . * .              . *                . * . *
line 1 (* . *).     does        (* . *).           (* . *).           (*)(. *)(. *)
line 0 (*)(* *)(**) ─PTL→ not    (*)(* *)(**)        (*)(* *)(**)       (*)(. *)(. *)
       wayyadabberuu     apply   wayyadabberuu ─(37)→ wayyadabberuu ─(38)→ wayyadabberuu ⟶ [wàyy'dabb'rúu]
                                                                       (*)(* *)(**)
line 0                                                                 * . * . *
line 1
```

All forms derived in (39) show the correct pattern of reduced vowels and placement of main stress. However, they contain a number of secondary stresses that are systematically not recorded in the Masoretic text. Rappaport points out (p. 155) that Tiberian Hebrew is subject to a rule of Prestress Destressing that deletes a line 1 asterisk directly before main stress (that is, before a line 2 asterisk). This rule does not apply to asterisks of syllables of the form CVVC. Hence, the stress on the first syllable of *yikt'buu* (39c) is removed, whereas that on the first syllable of *kaat'buu* is retained (compare (32c,d), (34)).

In summary, this account to Tiberian Hebrew stress has been crucially based on the following three assumptions: (1) that more than one metrical constituent structure may be associated with a given central line of phonemes, (2) that metrical constituent structure need not always be interpreted in stress terms, and (3) that a special relationship holds between the head of a metrical constituent and the rest of the elements in the constituent. Rappaport (1984) has shown that descriptions that fail to make these assumptions or that, like the description of Prince (1983), specifically deny assumptions 2 and 3 are unable to deal with the facts in an equally perspicuous fashion.

2.4 More on Accented Elements

In the cases examined so far we have always encountered pairs of rules, of which one constructed the constituent boundaries and the other marked their heads on the line immediately above in the grid. We inquire here whether or not this joint appearance of the two rules is obligatory. It will turn out that an interesting class of stress patterns is generated by a system that does not include the rule constructing constituent boundaries on a given line in the gird.

2.4.1 Stress Patterns with Main Stress on the First (resp. Last) Accented Element

In the discussion of Koya in section 1.1 we distinguished between constructed and obligatory constituents. Constructed constituents result from the application of a rule constructing constituent boundaries, whereas obligatory constituents are associated with the accented elements in the string. Consider now a language like Koya whose stress patterns are captured by the rules in (30) of chapter 1, supplemented by a set of rules constructing an unbounded left-headed constituent on line 1, but not including the rule (30c) that constructs constituent boundaries on line 0. We give the rules in (40).

(40)

a. Assign a line 1 asterisk to a vowel in a closed or long syllable.

b. Line 0 parameter settings are [+HT, −BND, left].

c. Locate the heads of line 0 constituents on line 1.

d. Line 1 parameter settings are [+HT, −BND, left].

e. Construct constituent boundaries on line 1.

f. Locate the heads of line 1 constituents on line 2.

To illustrate the functioning of the rules in (40), we need to investigate only the two cases in (41): words that contain a long or closed syllable (41a) and words that contain no such syllable (41b).

(41)

```
a. . .  *  . .  * .       b. . . . . . . .      line 1
   1 2 3 4 5 6 7            1 2 3 4 5 6 7    line 0
```

Applying the rule set (40) to the forms in (41) results in the following forms,

(42)

```
a. . .   *  . . . .        b.         ?          line 2
   . . (*  . .  * .)          (. . . . . . .)    line 1
   * * (* * *)(* *)           * * * * * * *      line 0
```

where the question mark on line 2 of example (42b) indicates that the conventions developed to this point do not determine the output.

The first two elements in (42a) are not enclosed in constituent boundaries because we have no rule constructing such boundaries on line 0. For the same reason there are also no constituent boundaries on line 0 in (42b). The metrical boundaries that appear on line 1 in (42a) are those induced by the accented elements (see section 1.1 and chapters 4 and 5). The rules of (40) make a definite prediction about the location of stress in (42a), namely, that main stress will be placed on the leftmost closed or long syllable. They make no prediction about placement of stress in (42b), that is, in words that have no long or closed syllables.

We have already dealt with languages where stress is placed on the leftmost (Turkish) or the rightmost (Eastern Cheremis) syllable containing a particular mark. In these languages stress on words without marked elements goes to the opposite end: to the word-final syllable in languages like Turkish and to the word-initial syllable in languages like Eastern Cheremis.

However, there exist languages of this type where stress on words without marked elements goes to the same end as in words with marked syllables. For instance, in Khalkha Mongolian (Street 1963; Hayes 1980/1, 63) stress falls on the leftmost long syllable or on the word-initial syllable, whereas the mirror-image situation is found in Aguacatec Mayan (McArthur and McArthur 1956; Hayes 1980/1, 65). We could account for this class of languages by assuming that they differ from the Turkish/Eastern Cheremis type by lacking a head-marking rule for line 0 constituents. The only additional machinery required would be an interpretive convention that would assign a line 2 asterisk to the terminal syllable in structures of the type illustrated in (42b). The required convention is given in (43).

(43) In a left-headed (resp. right-headed) constituent the head is marked over the leftmost (resp. rightmost) asterisk in the line. In cases where the line contains no asterisks the head is placed over the leftmost (resp. rightmost) asterisk of the next lower line.

When applied to (42b), convention (43) will then generate (44).

(44) * . . . . . .   line 2
   (. . . . . .)   line 1
    * * * * * * *   line 0

This representation is ill formed since there is no position on line 1 that can be projected up to line 2. We shall assume that by convention the gap in the asterisk column is automatically filled, thus inducing constituent structure on line 0 as shown in (45).

(45) * . . . . . .   line 2
   (* . . . . .)   line 1
   (* * * * * * *) line 0

It is worth noting that the headedness of the line 0 constituents will not affect the location of the surface stress. To see this, consider an input string identical to (41a) where the line 0 constituents are specified as right-headed (rather than as left-headed). Instead of (42a), this will produce the output grid (46), which has the same stress contour.

(46) . . * . . . .   line 2
   (. . * . . *) .   line 1
   (* * *)(* * *) *   line 0

Formally this means that replacing (40b) with (47) will have no effect on the surface stress distribution.

(47) Line 0 parameter settings are [+HT, −BND, right] (that is, unbounded and right-headed).

Although yielding identical stress contours, the grids in (42a) and (46) do
not have identical consequences in all cases. The two grids make different
predictions about the effects that the deletion of a stressed element would
have on the stress contour of the word. Words with the grid (42a) would
undergo stress shift to the right if a stressed syllable were deleted, whereas
words with the grid (46) would undergo stress shift to the left. It is
therefore interesting to note that contrasts of this type are found in actual
languages. The basic stress pattern of the Indo-European protolanguage is
rather similar to that of Khalkha Mongolian (Kiparsky and Halle 1977).
The major difference from the point of view of stress is that in Indo-
European each morpheme may or may not have a line 1 asterisk (or
"accent") in its lexical representation, whereas in Khalkha line 1 asterisks
are supplied to long or closed syllables by rule (40a). The basic principle of
stress distribution in Indo-European words is that stress surfaces on the
first (leftmost) accented morpheme or, in the absence of accented morphemes, on the first syllable. This distribution of stress can be obtained
with the rules in (40).[9]

Among the languages that continue the Indo-European stress pattern
basically unchanged are Sanskrit and modern Russian. The languages
differ, however, with regard to the effects that deletion has on stress
placement. As we have shown in (58) and (59) of chapter 1, in Russian
deletion causes stress to move toward the beginning of the word, whereas
in Sanskrit stress moves toward the end of the word when the syllable
becomes incapable of bearing stress. Formally, this means that Sanskrit is
subject to (40b), whereas Russian is subject to (47).[10]

We may finally explore what would happen if a system like (40) had
bounded rather than unbounded constituents on line 0. Since bounded
constituent boundaries are invariably constructed by rule, no constituent

---

9. D. Steriade (personal communication) notes that the development of initial stress
in many Indo-European languages (for instance, early Latin, West Slavic) suggests
that these languages systematically eliminated stress (that is, line 1 asterisks) in
their lexical representations. If the Indo-European stress rules are maintained
intact, they would assign initial stress to all words. That all the rules should survive
intact for any length of time under such circumstances is unlikely. Since there would
be no occasion for rules (40b,c) to be applied, these rules would never be learned
by speakers of generations born subsequent to the elimination of lexical stress.
10. We unfortunately do not possess any evidence other than the different behavior
under deletion for this difference between Russian and Sanskrit.

could appear on line 0 in such a case. It is significant, therefore, that in languages with stress systems such as those of Sanskrit or Russian, line 0 constituents are never binary.

We conclude this section by contrasting our treatment of the Khalkha Mongolian/Aguacatec Mayan type of stress pattern with the treatment given in the Hayes/Hammond framework. In that framework these stress patterns are formally expressed by recourse to a special constituent type, called obligatory branching. In obligatory branching constituents the head must dominate a branching rime; if no branching rime is to be found in the word, no constituent is constructed.[11] To capture the Khalkha/Mayan stress pattern, Hayes proposes that on the foot level—the equivalent of our line 0—obligatory branching constituents are constructed, whereas on the word level—the equivalent of our line 1—a quantity-insensitive un-bounded constituent is constructed. If the word contains branching rimes —or their "honorary" equivalents, that is, rimes supplied with the diacritic feature [+H]—then the element heading the leftmost (resp. rightmost) foot will be designated the head of the word. On the other hand, if the word contains no branching rime, no feet will be constructed. "Thus, the only metrical structure that is created is the word tree..." (Hayes 1980/1, 64).

Since this derivation is quite similar to the one described in the first part of this section, it might appear that the two frameworks are notational variants of one another. But in spite of the similarity of the derivations, there is a fundamental difference between the types of theoretical machinery employed in the two cases. Our procedure does not require adding any new theoretical machinery and instead exploits the consequences of omitting the rule of Constituent Construction. By contrast, the Hayes/ Hammond solution depends crucially on the introduction of a new type of constituent, one that obeys the condition that its head must dominate a branching rime. The primary objection to introducing this type of condition into the theory is its arbitrariness. If we may require that constituent heads dominate branching rimes, what prevents us from imposing the same or a similar condition on nonheads, as proposed by both Hayes (1980/1) and Hammond (1986)? In the framework advocated here, conditions can-not be imposed on nonheads at all, and conditions can be imposed on heads only indirectly—that is, by labeling certain elements in a string as heads, which is the equivalent of Hayes's diacritic feature [+H]. The absence of these options in our framework does not affect its empirical coverage; in the

---

11. We disregard for the moment whether or not in obligatory branching con-stituents the nonheads should be required to dominate only nonbranching rimes.

numerous cases that we have had an opportunity to examine, the solutions provided within our framework must be valued at least as highly as those provided by others that have been proposed. This is well illustrated by a brief examination of the Klamath stress pattern.

2.4.2 The Stress Pattern of Klamath

The facts of stress in Klamath are summarized by Hammond (1986, 219) as follows.[12]

(48)

a. The rightmost long vowel receives primary stress.

b. Otherwise, stress a closed penult.

c. Otherwise, stress the antepenult if there is one.

d. Otherwise, stress the penult.

The Klamath stress pattern is in some respects similar to that of foreign loans in Turkish, for in both cases stress is assigned to the penult except in clearly defined classes of forms. We shall therefore postulate the system of rules in (49).

(49)

a. Mark a word-final short syllable extrametrical.

b. Assign a line 1 asterisk to long vowels.

c. Line 0 parameter settings are: [+HT, −BND, right].

d. Line 1 parameter settings are [+HT, −BND, right].

e. Construct constituent boundaries on line 1.

f. Locate the heads of line 1 constituents on line 2.

g. Conflate lines 1 and 2.

h. Delete line 0 asterisk on the penultimate syllable if its rime is non-branching and the word has at least three syllables.[13]

---

12. We disregard secondary stresses here because these are not established with sufficient reliability in our primary sources of information on Klamath (Barker 1963, 1964).

13. The context for the deletion rule (49h) will be characterized by means of a mechanism similar to that introduced for Tiberian Hebrew in section 2.3.3. Specifically, we would posit an independent reduction plane in which all syllables with a branching rime are accented and in which bounded left-headed constituents are constructed from right to left. A line 0 asterisk on the stress plane is deleted whenever it corresponds to a governed position on the reduction plane.

Rule (49a) renders the word-final syllable invisible to the stress rules. As a result, Klamath stress assignment becomes essentially identical to that of Aguacatec Mayan, where stress falls on the rightmost long vowel, if there is one, and otherwise on the last vowel. Rules (49b–g) then place stress on the rightmost long vowel, if there is one, and otherwise on the penult. Thus, stress is assigned correctly in all cases except (48c). These cases are handled by rule (49h), which renders a penultimate nonbranching rime non-stress-bearing. If the penult is unstressed, the rule will apply vacuously. If, on the other hand, the penult has received stress by rules (49b–g), the application of (49h) will have the effect of shifting stress to the left since by virtue of (49d) the syllable that has become non-stress-bearing is the head of a right-headed constituent.

This account should be compared to the one offered by Hammond (1986). As noted, Hammond's account crucially depends on allowing rules that construct metrical constituents to have direct access to the internal structure of syllables. In spite of this additional power of the rules, Hammond must devote seven printed pages (pp. 219–226) to accounting for the Klamath data discussed above in about a page.

Theories such as that of Hayes and Hammond, which admit a category of constituents with obligatory branching heads, also predict stress patterns that have never been encountered. For instance, their theory predicts the stress distributions in (50) with the help of the relatively simple set of rules in (51).[14]

(50)

a. Heavy syllables are stressed.

b. Stress falls in addition on odd-numbered light syllables, where the numbering of the syllable in a word is established by counting from left to right but *omitting in the count every light syllable immediately preceding a heavy syllable.*

(51)

a. Construct right-headed binary obligatory-branching feet.

b. On the next higher layer construct left-headed binary feet from left to right.

We illustrate this in (52).

---

14. We are grateful to D. Steriade for drawing our attention to this example.

(52)

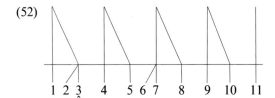

Clearly, stress distributions such as those in (50) are highly implausible, and the fact that they are readily expressed in terms of the Hayes/Hammond framework must be taken as an indication that the framework is flawed.

Chapter 3
Stress and the Cycle

3.1 Cyclic and Noncyclic Affixes

All examples studied in chapter 1 were instances of noncyclic stress placement. In this chapter we examine cases where stress is assigned cyclically. In attempting to deal with cyclic stress assignment, we have been much influenced by the ideas of Pesetsky (1979), Kiparsky (1982a, 1983, 1984, 1985), Mohanan (1982), Halle and Mohanan (1985), and other workers on what has become known as Lexical Phonology, as well as by such critics of this approach as Aronoff and Sridhar (1983) and Sproat (1985). We adopt from Lexical Phonology the organization of phonological rules into a number of blocks called *strata* and allow a given rule to be assigned to more than one stratum (Mohanan 1982; Halle and Mohanan 1985). We also follow Lexical Phonology in distinguishing *lexical* from *postlexical* strata, but we see this distinction in the light of the interpretation proposed by Sproat as being one between phonological processes that are word-internal and processes that are not limited to the word but apply freely to word sequences as well. We therefore speak not of *lexical* and *nonlexical* strata but of *word-internal* and *word-sequence* strata. Ordered before the first word-internal rule stratum is the allomorphy component, a block of rules concerned with the shape of individual morphemes in specific morphological contexts. For example, the different inflected forms of the English "strong" verbs are determined by rules of the allomorphy component.

In figure 3.1 we illustrate this view of the organization of the phonology. Since most of the facts we deal with in this book concern word-internal processes, we assume that unless otherwise indicated, the rules we discuss belong to strata 2 and 3.

As indicated in figure 3.1, strata are stipulated as being *cyclic* or *noncyclic*. What primarily differentiates cyclic from noncyclic strata is the manner in which the rules in a stratum take account of the morphological

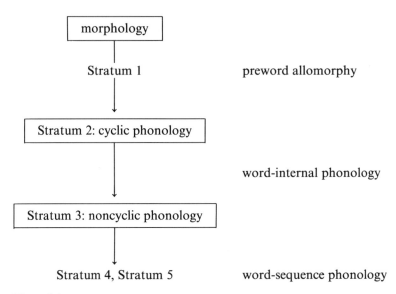

Figure 3.1

composition of the string. As noted by Halle and Mohanan (1985), in a cyclic stratum "the relevant phonological rules apply to every morphological constituent in the stratum—to the basic stem ... as well as to every constituent created by morphological processes" (p. 66), whereas in a noncyclic stratum "phonological rules ... apply ... only *after* all morphological processes" (p. 67). Moreover, *Strict Cyclicity* governs the application of rules in cyclic strata but not elsewhere.[1]

We deviate from most proponents of Lexical Phonology in that, following Sproat (1985), we do not assign the rules of morphology—prefixation, suffixation, reduplication, compounding, and so on—to particular phonological strata. Instead, we make the traditional assumption that these rules are the province of a special module, the *morphology*. In our theory, then, as in *SPE*, morphology is distinct and separate from phonology. Morphology interacts with phonology in that it creates the objects on which the rules of phonology operate. We have represented stress on a separate plane from the rest of the phonological structure. It has been proposed elsewhere that other properties of morphemes, such as tone (Goldsmith 1976) and syllable structure (Halle 1985), are also to be represented on separate

1. For a detailed discussion of strict cyclicity, see Mascaró (1978) and Kiparsky (1984) and literature cited there.

planes. A morpheme thus will in general be represented by a family of planes intersecting in a central line. Given this formalization, the combination of morphemes into words will involve a combination of planes.

McCarthy (1986) has proposed that the separate autosegmental planes of Semitic morphology are the result of the fact that distinct morphemes must be represented on separate planes as in (1).

(1)

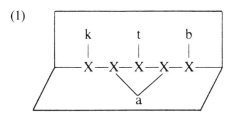

We propose to extend this idea to concatenative morphology as well. A sequence of morphemes will then be represented as in (2), where each plane stands for the entire family of planes associated with the particular morpheme.

(2)

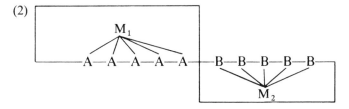

We assume further that not all morphemes give rise to independent planes (families of planes). Morphemes of a certain class—to be detailed directly below—do not give rise to independent planes, as shown in (3).

(3)

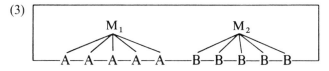

It has been observed that in many languages affixes fall into two major classes with regard to their interaction with the rules of phonology. Thus, Kiparsky (1982b) has shown that the suffixes of Vedic Sanskrit must be categorized as *dominant* or *recessive* in order to account for their stress behavior. Similarly, Siegel (1974) and Allen (1978) have shown that in English a distinction must be made between stress-sensitive suffixes such as

-ity, -al, -ous and stress-neutral suffixes such as *-ness, -hood, -ly*. Halle and Mohanan (1985) have argued that these distinctions in both Sanskrit and English correspond to the distinction between cyclic and noncyclic affixation. In English, for instance, a cyclic rule such as Trisyllabic Shortening, which is subject to Strict Cyclicity (which prevents the rule from applying to such underived forms as *ivory, dynamo, apricot*), is triggered only by the stress-sensitive suffixes (such as *-ity* in *divinity*) but not by stress-neutral suffixes (such as *-hood, -ly* in *maidenhood, miserly*).[2] We propose that the distinction between cyclic and noncyclic affixation is formally reflected in the morphology by the distinction between (2) and (3); that is, cyclic morphemes are affixed on a plane (family of planes) distinct from that of the stem, whereas noncyclic morphemes are affixed on the same plane (family of planes) as the stem.

We shall assume that the rules of phonology can operate only on a single family of planes. Following the suggestion of Younes (see McCarthy 1986), we postulate that cyclic affixation is accompanied by a process that copies the content of the stem onto the plane of the affix, leaving the content of the stem plane intact and hence subsequently accessible to other rules. The cyclic copying process thus does not reduce the number of cyclic planes in the representation; it only changes the content of the plane of each cyclic affix by transcribing onto the affix plane the content (or part of the content) of the adjoining stem. (4) graphically illustrates plane copying as it might affect (3).

(4)

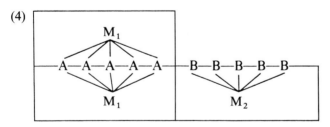

The plane on the bottom of (4) is not identical with that shown in (2), which corresponds to the plane of noncyclic affixation. In the process of plane copying not all information available in the plane to be copied is transferred. We assume in particular that the information contained in the metrical grid is not copied, except under special circumstances. The rules of the cyclic stratum then apply in the plane below the central line of

2. For some additional discussion of this shortening process, see section 7.8.2.

phonemes in (4), and the operation is repeated for each cyclic affix in turn. If a noncyclic affix is adjoined to a bare stem or to one ending (resp. beginning) with a cyclic affix, no new plane is created and the noncyclic affix is represented directly on the plane of the stem to which it is adjoined. Hence, the stem's metrical grid remains intact. The newly created sequence is not subject to the rules of the cyclic stratum—or, for that matter, to the rules of the noncyclic stratum—unless the affix happens to be the outermost constituent of the word. Thus, the rules of the noncyclic stratum are applied only once in the derivation of a word, at the very end.

We illustrate the preceding with the derivation of the stress contour of the English noun *ungrammaticality*, to which—pace Pesetsky (1985)—we attribute the traditional constituent structure (5).

(5) $[[\text{un-}[\text{grammat}+\text{ic}+\text{al}]_A]_A+\text{ity}]_N$

We postulate that the prefix *un-* is noncyclic whereas the suffixes *-ic*, *-al*, and *-ity* are cyclic and, moreover, that the Main Stress Rule of English is in the cyclic stratum. (For details, see chapter 7.) The Main Stress Rule of English will therefore assign antepenultimate stress to the adjective *grammatical*.[3] In the next cycle the noncyclic prefix *un-* is brought into the purview of the phonological rules. Since the prefix is noncyclic, the stress assigned on earlier cycles is preserved, but at the same time we cannot apply the rules of the cyclic stratum. Nor can we apply the rules of the noncyclic stratum, since these only apply when the outermost constituent of the word has been reached. On the next and final pass through the cycle the entire word is considered. Since *-ity* is a cyclic suffix, previously assigned stresses are wiped out and the cyclic Main Stress Rule assigns stress to the antepenultimate syllable. Subsequently the string with main stress in place is submitted to the rules of the noncyclic stratum, which distribute the subsidiary stresses and affect the string in various ways that are not relevant to the matter at hand. The point of this demonstration is that given the conventions developed above on the application of cyclic and noncyclic rules, stress is correctly assigned to words like *ungrammaticality* without leading to "bracketing" paradoxes of the kind that have been encountered in other theoretical frameworks (see Pesetsky 1979, 1985; Kiparsky 1983).

The analysis just presented carries over to the other major class of "bracketing paradox" discussed by Pesetsky (1979), that of the so-called

---

3. Since, as shown below, each cyclic affix eliminates the stresses assigned on earlier passes through the cyclic stress rules, we need not consider here the effects of earlier passes through the cyclic stratum.

yer rules of Russian. Like all Slavic languages, Russian includes a pair of vowels, traditionally called *yers*, which surface as /e/ or /o/ when followed by another yer and are deleted elsewhere.[4] What is especially intriguing about these "abstract" vowels is that their surface manifestation is heavily influenced by the morphology of the word in which they appear. A standard example of this influence is found in prefixes, illustrated in (6) with the masc.sg. and fem.sg. past tense forms of the prefixed verb meaning 'burn'. (*Y* represents both yers of Russian.)

(6) $[[[sY + [žYg]] + l] + Y]$ → s + žog
   $[[[sY + [žYg]] + l] + a]$ → so + žg + l + a

The forms consist of the prefix /sY/, the verb root /žYg/, the past marker /l/, and the gender/number suffix /Y/ (masc.sg.) or /a/ (fem.sg.). We shall assume that in Russian unstressed prefixes are noncyclic and suffixes cyclic. Like Pesetsky, we follow Lightner (1972) in postulating a "lowering" rule that turns yers into /e/ or /o/, and a separate rule that deletes yers. We deviate from Pesetsky in that we assign the "lowering" rule both to the cyclic and to the noncyclic strata, whereas the rule deleting yers is assigned to the noncyclic stratum. Finally, we assume that all words have the expected left-branching constituent structure indicated in (6); hence, there is no "bracketing paradox." On the innermost root cycle the "lowering" rule cannot apply since the root yer is not followed by a yer in the next syllable. On the next cycle the constituent [sY + žYg] is operated on. Although the constituent satisfies the "lowering" rule, the rule cannot be applied since in Russian prefixes are noncyclic; that is, they generate constituents to which a rule of the cyclic stratum cannot apply. The noncyclic "lowering" rule cannot apply here either, since we have not yet reached the outermost constituent of the word. Nothing of interest transpires in the next cycle, where the past tense marker /l/ is added to the string under consideration.

In the final pass through the cyclic stratum we analyze the strings [sY + žYg + l + Y] and [sY + žYg + l + a]. The former contains two yers that are followed by a yer and hence subject to the "lowering" rule. The rule cannot apply to the substring [sY + žYg ..., however, because Strict Cyclicity prohibits a cyclic rule from applying to a string that was already present on the preceding cycle. Hence, the "lowering" rule can apply only to the substring ... žYg + l + Y]. This will yield the output

---

4. The best treatment of the yer problem known to us is that of Kenstowicz and Rubach (1986).

[sY + žog + l + Y]. The situation is somewhat different in the case of the feminine form [sY + žYg + l + a]. Here too Strict Cyclicity prevents the cyclic "lowering" rule from applying to the substring [sY + žYg. . . . Hence, the form enters the noncyclic stratum essentially unchanged: [sY + žYg + l + a]. The "lowering" rule, which is also assigned to the noncyclic stratum, can apply to the string [sY + žYg + l + a] yielding [so + žYg + l + a], from which the correct output string is readily derived. The noncyclic "lowering" rule does not apply to the string [sY + žog + l + Y] because the string does not meet the structural description of the rule. The string is then subject to yer deletion, which yields the correct output.

We have thus shown that the correct outputs can be derived without any assumptions about "bracketing" paradoxes, provided that the morphological operations of affixation are not made an integral subpart of the different phonological strata. We therefore take the above facts to be evidence against the standard version of Lexical Phonology, where each rule stratum includes a set of affixation rules.

We have assumed that stresses generated on earlier passes through the cyclic rules are not transferred to the plane of a cyclic affix. However, this is not always the case. Instead, stress erasure applies only when the affix itself is not a domain for the stress rules; when the affixed substring itself undergoes the cyclic stress rules, no stress erasure takes place. This is why stress erasure is not found in compound words despite the fact that compound words are clearly cyclic constituents. Though most common affixes in English are not domains for the stress rules, English has a number of suffixes, such as -oid, -ode in *molluscoid, electrode*, that constitute stress domains. We shall show in section 3.2.2 that all affixes in Diyari constitute domains for the stress rules.

We incorporate the preceding observations formally into our framework by means of the convention (7).

(7) *Stress Erasure Convention*
    In the input to the rules of cyclic strata information about stress generated on previous passes through the cyclic rules is carried over only if the affixed constituent is itself a domain for the cyclic stress rules. If the affixed constituent is not a domain for the cyclic stress rules, information about stresses assigned on previous passes is erased.

We shall argue in section 3.3.2 that when stresses assigned on earlier passes through the cyclic stress rules appear in the output in forms with cyclic affixes that are not domains for stress rules, as they do in certain well-known cases in English, this is due to a special rule that copies asterisks from one stress plane onto another.

Since a noncyclic affix is represented on the same plane as the stem to which it is adjoined, none of the phenomena accompanying cyclic affixation are observed there. In particular, in the case of noncyclic affixation the metrical grid of the stem generated by the cyclic stress rules is preserved intact and serves as input to the stress rules of the noncyclic stratum.

3.2 Consequences of the Stress Erasure Convention

3.2.1 Stress in Vedic and Lithuanian

Vedic stress has been analyzed in an important paper by Kiparsky (1982b), which was also discussed by Halle and Mohanan (1985). Kiparsky and Halle (1977) have shown that in Vedic—as in a number of other languages, both Indo-European and non-Indo-European—the location of word stress is governed by the Basic Accentuation Principle (BAP).

(8) *Basic Accentuation Principle*
Stress the leftmost accented vowel or, in the absence of accented vowels, the leftmost vowel.

We showed in section 2.4 that this stress pattern is accounted for by the set of rules in (9).

(9)
a. Line 0 parameter settings are [+HT, −BND, left].

b. Line 1 parameter settings are [+HT, −BND, left].

c. Construct constituent boundaries on line 1.

d. Locate the heads of line 1 constituents on line 2.

e. Conflate lines 1 and 2.

Kiparsky drew attention to the fact that from the viewpoint of stress assignment the suffixes of Vedic must be divided into two classes: recessive and dominant. We illustrated in section 2.4 how the rules given in (9) apply in words that contain only recessive suffixes. In Vedic and in other languages that continue the stress system of the Indo-European proto-language, stress is distinctive: morphemes may or may not be accented—supplied with line 1 asterisks—in their underlying representations. In words containing no dominant suffixes the rule set (9) then places main stress on the leftmost syllable with a lexically assigned line 1 asterisk. Stress assignment is somewhat less transparent in the case of words that contain dominant suffixes. In such words the last dominant suffix determines the surface stress. In particular, if the last dominant suffix is underlyingly accented (has a line 1 asterisk in its underlying representation), the surface stress is located on this suffix; if the last dominant suffix lacks a line 1 asterisk in its underlying representation, the surface stress is invariably located on the initial syllable. Thus, in Vedic words formed with the underlyingly accented dominant suffix *-in-* stress falls on the suffix both when the stem is accented and when it is not. We illustrate this in (10), where the stem *rath* but not *mitr* is accented, but this difference in underlying representation does not result in a difference in surface stress: in both words surface stress appears on the underlyingly accented dominant suffix *-in*.

(10) rath + íṇ + e   'charioteer' (dat.sg.)
      mitr + íṇ + e   'befriended' (dat.sg.)

In words where the last dominant suffix is underlyingly unaccented (without a line 1 asterisk), stress falls on the initial syllable regardless of the inherent accentual properties of the morphemes that follow it. We illustrate this in (11), where the stem ending with the last dominant suffix is enclosed in parentheses.

(11)
a. (sár + as) + vat + i + vant   'accompanied by Sarasvati'
b. (práti + cyav + iyas) + i   'more compressed'
c. (cí + kar + ay + iṣa) + ti   'wants to cause to make'

(11a,b) contain only a single dominant suffix, which is underlyingly unaccented. This is self-evident for (11a) and becomes self-evident for (11b) as soon as it is realized that *prati* is a prefix and *cyav* is the verb stem.[5] In (11c) the stem *kar* is followed by two dominant suffixes, of which the first is underlyingly accented and the second is not. Since the last dominant suffix is underlyingly unaccented, the surface stress appears on the first syllable.

  Halle and Mohanan (1985) have suggested that in order to capture these facts formally it must be assumed that dominant suffixes are cyclic, whereas

---

5. The adjective *práticyaviyasi* has fixed stress on the initial syllable in all case forms including forms such as the gen.pl. where the case ending is inherently accented. This fact indicates that the prefix must be in a constituent internal to the last dominant suffix. It therefore constitutes counterevidence to the proposal (see, for instance, Kiparsky 1983) that prefixes in Vedic are the outermost constituent of the word.

recessive suffixes are noncyclic. In order to obtain correct outputs, Halle and Mohanan also had to postulate a rule that deletes any underlying or previously assigned stresses in position before a dominant suffix. Given the Stress Erasure Convention (7), such a rule is unnecessary. All that needs to be assumed is that Vedic has two strata of rules in its word phonology, cyclic and noncyclic, and that the stress rules in (9) are assigned to both strata. Once this assumption is made, the rule deleting previously assigned stresses can be dispensed with, because in conformity to condition (7) previously generated stresses in the stem are not carried over to the next cycle since the dominant affixes are by themselves not domains for the stress rules. By eliminating the rule of accent deletion, we imply that the peculiar stress assignment facts of Vedic are not due to an idiosyncrasy of this language but are rather consequences of Universal Grammar. If correct, this is a result of some significance.[6]

We now illustrate in some detail the workings of the theoretical framework outlined above. Consider first the simplest cases, where an underlyingly accented stem is followed by a single dominant suffix that is also underlyingly accented. Since dominant suffixes are cyclic, two metrical planes will be generated, one containing the stem alone and one containing nothing but the suffix. The application of the cyclic stress rules is subject to the principle of Strict Cyclicity. Since stress is distinctive in Vedic—that is, a Vedic morpheme may or may not have stress in its underlying representation—Strict Cyclicity prevents the stress rules (9) of the cyclic stratum from applying to underived strings, in particular, to the innermost stem of a word. At the end of the first pass through the cyclic rules the stem will therefore retain unchanged the metrical grid of its underlying representation. However, when the stem is subsequently copied onto the plane of the first cyclic (dominant) suffix, asterisks above line 0 will not be copied. As a result, the contrast between underlyingly accented and unaccented stems is neutralized before dominant suffixes. A word consisting

---

6. There are additional differences between the theory developed here and that of Halle and Mohanan. Suppose, for example, that in addition to accented cyclic (dominant) suffixes, Sanskrit also had accented cyclic prefixes. If such a prefix were adjoined to an accented stem, Halle and Mohanan's theory predicts that the prefix would lose its accent, whereas the present theory predicts instead that the element that would lose its accent is the stem. (This consequence was pointed out to us by B. Hermans.) Unfortunately we have been unable to find relevant examples in Vedic.

of a stem followed by an accented dominant suffix will therefore appear at the beginning of the second cycle in the form (12).

(12)

In (12) S represents a bisyllabic stem and D a monosyllabic dominant suffix that is underlyingly accented (as shown by the asterisk on line 1). It is obvious that the stress rules in (9) will assign main stress to the dominant suffix. The subsequent reapplication of the stress rules in (9) in the noncyclic stratum will be vacuous; it will effect no changes in the metrical grid.

The example in (12) should be compared with the treatment of the minimally different string (13) consisting of an accented stem followed by an accented recessive suffix. Once again Strict Cyclicity prevents the stress rules in (9) from applying to the stem on the cyclic stratum, for this is a nonderived environment and stress in Vedic is distinctive. Since the string contains no dominant suffixes, no cyclic metrical planes are generated; instead, the recessive suffix is represented directly on the plane of the stem, and the input to the stress rules of the noncyclic stratum is of the form (13).

(13)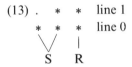

The stress rules in (9) place main stress on the second stem syllable. If these rules had not been assigned to the noncyclic stratum, we would have no way of assigning main stress in (13). The examples just discussed therefore show that in Vedic the stress rules in (9) must be assigned both to the cyclic stratum and to the noncyclic stratum.

Consider now the case where more than one dominant suffix is adjoined to the stem. Since each cyclic affix creates a stress plane of its own and since stresses generated on earlier planes are not carried over to later planes, the accentual properties of dominant suffixes other than the rightmost are irrelevant for the location of stress in Vedic words. Here again stress falls on the last dominant suffix if it is underlyingly accented, and on the word-initial syllable if that suffix is not underlyingly accented, because the only two possible input strings on the outermost cyclic constituent are those in (14a) and (14b).

(14)

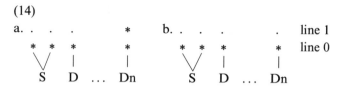

In (14a) the cyclic stress rules in (9) will assign stress to the syllable dominated by Dn; in (14b) they will assign stress to the word-initial syllable.

As noted previously, recessive (noncyclic) suffixes do not create new metrical planes but are represented on the same stress plane as the constituent containing the last cyclic suffix. Since in Sanskrit the recessive suffixes invariably follow the dominant suffixes and since the rules in (9) assign stress to the leftmost accented syllable, the accentual properties of the recessive suffixes can have no effect on the location of stress in words also containing dominant (cyclic) suffixes. In such words the noncyclic application of the rules in (9) will vacuously assign stress to the syllable on which stress was placed on the last cyclic pass through the stress rules. The conflation rule (9e) eliminates the line 1 asterisks present in the lexical representation of inherently accented recessive suffixes.

There is an interesting difference between the stress pattern of Vedic and that of Lithuanian, another Indo-European language that, like Vedic, is known to have preserved important aspects of the stress system of the Indo-European protolanguage. Lithuanian stress is governed essentially by the same set of stress rules as Vedic; in fact, the similarities between Vedic and Lithuanian stress are so great that for purposes of the present discussion we shall assume that the rules in (9) are valid for both languages. (For additional details on Lithuanian stress, see section 6.2.1)

It is traditional to distinguish four accentual classes in the Lithuanian nominal declension. As detailed in chapter 6, the stems of nouns in classes I and II have an underlying accent, whereas the stems of nouns in classes III and IV are underlyingly unaccented. Except for the effects of Saussure's Law, which are accounted for by a rule of the noncyclic stratum ordered after the stress rules (for details, see section 6.2.1), the distinction between classes I and II, on the one hand, and III and IV, on the other, plays no role in stress placement. As expected, in nouns of classes I and II stress surfaces on the stem, whereas in nouns of classes III and IV stress surfaces on the case ending if the latter is inherently accented and on the initial syllable if the case ending is unaccented. Like Vedic, Lithuanian has both dominant and recessive suffixes, and as far as words without dominant suffixes are concerned, the two languages behave identically; that is, stress falls on the leftmost syllable with a lexically assigned line 1 asterisk or, in words without such asterisks, on the leftmost syllable. As expected, Lithuanian dominant suffixes, like those of Vedic, eliminate contrasts in the previously assigned stress of the stems to which they attach. As shown in (15), when the dominant suffix is underlyingly accented, surface stress is located on the dominant suffix without regard to the stress of the following recessive suffixes. The derived nouns therefore all belong to the accentual class I.

(15) eln + íen + a   I   'venison'   cf. éln + ias   I   'stag'
     kišk + íen + a   I   'rabbit meat' cf. kìšk + is   II   'rabbit'
     ož + íen + a   I   'goat meat'   cf. ož + ỹs   III   'goat'
     vilk + íen + a   I   'wolf meat'   cf. vil̃k + as   IV   'wolf'

In (16) we give forms of words derived from the same roots as those in (15). The suffix -en- is also a dominant suffix, as shown by the fact that nouns derived with this suffix exhibit no effects in their stress pattern that might be attributed to the accentual class of the stem. As illustrated in (16), words derived with this suffix differ from those in (15) in that if the following recessive suffix is underlyingly unaccented, the word stress falls on the initial syllable, whereas if the following recessive suffix is underlyingly accented, the surface stress falls on the recessive suffix.[7]

(16) Dat.Sg.   Nom.Sg.
     éln + en + ai   eln + en + à   'deer skin'
     kìšk + en + ai   kišk + en + à   'rabbit skin'
     óž + en + ai   ož + en + à   'goat skin'
     vil̃k + en + ai   vilk + en + à   'wolf skin'

There is no counterpart to (16) in Vedic. In Vedic, unaccented dominant suffixes invariably result in words with fixed stress on the initial syllable.

In sum, in both Vedic and Lithuanian, if the dominant suffix is underlyingly accented, the surface stress falls on the suffix. In Vedic, if the dominant suffix is underlyingly unaccented, the surface stress invariably falls on the word-initial syllable. By contrast, in Lithuanian, if the dominant suffix is underlyingly unaccented, surface stress falls on the word-initial syllable only if the recessive suffix(es) following are also underlyingly unaccented. If one or more of the following recessive suffixes

---

7. Lithuanian case suffixes are recessive (noncyclic): the fem.dat.sg. is unaccented, the fem.nom.sg. is accented.

are underlyingly accented, the surface stress falls on the leftmost of these, rather than on the word-initial syllable.

We can readily account for this difference between Vedic and Lithuanian, if we assume that in Lithuanian the stress rules are assigned only to the noncyclic stratum, whereas in Vedic the stress rules must be assigned both to the cyclic stratum and to the noncyclic stratum. Given the Stress Erasure Convention (7), the fact that a suffix is cyclic suffices to ensure that all stresses—all asterisks above line 0—of the stem will be eliminated. Since in Vedic the stress rules are assigned to the cyclic stratum, they will—on the last pass through the cycle—place stress either on the (dominant) suffix or on the word-initial syllable. The subsequent application of the stress rules assigned to the noncyclic stratum will be vacuous: it cannot change the location of the stress because the stress rules in (9) assign main stress to the leftmost syllable with a line 1 asterisk, and recessive suffixes in Vedic are added after (to the right of) all dominant suffixes. In Lithuanian, where the stress rules are assigned only to the noncyclic stratum, stress will be placed in accordance with the rules of (9) on the last dominant suffix if it is underlyingly accented (as in (15)). If the dominant suffix is underlyingly unaccented and there are other suffixes in the word with underlying accent, stress will be placed on the leftmost of these (as in the right column in (16)). Finally, if the dominant suffix is underlyingly unaccented and there are no other underlyingly accented morphemes in the word, surface stress will be initial (as in the left column in (16)).

3.2.2 Stress in Dakota and Diyari

The Stress Erasure Convention (7) was restricted to rules assigned to the cyclic stratum in the word-internal rule block. The stress facts of Dakota and Diyari appear at first sight to demand additional restrictions. In fact, however, none is required; the facts can be accounted for with the machinery standardly available.

In Dakota, stress is generally placed on the second syllable of the word (Shaw 1985). There are, however, three types of exception.

(17) Stress falls on the first syllable
    a. in monosyllabic words
       zí 'yellow'

    b. before certain suffixes the so-called postnominal and postverbal clitics
       ʔú-pi-kte-šni 'they are not going to use' (use-Pl-Fut-Neg)
       cf. *o-wičha-ya-kte* 'you kill them there' (Loc-them-you-kill)

c. in syntactic compounds whose first member is monosyllabic
mní-wa-xčà-xča 'water flower' (water-[Nom-to blossom-Redup])
cf. *mni-wá-xča-xča* 'water lily' (water-Nom-to blossom-Redup)

(17a) poses no special problem: we expect a rule assigning stress to the
second syllable to assign stress to the only syllable in monosyllabic words.
The pattern in (17b) is accounted for if we assume that the Dakota stress
rule is cyclic and that these clitics are noncyclic suffixes.

To account for the examples in (17c), we must note that Dakota has two
kinds of compounds: "syntactic" and "lexical." The word glossed 'water
flower' is a syntactic compound, whereas 'water lily' is a lexical compound.
The main phonological difference between lexical and syntactic compounds is that lexical compounds are stressed on the second syllable like
other, noncompound words of the language. In syntactic compounds, on
the other hand, each word has its own stress. Thus, *mni* in 'water flower',
being monosyllabic, is stressed on its only syllable, whereas the trisyllabic
wa-xča-xča has stress on its second syllable.

The syntactic compounds present no problem: they are instances of
compounding, where stress erasure does not take place since the affixed
morpheme is a domain of the stress rules. The problem is the lexical
compounds. It is to be noted that stress will be placed correctly on the
second syllable of the lexical compound *mniwaxcaxca* if either *mni* or
waxcaxca is a cyclic affix. The constituent will then not be the domain for
the stress rules and will also wipe out the stress placed on the other
constituent on previous passes through the cyclic rules. Hence the last
pass through the cyclic rules will assign stress to the second syllable of
mniwaxcaxca.

This assumption seems to be implicit also in Shaw's representation of
the lexical compound, reproduced in (17c), as a sequence of morphemes
without internal constituent structure. But if words can thus be "demoted"
to the rank of affixes, then the morphology must include a rule or other
device capable of implementing this "demotion." The existence of such a
device in the morphology of a language is made plausible by the contrasting
stress patterns of the English words in (18).

(18)
a. garbage man   front man   Kennedy man   garage man
b. infantryman   salesman   outdoorsman   postman
   doorman

The forms in (18a) are ordinary compounds with the falling stress contour typical of such words in English. The forms in (18b), on the other hand, are compounds whose second constituent is treated not as a full word but as an affix. This is shown by the fact that *man* surfaces without stress. The examples in (18b) are the English counterparts of the lexical compounds of Dakota; in both languages stems and words are demoted to the status of affixes. The only difference between the Dakota compounds and those of English is that in Dakota the demoted morphemes are treated as cyclic affixes whereas in English they are treated as noncyclic affixes.

The Dakota facts can thus readily be dealt with by the machinery developed here, provided that the morphology is assumed to include a device that in particular contexts can turn words or stems into affixes that are not domains for the stress rules.

We have noted that in the neutral case affixes are not by themselves domains for stress rules. The facts to be examined next suggest that this is not true everywhere: there are languages where in addition to stems and words, affixes regularly constitute domains for the stress rules.

Poser (1986) has examined stress distribution in the words of Diyari, a language of southern Australia. The basic stress rule of this language assigns stress to each odd-numbered syllable of the word, with main stress falling on the first syllable. Word-final syllables are universally stressless even if they are odd-numbered. We shall assume with Poser that this is accounted for by a rule deleting stress in nonbranching metrical constituents (feet). The relevant problem arises with respect to the examples in (19).

(19)

a. púluri-ni   'mud-Loc'

b. máda-la-ntu   'hill-Characteristic-Proprietive'

c. púluru-ni-màta   'mud-Loc-Ident'

d. pínadu-wàra   'old man-Pl'

e. nánda-na-màta   'hit-Participle-Ident'

f. kána-na-màta   'man-Loc-Ident'

g. yákalka-yìrpa-màli-na 'ask-Ben-Recip-Participle'

As Poser notes, these patterns "may be succinctly described. Each morpheme in Diyari is stressed separately [on its odd-numbered syllables]" (p. 1). The noncyclic stratum then includes a rule assigning main stress to the initial syllable and another rule deleting secondary stresses on nonbranching (monosyllabic) metrical constituents.

We can account for the Diyari facts by assuming that the rule placing stress on odd-numbered syllables treats each morpheme as a stress domain. The fact that a cyclic affix constitutes an independent domain for the assignment of stress in turn entails that it carries over intact stresses generated on previous passes through the stress rules (see condition (7)).

Poser considers this solution but rejects it on the grounds that "the theory permits cycles to be initiated only by stems, not by arbitrary morphemes" (p. 9). To deal with the Diyari facts, he postulates that in Diyari "metrical structure construction is cyclic and that feet once constructed may not be modified by subsequent applications of the foot construction rule" (p. 4). He notes that "the literature contains cases in which stress rules apparently modify existing structure" and concludes from this that "there can be no hard and fast principle to the effect that metrical structure construction rules never modify existing structure" (p. 6). Hence, "whether or not a stress rule modifies existing structure is to some extent an idiosyncratic property of that rule." This conclusion does not differ radically from the one we have arrived at above. The two solutions differ in the implementation of the insight that previously assigned metrical structure may or may not be modified by later rules. Whereas Poser considers this an idiosyncratic property of each stress rule, we believe it is correlated with the somewhat more general property of whether or not a morpheme adjoined to a stem is itself a domain for the stress rules.

The preceding discussion brings out the fact that the property of being a stress domain is not necessarily coextensive with that of being a word. In a language like Diyari affixes turn out to be stress domains, whereas in a language like Dakota or English certain words may cease to be stress domains, as illustrated in (17c) and (18b), respectively.

3.3 Exceptions to Stress Erasure

We have argued that cyclic affixes obliterate stresses assigned on earlier passes through the cyclic rules. In this and the following section we deal with certain apparent exceptions to the Stress Erasure Convention (7).

3.3.1 Main Stress in Spanish
Spanish includes a rule of diphthongization that applies to certain stressed mid vowels (see Harris 1969), as shown by the alternations in (20).

(20) pensámos   (1pl.)   piénso   (1sg.)   'think'
      venímos   (1pl.)   viéne   (3sg.)   'come'
      soltámos   (1pl.)   suélto   (1sg.)   'release'
      olémos   (1pl.)   huéle   (3sg.)   'smell'

However, Spanish also includes forms such as those in (21), where the vowel is diphthongized even though unstressed.

(21) buenísimo   'very good'
      pueblíto   'little town'
      adiestrár   'to train (as in a craft or skill)'

To account for such forms Harris, (1969, 125–126) postulates that the rule of main stress assignment applies cyclically. Vowels with cyclically assigned stress undergo diphthongization. Harris notes, however, that the stresses assigned before the last cycle do not surface. To account for this fact, he posits a rule that deletes all but the rightmost primary stress (p. 95). Such a rule is unnecessary within our framework. Once the assumption is made that the Spanish stress rule is assigned to the cyclic stratum, it follows automatically from condition (7) that stresses generated on previous cycles do not surface. To account for diphthongization in cases such as those in (21), we must postulate that the rule of diphthongization is also assigned to the cyclic stratum and is ordered after the rule that assigns main stress.[8]

J. Harris (personal communication) has drawn our attention to the following facts of Spanish that have direct bearing on the issue at hand. The fem.sg. definite article has two allomorphs: *la*, which occurs in the overwhelming majority of cases, and *el*, which occurs only when followed by a noun beginning with a stressed /a/.

(22)
a. la armadúra   'the weaponry'
    la avenída   'the avenue'
b. el áma   'the mistress'
    el álma   'the soul'

To account for these facts, we shall assume that Spanish has a rule replacing *la* with *el*.

(23) *la* → *el* / $_{NP}$[—— $_N$[á

We shall assume that like diphthongization, rule (23) is part of the cyclic

---

8. On the assignment of secondary stress in Spanish, see section 3.4.1.

stratum of the word phonology of Spanish. We note that although the article is a cyclic affix, it does not trigger stress erasure. We shall account for this fact by assuming that in Spanish determiners are cyclic domains and that they bear stress at the beginning of the cycle at which they are sisters of the following noun.[9] We assume that the process of cliticization adjoins the determiner to the noun on its right, rather than to the noun phrase, transforming a phrase such as $[[la][[Italia][de[Mussolini]]]]$ into $[[[la]$ $[Italia]][de[Mussolini]]]$. These determiners—in particular, the article—are destressed by a rule of the cyclic phonology.

We owe to Harris the important observation that rule (23) applies in a number of instances where the noun-initial /a/ is stressless on the surface—for example, in the diminutives of the nouns in (22b), which contrast directly with the nouns in (22a).

(24) el amíta   'the mistress'
     el almíta   'the soul'

As Harris points out, these "exceptions" become perfectly regular if the diminutive forms are assumed to have the constituent structure in (25).

(25) [[[la][am]] ita]
     [[[la][alm]] ita]

In order to generate the structures in (25), we propose that the strings under discussion undergo a special restructuring so that the article is a sister not of the noun but of the head of the noun. Since in the framework developed here the morphology is a separate component from the phonology, both cliticization and the restructuring will take place before the rules of the phonology become operative. We shall take this morphological restructuring rule to be part of the process of cliticization. The rule of the phonology have as their input the structures in (25).

It should be noted that the choice of diminutive affix, which depends on the number of syllables in the head noun, is implemented by a rule of the allomorphy stratum (see figure 3.1) that has as input the head noun without the article. This somewhat unusual accessibility of a constituent head to an adjoining affix that is not a sister of the head is encountered elsewhere. For

---

9. The fact that articles are cyclic domains is further confirmed by the behavior of the syllabification rule and of the well-known rule of "aspiration," which replaces /s/ by /h/ in rime-final position. In order for "aspiration" to affect the article in, say, *las avenidas*, it is necessary that syllabification and aspiration both be non-neutralizing cyclic rules and that the article be a cyclic domain.

instance, Pesetsky (1979) noted that the rules governing ablaut in the English strong verbs must be able to affect the head of the verb directly even when the verb is prefixed or derived, as in *understood, spoonfed*. These cases have usually been analyzed as instances of restructuring of the type illustrated in (26).

(26) [[[spoon][feed]] Past] → [[spoon][[feed] Past]]

But this is no longer necessary if heads may be accessible to nonsister morphemes. The choice of the comparative/superlative suffix of negative adjectives such as *unhappy, unlucky* will also be handled by the same device. If our proposal is correct, restructuring is not involved in any of these instances, though it is still required to generate the structures in (25).

3.3.2 The Stress Pattern of Damascene Arabic and the Rule of Stress Copy

A somewhat more complicated example of a language where the information about stress generated on earlier passes through the cycle is utilized by later rules is provided by Damascene Arabic. According to Bohas and Kouloughli (1981), in Damascene a noncyclic rule of Schwa Deletion does not apply to vowels that would have received stress during an earlier pass through the cyclic stress rules of the language. In Damascene a word has only a single surface stress, which is assigned to the final syllable if it is superheavy (see section 2.3.2); otherwise to the penult, if the latter is heavy; otherwise to the antepenult. We propose to account for this distribution of stresses, which resembles that of Latin and of Cairene Arabic, by the set of rules in (27) (see sections 2.2.2 and 2.3.2).

(27)
a. Vowels that are heads of rimes are stress-bearing.
b. Mark the last rime of the string extrametrical.
c. Assign a line 1 asterisk to the head of each branching rime.
d. Line 0 parameter settings are [+HT, +BND, left, right to left].
e. Construct constituent boundaries on line 0.
f. Locate the heads of line 0 constituents on line 1.
g. Line 1 parameter settings are [+HT, −BND, right].
h. Construct constituent boundaries on line 1.
i. Locate the heads of line 1 constituents on line 2.
j. Conflate lines 1 and 2.

If we now assume that the rules in (27) are part of the cyclic stratum, they will correctly assign the stress in Damascene words. Since stresses assigned on earlier cycles are not carried over, the surface stress will be the one assigned on the last pass through the cyclic stress rules.

Though not phonetically interpreted as stress, the asterisks assigned on earlier passes through the cycle must be available for Schwa Deletion to apply properly. Since Bohas and Kouloughli show that Schwa Deletion is noncyclic, we cannot utilize here a variant of the solution proposed above for Spanish. Instead, we postulate that Damascene Arabic is subject to the special Stress Copy rule (28).

(28) *Stress Copy*
      Copy the line 1 asterisks from the metrical planes of earlier cycles.

We assume further that this rule is assigned to the noncyclic stratum so that the asterisks it copies will appear on the metrical plane of the last pass through the cyclic stratum. Schwa Deletion can then be ordered after (28) and stated quite simply as (29).

(29) *Schwa Deletion*
      Delete a schwa without a line 1 asterisk.

This procedure yields the correct results for schwa deletion but at a cost of generating a series of unattested subsidiary stresses (line 1 asterisks). They can be readily eliminated by postulating that the line conflation rule (27j) is assigned to both the cyclic stratum and the noncyclic stratum; all other rules in (27) are assigned exclusively to the cyclic stratum. If in the noncyclic stratum (27j) is ordered after (29), the correct stress contours are readily generated.

The introduction of stress copy rules such as (28) into a phonological description constitutes a significant modification of the theory, for it provides later rules with information about earlier stages in the derivation that would otherwise not be accessible to them. We believe that the facts of Chamorro (section 6.3), Lenakel (section 6.4), and, to a somewhat lesser extent, English (section 3.5 and chapter 7) provide the required motivation for introducing limited transderivational power into the theory in this way.

3.3.3 Stress Copy and the Stress Rules of Russian
Interesting light is shed on the role of stress copy by certain aspects of Russian stress. Russian stress, like that of Vedic and Lithuanian, is governed by the BAP of Indo-European (8), which locates the word stress on the first accented syllable or, in the absence of accented syllables, on the initial syllable. Moreover, desinences—the obligatory suffixes such as case

endings and gender, number, and person markers—are invariably cyclic in Russian. We have demonstrated this with respect to the gender/number suffix of Russian past tense verbs in section 3.1, and we know of no evidence that would motivate a different treatment for the other desinences. If desinences are cyclic, they should be stress-deleting. This is not the case, however: like those of Vedic and Lithuanian, Russian desinences are never stress-deleting. In Vedic and Lithuanian we assumed that the desinences were noncyclic, but this clearly is not possible in Russian. We can account for the fact that the desinences are not stress-deleting by assuming that Russian has a stress copy rule that is assigned to the cyclic stratum. This rule will ensure that stresses assigned on the penultimate pass through the stress rules will be present in the representation to which the stress rules apply on the last pass through the cyclic stratum.

In Russian, unsuffixed stems generate paradigms in which stress alternates between the desinence and the word-initial syllable, whereas suffixed stems do not generate such paradigms with mobile stress (J. Melvold, personal communication). This demonstrates that in Russian, as in Vedic, the stress rules must be assigned to the cyclic stratum. Since the rule of Stress Copy is cyclic, we would expect that in suffixed words with inherently accented roots stress would fall on the root, whereas in suffixed words with inherently unaccented roots it would fall on the initial syllable. Such cases do exist, as illustrated in (30) with the nominalizing suffix -ost'.

(30) suróv-ost'   'severity'   (cf. suróv-yj 'severe')
     korótk-ost'   'shortness'   (cf. korótk-ij 'short')
     but
     mólod-ost'   'youth'   (cf. molod-ój 'young')
     rázvit-ost'   'maturity'   (cf. razvit-ój 'developed')

However, there are also suffixes such as the one in (31) that result in paradigms with initial stress regardless of whether the root is accented or not. We shall account for such suffixes by saying that they are exceptions to the cyclic rule of Stress Copy.

(31) skóvorod-en'   'dovetail'   (cf. skovorod-á 'pan')
     óborot-en'   'werewolf'   (cf. oborot-ít' 'to turn')

3.4 Noncyclic Secondary Stress

3.4.1 Noncyclic Secondary Stress in Spanish
In the examples discussed so far secondary stresses in the word were invariably assigned as a by-product of assigning main stress. Thus, in

Koya, Maranungku, and other languages examined in chapter 1 the main stress was assigned to one of the syllables to which (secondary) stress had been assigned by a prior rule. However, there are also languages in which secondary stresses in the word depend on the prior assignment of primary stress. A typical example would be a language where subsidiary stresses are assigned to even-numbered syllables counting from the end of the word if main stress falls on the penult, but to odd-numbered syllables if it falls on the last syllable—in other words, on every other syllable preceding the main stress. Modern Spanish exemplifies this type of secondary stress distribution (see Roca 1986, on which the following brief discussion is based).

As illustrated in (32), subsidiary stresses in Spanish are placed on every other syllable preceding the main stress of the word.

(32) natùralìzación   nàturàlizár
      cònstantìnopòlitáno   constàntinòpolitanísmo

We have noted that main stress in Spanish is assigned in the cyclic stratum. Since main stress in Spanish falls on one of the last three syllables of the word, we assume with Roca that it is assigned by a set of rules that are essentially identical with those for Latin (see section 2.2.2). Central among these are a rule specifying that line 0 constituents are left-headed and the rule constructing bounded constituents on line 0 from right to left. Obviously, the distributions of stresses in the words in (32) cannot be readily generated with the help of left-headed binary constituents constructed from right to left. Following Roca, we shall therefore assume that the rules of the noncyclic stratum of Spanish include a rule specifying that line 0 constituents are right-headed.

In sum, Spanish must be supposed to include the following rules, which are assigned to the cyclic (*c*) and noncyclic (*n*) stratum as indicated by the letter preceding the rule.

(33)

a. c   Line 0 parameter settings are [+HT, +BND, left, right to left].

b. n   Line 0 parameter settings are [+HT, +BND, right, right to left].

c. c/n Construct constituent boundaries on line 0.

d. c/n Locate the heads of line 0 constituents on line 1.

e. c   Line 1 parameter settings are [+HT, −BND, right].

f. c   Construct constituent boundaries on line 1.

g. c   Locate the heads of line 1 constituents on line 2.

h. c   Conflate lines 1 and 2.

i. c   Diphthongization

j. c   *la* → *el* (rule (23))

We have found that many languages include a set of rules such as (33a/b–d) in their noncyclic stratum. It is convenient to have a special term to refer to this set of noncyclic rules, and we have adopted the word *Alternator* for this purpose.[10]

3.4.2 The Stress Pattern of Seneca

Attention was first drawn to the intricate stress pattern of Seneca by Stowell (1979), who gives the following algorithm for main stress assignment in that language (p. 62).

(34) Stress the last nonfinal even-numbered syllable (counting from the beginning of the word) that is either closed itself or immediately followed by a closed nonfinal syllable.

In addition to main stress, Seneca has secondary stresses distributed according to the algorithm in (35).

(35) The syllable bearing main stress is preceded by alternating secondary stresses arranged in an iambic pattern.

To account for this distribution of stresses, we shall first assign main stress to the rightmost closed syllable that is nonfinal. We shall then assign secondary stresses to the even-numbered syllables preceding main stress. In cases where main stress is assigned to an odd-numbered syllable, we shall shift the main stress to the left. Formally, this procedure requires the following rules.

(36)

a. Mark the last syllable extrametrical.

b. Assign a line 1 asterisk to all closed syllables.

c. Line 0 parameter settings are [+HT, −BND, left].

d. Construct constituent boundaries on line 0.

---

10. The distribution of secondary stresses in the style of pronunciation of Polish described in Rubach and Booij (1985) strikingly resembles that of Spanish and is treated in essentially the same manner.

e. Locate the heads of line 0 constituents on line 1.

f. Line 1 parameter settings are [+HT, −BND, right].

g. Construct constituent boundaries on line 1.

h. Locate the heads of line 1 constituents on line 2.

i. Conflate lines 1 and 2.

j. Line 0 parameter settings are [+HT, +BND, right, left to right].

k. Construct constituent boundaries on line 0.

l. Locate the heads of line 0 constituents on line 1.

m. Delete a line 1 asterisk in the environment   *   _____   line 1
                                           *   *   line 0.

In (37) we illustrate the effects of applying rules (36a–h) to two nine-syllable strings, where closed syllables are marked with an arrowhead.

(37)

a.   .   .   .   .   *   .   .   .   .   line 2
     (*   *   .   .   *).   .   .   .   line 1
     (*)(*   *   *)(*   *   *   *)   .   line 0
     1   2   3   4   5   6   7   8   ⟨9⟩

b.   .   .   .   .   .   *   .   .   .   line 2
     (*   .   *   .   .   *).   .   .   line 1
     (*   *)(*   *   *)(*   *   *)   .   line 0
     1   2   3   4   5   6   7   8   ⟨9⟩

In (38) we show the effects of the conflation rules (36i).

(38)

a.   .   .   .   .   *   .   .   .   .   line 2
     (.   .   .   .   *).   .   .   .   line 1
     *   *   *   *(*   *   *   *)   .   line 0
     1   2   3   4   5   6   7   8   ⟨9⟩

b.   .   .   .   .   .   *   .   .   .   line 2
     (.   .   .   .   .   *).   .   .   line 1
     *   *   *   *   *(*   *   *)   .   line 0
     1   2   3   4   5   6   7   8   ⟨9⟩

Note that as a result of conflation, a given syllable constitutes the head of two distinct metrical constituents. In (39) we illustrate the effects of rules (36j–l).

(39)

a. . . . . *. . . .   line 2
    (. * . * *). . . .   line 1
    (* *)(* *)[(*) * * *] .   line 0
     1 2 3 4 5 6 7 8 ⟨9⟩

b. . . . . . *. . .   line 2
    (. * . * . *). . .   line 1
    (* *)(* *)(* [*) * *] .   line 0
     1 2 3 4 5 6 7 8 ⟨9⟩

where the square brackets represent the boundaries of the unbounded line 0 constituent.

In both representations in (39) the rightmost bounded constituent on line 0 shares its head with the unbounded constituent that includes the rest of the string. Such sharing of heads has been encountered repeatedly as the result of line conflation (see, for example, (38)). However, previous instances have always involved constituents on different lines in the grid. The Seneca example shows that head sharing is admissible between constituents constructed on the same line of the grid. We have noted repeatedly that previously assigned structure must be respected in constructing constituents. It is for this reason that rule (36k) stops constructing binary constituents when it reaches the main stress of the word.

The metrical grid in (39b) fails to satisfy the context for rule (36m); it represents the correct surface stress contour of the form. By contrast, the metrical grid in (39a) is subject to the rule, which deletes the line 1 asterisk associated with syllable 5. As a result, syllable 4 becomes the rightmost element on line 1 and the line 2 asterisk shifts to syllable 4. This produces the correct surface stress contour of the form.

3.5 English Stress

In the course of our research we have been interested to note that the specific proposals of Hayes (1980/1) concerning English stress can easily be translated into our framework. Hayes's most important result with regard to the treatment of English stress is that there are two stress rules rather than one. One of these, the *English Stress Rule*, is sensitive to rime structure and determines the placement of primary stress. The other, *Strong Retraction*, is not sensitive to rime structure and determines the placement of subsidiary stresses—completely in nonderived words, and partially in derived words. Hayes observes that "the English Stress Rule must precede

Strong Retraction, because it [Strong Retraction] begins its right-to-left binary count at the left boundary of the foot constructed by the English Stree Rule: compare *Àpalàchicóla*, where the secondary stresses fall on even numbered syllables from the end, with *hàmamèlidánthemum*, in which they fall on odd numbered syllables from the end" (p. 158). This is identical with the situation described in section 3.4.1 for Spanish. We conclude, therefore, that Hayes's rule of Strong Retraction is a special case of the Alternator rules (33). English differs from Spanish in its treatment of word-initial stress; in English the word-initial syllable is generally stressed except in special contexts where stress is deleted (for details, see chapter 7). The English Alternator rules must therefore read as follows.

(40)
a. Line 0 parameter settings are [+ HT, + BND, left, right to left].

b. Construct constituent boundaries on line 0.

c. Locate the heads of line 0 constituents on line 1.

In discussing derived words with internal constituent structure, Hayes remarks that "the English Stress Rule and Strong Retraction differ in whether they must respect the boundaries of feet constructed earlier in the derivation: Strong Retraction obeys these boundaries, while the English Stress Rule obliterates earlier metrical structure" (p. 165). In the framework developed here, this difference would fall out automatically if the English Stress Rule were assigned to a cyclic stratum and the rule of Strong Retraction to a noncyclic stratum. But this is not all. Both the English Stress Rule and Strong Retraction construct binary constituents from right to left. We suggest, therefore, that they are the same rule—in other words, that (40) is assigned to both the cyclic stratum and the noncyclic stratum. In the cyclic stratum (40) represents the English Stress Rule, whereas in the noncyclic stratum it represents Strong Retraction.

There is a further difference between the English Stress Rule and Strong Retraction. The English Stress Rule assigns but a single stress, whereas Strong Retraction assigns an unlimited number of stresses. We capture this difference by postulating that the cyclic stratum includes a rule of main stress (line 1 constituent) assignment as well as a rule conflating lines 1 and 2 in the metrical grid.[11]

---

11. An anonymous reviewer has observed that "the theory predicts that only the strongest foot in a line may be constructed by a process distinct from that which constructed the other feet." The reviewer comments that "the authors fail to note that in Hayes's (1980/1) analysis of English word stress, the main stress is sometimes

It is well known that certain subsidiary stresses of English words reflect the main stresses that would have been assigned to their subconstituents if these had surfaced as full words. Some well-known examples are cited in (41).

(41) ìnstrumèntálity èlèctrícity ìnfèstátion còndènsátion

When the Alternator rule (40) functions as Hayes's Strong Retraction, it is a noncyclic rule and applies after the last pass through the cyclic rules. Its effects will therefore be recorded on the same metrical plane as those of the last pass through the cycle. Since only a single syllable is stressed by our counterpart of the English Stress Rule, we must provide some additional machinery so that the Alternator will respect stresses assigned on previous passes through the cycle. We can readily achieve this result by postulating that English is subject to the rule of Stress Copy (42), which is assigned to the noncyclic stratum.

(42) Copy line 1 asterisks assigned on preceding cycles.

Words such as *instrumentality* and *condensation* will then emerge from Stress Copy with the metrical grid shown in (43).

```
(43)  .    .   . *. .         .   . * .    line 2
      (*   .  * *). .       (.   * *) .    line 1
      *   * * (* *)*         *   * (*) *    line 0
      instrumental i ty      condensation
```

The line 1 asterisks in *instrumentality* represent the main stresses of the subconstituents *instrument* and *instrumental*, whereas those of *condensation* represent the main stress of the subconstituent *condense*. The effects of applying the Alternator to the words in (43) are shown in (44).

```
(44)  .    .   . *. .         .   . * .    line 2
      (*   .  * *) *.        (*   * *) .    line 1
      (*   *)(*)(*)(* *)      (*) (*)(* *)  line 0
      instrumenta lity        condensation
```

laid down by the 'noniterative' stress rule (the English Stress Rule, in words like *America*), and sometimes by the 'iterative' stress rule (Strong Retraction, in words like *assimilate*). Under the authors' theory we can only derive **assimiláte*." In chapter 7 we argue that these verbs with main stress on the antepenult do indeed emerge from the stress rules given here with final stress. They are, however, subsequently subject to a rule of stress retraction that moves the topmost asterisk in a word to the left, provided that this asterisk is located on the word-final syllable. These words thus do not constitute counterexamples to the theory advanced here.

As shown in (44), the Alternator adds a line 1 asterisk over the penultimate syllable of *instrumentality* and over the initial syllable of *condensation*. This extra asterisk in *instrumentality* is subsequently deleted by Poststress Destressing (see chapter 7 and *SPE*, pp. 119–125).

In possessing two kinds of suffixes—cyclic and noncyclic—English resembles Vedic with its dominant and recessive suffixes. As illustrated in (45), in English only cyclic suffixes like *-ity* affect the placement of main stress in the word; noncyclic suffixes like *-ness* do not.

(45) grammátical   grammaticálity   grammáticalness
     sólemn   solémnity   sólemnness

English thus differs from Vedic in that in Vedic noncyclic (recessive) suffixes determine stress placement except in words that also contain cyclic (dominant) suffixes, whereas—as shown by the stress of words such as *solemnness*, which contains no cyclic suffixes—in English noncyclic suffixes have no effect on main stress placement. The word *solemnness* brings out a further difference between Vedic and English. Whereas in Vedic Strict Cyclicity blocks the application of the cyclic stress rules to the underived stem of a word, in English the cyclic rule of main stress assignment must apply to the underived stem of *solemnness*, for there is no rule of main stress assignment in the noncyclic stratum of English. That the cyclic main stress rule in English must apply to underived stems is shown also by the fact that underived words have main stress just like derived words.

At first sight, this might seem to point to a serious shortcoming in the important concept of Strict Cyclicity. This difficulty is only apparent, however, for (as noted in Halle and Mohanan 1985, 70) word stress rules in English apply to underived forms, because, unlike those of Vedic, the English stress rules are not structure-changing but structure-building, and only structure-changing rules are prevented by Strict Cyclicity from applying to an underived stem. The stress rules are structure-changing in Vedic but not in English because stress (that is, line 1 asterisks) must systematically be indicated in the lexical representations of Vedic but not in those of English. It is this need for systematic recording of stress in the lexical representation of morphemes that makes stress distinctive. In languages such as English or Spanish, where stresses need to be indicated in lexical representations only exceptionally, not systematically as in Vedic or Lithuanian, stress is not distinctive and the cyclic stress rules of English therefore apply freely to underived stems.

PART II
Formalism

Chapter 4
Constituent Construction and Natural Boundaries

4.1 The General Constraints on Constituent Construction

In chapter 1 we observed that the application of the rules of metrical constituent construction is governed by certain general conditions, which determine the relation between the form of the rule and the mapping it effects. One of these, the *Exhaustivity Condition*, reflects the fact that rules of metrical constituent construction apply in an exhaustive fashion. This condition applies both to rules constructing unbounded constituents, such as the stress rules of Latvian and Koya in (23) and (30) of chapter 1, and to rules constructing bounded constituents, such as those of Maranungku, Weri, Warao, Southern Paiute, Garawa, Aklan, and Winnebago; such rules are always interpreted as erecting continuous sequences of constituents over the whole input string.

A second characteristic condition on the application of metrical rules is the *Maximality Condition*: the rules of metrical construction build constituents that are maximal with respect to the specifications of the metrical structure. Thus, given the input structure for Koya shown in (1a), the output structure displayed in (1b) violates the Maximality Condition. This is because there exists an output that can be associated to (1a) and that has more inclusive constituents than (1b), namely, (1c).

(1)

a. . . * . . . * . .
   * * * * * * * * *

b. * . * . * . * * .
  (* *)(* *)(* *)(*)(* *)

c. * . * . . . * . .
  (* *)(* * * *)(* * *)

Since (1c) is the structure that can be associated with (1a) that has the most inclusive constituents, the pair (1a)/(1c) is well formed. Similarly, the Maximality Condition permits the pairing between (2a) and (2b) but excludes the pairing between (2a) and the output structure displayed in (2c).

(2)

a.   . . . .
     * * * *

b. * . . .
    (* * * *)

c. * . * .
    (* *)(* *)

In the case of unbounded constituents, imposing a maximality condition on the extension of each constituent constructed is equivalent to imposing a *minimality condition* on the number of constituents erected. We shall demonstrate that such a minimality condition is in fact a special instance of a more general principle stating that metrical construction must proceed according to a maximally simple deterministic procedure. This general principle, in turn, entails the Maximality Condition. However, the Maximality Condition cannot in general be reduced to the more special minimality constraint, because the minimality constraint will not in general yield the deterministic directional construction that is typical of patterns involving bounded constituents. To illustrate, consider the case of a structure with binary constituents; and consider an input form consisting of three positions, none of which is accented.[1] For such an input and for each direction of construction, there are two patterns that conform to the minimality constraint.

(3)

a. (* *)(*)

b. (*)(* *)

If, on the other hand, the Maximality Condition is imposed at each step in the iterative construction of the sequence of binary constituents, then (3a) will be unambiguously associated with the left-to-right structure, and (3b) will be unambiguously associated with the right-to-left one.

---

1. An accented position is one that is necessarily a head. An accented position is identified by being provided with an asterisk on line 1 in the input to the rules of metrical construction. See the example of Koya in (26)–(30) of section 1.1.

A third characteristic condition on the application of rules of metrical construction is the *Faithfulness Condition*, which states that the rules must respect the asterisks that mark the intrinsic heads; that is, they must erect the constituent structure in such a way that the marked elements will be at the appropriate position within the constituents. For example, in the case of the input for Koya displayed in (1a), the structure in (1c) and those in (4a,b) will conform to the Faithfulness Condition, but those in (4c,d) will not.

(4)

a. * . * . . . * . .
    (* *)(* * *) * (*) * *

b. * . * . . * * * .
    (* *)(* * *)(*)(*)(* *)

c. * . * . . . * . .
    (* * * * * * * * *)

d. * . * . * . * . .
    (* * * *)(* * * * *)

Of course, only the structure (1c) constitutes a well-formed output. The structures (4a,b), although they obey the Faithfulness Condition, are excluded by other conditions: (4a) because it violates the Exhaustivity Condition, and (4b) because it violates the Maximality Condition.

A fourth condition on the application of metrical rules, the *Directionality Condition*, specifically constrains those rules that build bounded constituents: bounded constituents are built either from left to right or from right to left. Thus, given an input such as (5a), two possible sequences of binary constituents can be constructed over it, namely, those in (5b) and (5c); but there is no mapping constructing bounded constituents that would associate (5a) with (5d) or (5e).

(5)

a. . . . .
    * * * * * * *

b. . . . .
    (* *)(* *)(* *)(*)

c. . . . .
    (*)(* *)(* *)(* *)

d. . . . .
    (* *)(* *)(*)(* *)

e. .   .   .   .
  (* *)(*)(* *)(* *)

For example, the structure (5d) could be obtained from (5a) by applying the following "flip-flop" algorithm: Construct a constituent at the left end of the string and another at the right end. Go back to the left extremity of the string and construct a constituent immediately to the right of the first constituent erected. Go back to the right extremity of the string and construct a constituent immediately to the left of the rightmost constituent. And so on. The symmetric algorithm would produce the structure in (5e). However, no such complex iterative algorithms are found in grammars: the only iterative processes actually encountered are the ones that conform to the Directionality Condition illustrated in (5b,c).

The final condition on metrical construction, the *Domino Condition*, is also specific to structures with bounded constituents and concerns the manner in which such structures are reconstructed when the alternating order is disturbed by the application of an epenthesis rule. This condition states that the introduction of a supplementary position inside a binary constituent will trigger the restructuring of *that constituent and of all those that were constructed after it by iteration in the directional procedure that gave rise to the constituent structure.* It would seem that this condition should bear an intimate relation to the preceding Directionality Condition. And in fact we shall demonstrate that, when the construction of metrical constituents is properly formalized, these two conditions turn out to be corollaries of a unique and more general principle.

Two questions arise at this point:

(6)

a. Why should we encounter this particular set of conditions, and not some other set?

b. Assuming that this set of conditions can be related to more general principles, by what independently motivated formalization could it be made to follow from these principles?

The five conditions described above are quite natural, and it is not obvious that they should not be taken as axioms. Still, we shall search for explanations.

4.2 Deterministic Procedures and Natural Boundaries

Consider the case of Latvian stress. The mere characterization of the Latvian stress rule as a rule constructing unbounded left-headed constituents will not in general be sufficient to formally identify the unique metrical structure that is associated with a given string of positions. Thus, many constituent structures that conform to the description of the rule can be associated with an input string such as the one in, say, (2a): the structures in (2b) and (2c), those in (7), and many others.[2]

(7)
a. * . . .
   (∗) ∗ ∗ ∗
b. . . ∗ . .
   ∗ (∗ ∗) ∗
c. ∗ . ∗ .
   (∗) ∗ (∗ ∗)
d. . . . . ∗
   ∗ ∗ ∗ (∗)
   and so on

The Exhaustivity Condition and the Maximality Condition ensure that the construction of a sequence of unbounded constituents over a string of positions devoid of intrinsic heads will take place in an unambiguous fashion. These two conditions act as principles that interpret the grammatical description of the metrical structure and that restrict the form of the output generated. In fact, these two principles entail that, in general, only one output will be associated to an input devoid of intrinsic heads by a rule constructing unbounded constituents. More specifically, the two principles ensure that such a rule will always apply to such inputs in a *deterministic fashion*.

Since determinism can be enforced in many different ways, we must still explain why metrical theory should implement the particular design encountered here. We note that, when an input is already endowed with some

---

2. In fact, the number of constituent structures that can be associated to an input string of length 4 is 34 (if we include the null structure, the one with no metrical constituent at all over the string). More generally, given an input string of length n, the number of different constituent structures that can be built over it is given by the formula (i).

(i) $K(1) + K(2) \cdot (n-1) + \cdots + K(p) \cdot C(n-1, p-1) + \cdots + K(n)$
   where $C(n-1, p-1)$ is the number of combinations of $n-1$ elements taken $p-1$ at a time and where $K(p)$ is given by the recursive (Fibonacci) equation $K(p) = K(p-1) + K(p-2)$, with $K(1) = 2$ and $K(2) = 3$.

The above number is inferior to the number $2 \cdot 3^{n-1}$.

initial constituent structure displaying no embedding, there is a trivial deterministic procedure that gives rise to unbounded metrical constituents, namely, (8).

(8) Interpret the constituents in the input as metrical constituents.

Every input to a metrical rule is in fact endowed with a minimal constituent structure, since it is necessarily characterized as a morphological constituent that has a beginning and an end. Let us refer to such previously given constituent structure as *natural constituent structure* and to the corresponding boundaries and bracketing as *natural boundaries* and *natural bracketing*, respectively.

(9) The leftmost and rightmost morphological boundaries of an input string to a metrical rule are defined to be *natural boundaries*.

By convention, we shall use square brackets to denote natural boundaries. Thus, a string like (2a) has the natural boundaries indicated in (10).

(10) . . . .
    [* * * *]

The notion of natural constituent gives rise to a special instance of the minimal deterministic procedure in (8), namely, (11).

(11) Interpret the natural constituents as metrical constituents.

The procedure in (11) meets the Exhaustivity Condition, as well as the Maximality Condition, in the case of simple inputs without accented elements. We can then take it to describe the mapping effected by a rule constructing unbounded constituents over such inputs. In other words, in the case of unbounded constituents and of inputs of the form in (10), the rule of metrical construction will not actually build any additional structure over the string, beyond the natural structure provided by convention (9). The role of the metrical rule will be merely to identify the latter structure as a "metrical structure": we observe the "minimality constraint" mentioned earlier in connection with the construction of unbounded constituents. We may formalize the rule (11) as in (12), where, in accordance with the notational conventions of section 1.1, the paired parentheses represent metrical brackets and the paired square brackets delimit natural constituents.

(12) [...] → (...)

In a grammar where constituents are left-headed, the output of rule (12) and of the Head Location rule (22) of section 1.1 applying to the input string (10) (= (2a)) will be the structure (2b).

We should emphasize that the brackets used in such rules as (12) are not autonomous symbols on a par with the asterisks that denote metrical positions. Brackets denote left or right limits of constituent substrings and as such have no meaning in isolation: a left bracket is necessarily adjacent as a symbol to some metrical position on its right, and, symmetrically, a right bracket is necessarily adjacent as a symbol to some position on its left. This interpretation of the brackets will in particular govern the application of the various rules and conventions encountered in this chapter. The fact that the symbols used in this discussion must be constrained by some supplementary convention of course indicates that we are not dealing here with an adequate formalization of the notions in question. The proper formalization will be presented in the next chapter.

We can thus provide a partial answer to the questions in (6). This partial answer concerns the simple case of a rule constructing unbounded constituents over inputs without accented elements. In this restricted situation the Exhaustivity Condition and the Maximality Condition turn out to express the fact that a metrical rule will apply according to a minimal deterministic procedure. Specifically, the mapping associated with a metrical rule constructing constituent boundaries is effected according to the particular minimal deterministic procedure (11), formalized in (12), where the notion of natural constituent is defined in (9). This partial result is summarized in (13).

(13) The procedure for constructing unbounded metrical constituents is the simplest possible deterministic procedure: it is the identity algorithm, which takes the already existing natural bracketing as input and merely interprets it as a "metrical bracketing."

At this point the question arises whether the observation in (13) can be extended to inputs that include accented elements (on the notion of accent, see footnote 1 and the discussion of Koya surrounding (26)–(30) in section 1.1). Consider for example the string in (1a), repeated here in (14).

(14) . . * . . . * . .
     * * * * * * * * *
     1 2 3 4 5 6 7 8 9

As in the string in (10), the leftmost and rightmost morphological boundaries in (14) constitute natural boundaries and will ultimately surface as metrical brackets. However, we know that, contrary to what happens in

(10), these two brackets belong to distinct constituents in the output and that other metrical boundaries will intervene between them. This is due to the Faithfulness Condition, which requires that metrical construction respect accented elements. Since unbounded constituents are [+HT] (see (14) in section 1.1), each of the two accented elements in (14) (= (1a)) will induce a constituent boundary, to its right, if the constituents are defined to be right-headed, or to its left, if the constituents are defined to be left-headed.

Actually, the formalism of chapter 1 permits a straightforward interpretation of the Faithfulness Condition. As stated there, the projection of the head of a given bracketed domain onto a higher line *is* the constituent that dominates that domain. The line 1 positions in such representations as (14) must then be viewed as *precursors* of metrical constituents. Depending on whether the grammar defines the constituents to be left-headed or right-headed, each precursor will be situated at the left boundary or at the right boundary, respectively, of the domain it ultimately dominates in the output representation. We are thus led to postulate that, in the case of unbounded constituents, accented elements induce constituent boundaries in the fashion indicated in (15).

(15) Each accented element is associated with a metrical boundary in the initial representation of the string. If the constituents are right-headed, the associated metrical boundary is a right boundary, located to the right of the accented element. If the constituents are left-headed, the associated metrical boundary is a left boundary, located to the left of the accented element.

Specifically, *the notion of natural boundary is extended so as to include the "precursor" metrical boundaries induced by the accented elements.* Given convention (15), the input in (14) will have the structure shown in (16) in a grammar with left-headed constituents, like that of Koya.

(16) . . * . . . * . .
       [* * (* * * * (* * *]
       1 2 3 4 5 6 7 8 9

As this example shows, the mere application of conventions (9) and (15) will not in general yield a constituent structure. These conventions must then be supplemented by some other principles. For the purpose of this discussion, it will be convenient to distinguish the brackets introduced by (9) and (15) from those introduced to supplement them. We shall refer to the former as the *intrinsic natural brackets*. In the case of the form (16), the simplest way of transforming the given sequence of positions and intrinsic brackets into a well-formed constituent structure is to introduce a right bracket to close the constituent opened by the intrinsic left bracket before position 1 and another one to close the constituent opened by the intrinsic left bracket before position 3. The simplest unambiguous rule for introducing such right brackets, in turn, is one that will insert them in positions adjacent to left brackets, where simplicity is measured by counting the number of metrical positions that must figure in the structural description of the rule. This can be expressed as the convention in (17a) and its symmetric counterpart (17b), where the square bracket in the contextual part of the rule denotes a natural bracket in the extended sense, that is, either a metrical bracket or a nonmetrical natural bracket.

(17)
a. $* \rightarrow *$] / ___ [
b. $* \rightarrow$ [$*$ /] ___

In effect, convention (17) means that a natural constituent starts (resp. ends) where the input string starts (resp. ends) or where another natural constituent ends (resp. starts). This convention is the simplest deterministic way of completing a string like (16) in which some brackets remain unmatched. The rule (17a) will then apply to the form in (16) to yield the structure in (18).

(18) . . * . . . * . .
      [* *](* * * *](* * *]
      1 2 3 4 5 6 7 8 9

The latter form may then undergo rule (12) and Head Location, giving rise to the surface metrical structure in (19).

(19) * . * . . . * . .
      (* *)(* * * *)(* * *)
      1 2 3 4 5 6 7 8 9

The Faithfulness Condition has been formulated in (15) as a principle inserting *metrical* boundaries. It is easy to see that, in the case of a language like Koya, the correct result could have also been obtained by formulating this condition as a principle inserting "square" natural boundaries. However, we have encountered grammars in which the metrical structure does not involve any rule of construction and in which the only metrical constituents that arise are those associated with accented elements; see section 2.4.1. Within such a grammar an input string of the form (14) will lead to the surface metrical structure in (20).

(20) . . * . . . * . .
   [* *](* * * *)(* * *)
   1 2 3 4 5 6 7 8 9

The difference between this structure and the one in (19) is that in (19) the natural constituent dominating the positions 1 and 2 in the string has been rewritten as a metrical constituent by rule (12), whereas in (20) it remains unaffected. We have assumed that languages with structures like (20) differ from languages like Koya in that their grammar does not include the "construction" rule (12). The constituents associated with accented elements, which we have called *obligatory constituents*, are then generated by the Faithfulness Condition, formulated as a condition inserting metrical boundaries (that is, as (15)), and by rule (17). To account for the full set of metrical boundaries in a string like (20), we must supplement rule (17) with the convention in (21).

(21) A left (resp. right) bracket that is paired with a right (resp. left) metrical bracket is interpreted as a metrical bracket.

It is important to distinguish such conventions as (9), (15), and (17) from the rules in (12) (= (11)) and (21), since these two types of principles fulfill very different functions within the theory. We shall say that the principles in (9), (15), and (17) are *licensing conventions* and that the rules in (12) and (21) are *interpretive rules*. Correspondingly, we shall say that natural boundaries are *licensed* in the contexts defined in (9), (15), and (17), whereas natural boundaries are *interpreted* as metrical boundaries by such rules as (12) and (21). Given this terminology, conventions (9) and (15) may be reformulated as (22a) and (22b), respectively.

(22)
a. The rightmost (resp. leftmost) element of the input string licenses a right (resp. left) natural boundary to its right (resp. to its left).
b. Within a grammar with right-headed (resp. left-headed) constituents, each accented element licenses a right (resp. left) metrical boundary to its right (resp. to its left).

Convention (17), in turn, may be formulated as in (23).

(23) An element that is adjacent to the right (resp. to the left) of a right (resp. left) boundary licenses a left (resp. right) boundary to its left (resp. to its right).

Convention (22) introduces what we have called the "intrinsic brackets."

Such brackets are defined in terms of properties of a bracket-free representation. By contrast, the brackets licensed by (23) are defined in terms of previously introduced brackets. We shall call brackets of the latter type *dependent brackets*. Thus, a dependent bracket is licensed *by another bracket*. For example, in the representation in (18) the right bracket to the right of position 2 is licensed by the intrinsic left bracket to its right, and the right bracket to the right of position 6 is also licensed by the intrinsic left bracket to its right. As we shall demonstrate, the notion of dependent bracket plays a crucial role in the account of the Domino Condition.

Convention (23) fulfills the roles of both the Maximality Condition and the Exhaustivity Condition for structures with unbounded constituents. This convention thus appears to be the true formal source of the two conditions in the case of structures with unbounded constituents.

To summarize, a rule constructing unbounded metrical constituents over a string may be formalized in general as a purely interpretive principle, namely, as (11) (= (12)). The input to that rule is endowed with a natural constituent structure generated by the rules (21), (22), and (23). The brackets licensed by (22) are to be distinguished from those licensed by (23). The former are "intrinsic" brackets, whose position is defined in absolute terms. The latter are "dependent" brackets, whose position is defined in terms of the previously defined intrinsic brackets. The replacement of (9) by the set of conventions (21), (22), and (23) allows us to extend to the case of inputs with accented elements the interpretation of (11) proposed in (13) in the case of inputs without accented elements. Specifically:

(24)

a. The procedure for constructing the natural unbounded constituent structure is the simplest possible deterministic procedure: the natural constituent demarcations are those licensed by the extremities of the input string and the accented elements, and only those.

b. The procedure for constructing unbounded metrical constituents, in turn, is the simplest possible deterministic procedure: it is the identity algorithm, which takes the already existing natural brackets as input and merely interprets them as metrical brackets.

The procedure for constructing unbounded metrical constituents thus involves three steps. The first step is the identification of the intrinsic natural boundaries licensed by (22). The second step is the construction of the natural unbounded constituent structure associated with the latter boundaries. This construction proceeds according to the simplest deterministic procedure, (23) and (21). The third step is the construction of the metrical constituent structure associated with the natural structure previously defined. Again, this construction proceeds according to the simplest deterministic procedure, the identity mapping in (11). One might want to argue at this point that this formalization is unnecessarily complex and cumbersome. Why have a three-step procedure for constructing metrical constituents? A two-step procedure in which the metrical structure was constructed directly from the set of boundaries licensed by (22) would appear to yield the same result in a simpler fashion. Within such a model the three conventions (23), (21), and (11) would be replaced by the single principle (25).

(25) Rewrite as metrical constituents the domains delimited by the boundaries defined in (22), and only those domains.

This convention would be taken to formalize the rule of metrical construction. A problem arises, however, concerning the characterization of metrical structures made up solely of obligatory constituents, like that illustrated in (20). Within the revised model the corresponding grammars would be described as not including the construction rule (25). On the other hand, we have shown that, even in these grammars, metrical constituents need to be characterized as maximal domains between natural boundaries. It appears, then, that the latter characterization should be separated from the rule of construction proper and should be stated as an independent principle, namely, as (23).

We have thus shown that within the formalization developed above, the Exhaustivity Condition and the Maximality Condition express the fact that the procedure for constructing natural constituents is the simplest deterministic procedure. Specifically, the two conditions immediately follow from convention (23). As for the Faithfulness Condition, it follows from the formal definition of the notion "constituent" adopted here, which states that the projection of the head of a given bracketed domain onto a higher line *is* the constituent that dominates that domain. The obligatory line 1 positions in an input representation must then be analyzed as precursors of metrical constituents. In the case of languages that are [+HT] each precursor will be situated at the left boundary or the right boundary of the domain it ultimately dominates in the output representation, depending on whether the grammar defines the constituents to be left-headed or right-headed.

We have thus answered the questions in (6) for structures with unbounded constituents. We must now determine whether these answers will also apply to bounded constituents.

4.3 Binary Constituents

The difference between bounded and unbounded constituents may be characterized as follows. The grammar for an unbounded structure identifies the constituents by merely identifying pairs of consecutive left and right brackets. Within such a grammar, each constituent is associated with a pair of brackets of the form [...] or (...), where "..." is characterized as containing no bracket; see the formalization of the rule (11) in (12), for example. This is why an unbounded metrical constituent structure over a given string is identical with the original natural structure of the string. By contrast, the identification of a bounded constituent must explicitly mention the extent of the substring dominated by the constituent, for it must provide a representation of the adjacency relation that holds between the head and governed positions. In a bounded structure, then, two consecutive natural brackets of the form [...] will not in general belong to the same constituent domain. Consequently, a bounded structure cannot be derived directly from the natural structure, as is the case with unbounded metrical constituents, but must be effectively constructed by a rule. Within the formal model put forth in this section, the difference between the two types of constituents will then be stated at the third stage of the three-stage derivation described earlier. In other words, in the case of bounded constituents the rule (11) (= (12)), which defines the metrical constituents in the case of unbounded structures, must be replaced by a construction rule that makes explicit the adjacency relation that must hold between the head and governed positions.

In the case of binary constituents a governed position must be adjacent to the head on its right or on its left, depending on the direction of government. Thus, the possible bracketings for binary constituents are those displayed in (26), and only those.

(26)
a. regular   b. degenerate

   (* *)   (*)

This pair of representations can be collapsed into a single schema by means of the parenthesis notation of *SPE*. We display this schema in (27), where the labeled parentheses correspond to the notation of *SPE* and should not be confused with metrical brackets.

(27) (* ($_a$ * $_a$))

The schema in (27) will characterize the notion "binary constituent." However, if we require the construction procedure to be deterministic, this schema, as it stands, cannot be used as a licensing convention generating metrical brackets, for the metrical positions it contains are not unambiguously identified within the input sequence. A rule licensing binary constituents will be deterministic only if at least one of the two paired brackets it mentions is a natural bracket in the input string. In other words, a deterministic formalization of the constraint of binariness requires that the mutual dependency that is established between the paired brackets in a formula such as (27) be analyzed into more elementary directional dependencies, in which one of the brackets is characterized as prior to the other in the construction algorithm. We then obtain exactly two deterministic licensing rules from the characterization of binariness.

(28)

a. Licensing of a right metrical bracket

$$[* \, (_a \, * \, _a) \, \rightarrow \, [* \, (_a \, * \, _a))$$

b. Licensing of a left metrical bracket

$$*(_a \, * \, _a)] \, \rightarrow \, (* \, (_a \, * \, _a)]$$

We assume that, by convention, a natural bracket mentioned in a rule may analyze metrical boundaries as well as simple "square" natural boundaries. Rule (28a) states that a metrical boundary is licensed when it is separated by at most two positions from some boundary on its left; rule (28b) states that a metrical boundary is licensed when it is separated by at most two positions from some boundary on its right. The metrical bracket licensed by (28a) or (28b) is thus a dependent bracket, in the sense defined above: it is licensed by the natural bracket mentioned in the structural description of the rule. In (28) the nondeterministic mutual dependency established between the brackets by (27) is analyzed into more elementary deterministic dependencies that are directional in nature. Specifically, rule (28a) establishes a left-to-right dependency between a natural bracket and a newly introduced metrical bracket, whereas rule (28b) establishes a right-to-left dependency. Accordingly, we shall call the first schema the *Left-to-Right Binariness Rule* and the second one the *Right-to-Left Binariness Rule*. We shall refer to the conjunction of the two as the *Binariness Rule*.

The initial input for the Binariness Rule in (28a) or (28b) is a string in the output of the rules (22) and (23), that is, a string endowed with natural brackets. The Binariness Rule must be construed as a rule that erects a metrical constituent, although it does not actually alter the natural boundary that is mentioned in it. When the latter boundary is not already characterized as a metrical boundary in the input (by rule (22b)), the effect of metrical construction is obtained by applying the interpretive convention (21) after the Binariness Rule. This convention applies only if the affected natural boundary has been paired with a metrical boundary by the Binariness Rule, in other words, if the metrical boundary that triggers the application of (21) is dependent on the affected boundary. We shall return to this aspect of the formalism in chapter 5.

Convention (23) will apply to the output of (28) and (21) and will introduce new natural brackets in positions adjacent to the metrical brackets inserted by (28). These new natural brackets in turn will provide a context for the reapplication of (28). If we assume that the system is deterministic, it follows that all the rules *will obligatorily apply*.

A deterministic licensing procedure involving rule (28) will be maximally simple if it makes use of only one of the two subclauses (28a) or (28b). Thus, in the case of binary constituents there are two maximally simple deterministic licensing algorithms, the one constituted by the set of conventions (22), (23), (28a), and (21), and the one constituted by the set (22), (23), (28b), and (21). We shall refer to the first algorithm as the *Left-to-Right Algorithm* and to the second as the *Right-to-Left Algorithm*, for reasons that will become obvious. To illustrate, consider the input string in (2a) and suppose that the licensing algorithm with the subclause (28a)—the Left-to-Right Algorithm—is applied. The application of (22a) to (2a) yields the representation in (10), repeated in (29).

(29) . . . .
    [* * * *]

The licensing convention (28a) will then apply to this form to yield the representation in (30).

(30) . . . .
    [* *) * *]

The application of (28a) is obligatory, because of the deterministic character of the procedure assumed here. The form in (30) in turn constitutes an input to convention (23), which requires that the right boundary of the constituent erected by the first application of (28a) be paired with the left boundary of a constituent adjacent to the right. Convention (23) thus inserts a left natural boundary to the right of this constituent and produces the representation in (31).

(31) . . . .
    [* *)[* *]

Convention (28a) will now reapply to the form in (31) and rewrite the rightmost bracket as a metrical bracket, yielding the structure in (32).

(32) . . . .

    [* *)[* *)

Finally, the interpretive principle (21) and Head Location rule will apply to (32) to produce the metrical constituent structure in (33).

(33) . * . *

    (* *)(* *)

To illustrate further the workings of convention (28) applied in the context of a deterministic procedure, let us consider an input with accented elements like (14), repeated in (34). We shall again consider the case of the Left-to-Right Algorithm—the case of the algorithm that includes (28a)—and we shall assume right-headedness.

(34) . . * . . . * . .

    * * * * * * * * *

    1 2 3 4 5 6 7 8 9

The numbers in (34) have been introduced for the sake of convenience, to facilitate the identification of the different positions in the string. Conventions (22a) and (22b) will apply to this input and will license the boundaries indicated in (35).

(35) . . * . . . * . .

    [* * *) * * * *) * *]

    1 2 3   4 5 6 7   8 9

The brackets marked in (35) are the intrinsic natural brackets, in the sense defined earlier. Under the left-to-right licensing procedure assumed here, a dependent right metrical bracket will now be introduced (by the Left-to-Right Binariness Rule (28a)) after position 2 in (35). At the same time convention (23) will introduce a dependent left natural bracket to the left of position 4 and of position 8:

(36) . . * . . . * . .

    [* *) *)[* * * *)[* *]

    1 2 3 4 5 6 7 8 9

Convention (23) then reapplies and introduces a dependent left natural bracket to the left of position 3. At the same time the Left-to-Right Binariness Rule (28a) introduces a right metrical bracket to the right of position 5 and licenses the right intrinsic natural bracket to the right of position 9 as a metrical bracket:

(37) . . * . . . * . .
    [* *)[*)[* *) * *)[* *)
    1 2 3 4 5 6 7 8 9

Convention (23) now applies, introducing a dependent left natural bracket to the left of position 6. At the same time the Left-to-Right Binariness Rule (28a) applies (vacuously) to the natural bracket to the left of position 3 and (vacuously) licenses the natural metrical bracket to its right. Note that in this case, it is the shorter version of (28a)—the version with only one position in the structural description—that applies. We now have the representation in (38).

(38) . . * . . . * . .
    [* *)[*)[* *)[* *)[* *)
    1 2 3 4 5 6 7 8 9

Finally, the Left-to-Right Binariness Rule (28a) licenses the right intrinsic natural bracket to the right of position 7 as a metrical bracket:

(39) . . * . . . * . .
    [* *)[*)[* *)[* *)[* *)
    1 2 3 4 5 6 7 8 9

The interpretive rule (21) and Head Location now apply, producing the left-to-right alternating pattern displayed in (40).

(40) . * * . * . * . *
    (* *)(*)(* *)(* *)(* *)
    1 2 3 4 5 6 7 8 9

The constituent structure in (40) includes four intrinsic brackets: the leftmost left bracket, the rightmost right bracket, and the right brackets after positions 3 and 7. The other brackets are dependent brackets. The right bracket after position 2 is licensed by the leftmost left bracket, by the Left-to-Right Binariness Rule (28a). This right bracket in turn licenses the left bracket before position 3, by convention (23). The left bracket before position 4 is licensed by the right bracket after position 3 (an intrinsic bracket), by convention (23). This left bracket in turn licenses the right bracket after position 5, by the Left-to-Right Binariness Rule (28a). And so on.

The Left-to-Right Algorithm would also give rise to a left-to-right pattern under the symmetric assumption of left-headedness. To see this, consider an input string like (41).

(41) . . . * . . . * .
     * * * * * * * * *
     1 2 3 4 5 6 7 8 9

Assuming left-headedness, convention (22) yields the intrinsic natural brackets in (42).

(42) . . . * . . . * .
     [* * * (* * * * (* *]
     1 2 3 4 5 6 7 8 9

Convention (23) now applies, introducing dependent right natural brackets to the right of position 3 and to the right of position 7. At the same time the Left-to-Right Binariness Rule (28a) introduces dependent right metrical brackets to the right of position 2 and of position 5. In addition, it licenses the right intrinsic natural bracket at the right extremity of the string as a metrical bracket:

(43) . . . * . . . * .
     [* *) *](* *) * *](* *)
     1 2 3 4 5 6 7 8 9

Convention (23) now introduces dependent left natural brackets to the left of position 3 and of position 6:

(44) . . . * . . . * .
     [* *)[*](* *)[* *](* *)
     1 2 3 4 5 6 7 8 9

Finally, the Left-to-Right Binariness Rule (28a) applies, licensing the right natural brackets after position 3 and position 7 as metrical brackets (note that the shorter version of the rule applies in the case of position 3):

(45) . . . * . . . * .
     [* *)[*)[* *)[* *)[* *)
     1 2 3 4 5 6 7 8 9

The interpretive rule (21) and Head Location apply to (45), yielding the metrical structure in (46), which corresponds to a left-to-right pattern.

(46) * . * * . * . * .
     (* *)(*)(* *)(* *)(* *)
     1 2 3 4 5 6 7 8 9

This concludes our demonstration that the Left-to-Right Algorithm generates left-to-right patterns. By symmetry, we also conclude that the Right-to-Left Algorithm will generate right-to-left patterns.

The *SPE* convention of disjunctive ordering plays a crucial role in derivations such as these. Thus, the shorter rule in the expansion of (28a) is applied in the case of position 3 in structures (37) and (44). On the other hand, the longer rule must be applied when the affected substring contains more than one position.

To summarize, we have argued that grammars with binary constituents are characterized as incorporating the condition in (27). A deterministic formalization of the binariness constraint requires the mutual dependency that links the paired brackets in a formula like (27) to be analyzed into more elementary directional dependencies, in which one of the brackets is characterized as prior to the other in the construction algorithm. Thus, two deterministic elementary licensing rules are associated with (27), namely, (28a) and (28b). The first establishes a left-to-right dependency and the second a right-to-left dependency, hence the appellations Left-to-Right Binariness Rule (28a) and Right-to-Left Binariness Rule (28b). The construction rules in (28) replace the interpretive convention (11) (= (12)), which characterizes structures with unbounded constituents.

It appears, then, that structures with binary constituents differ from structures with unbounded constituents in a fundamental way. The characterization of the former type crucially involves the notion of directionality, whereas the characterization of the latter type does not. The construction rules (28a,b) are supplemented by the conventions (21), (22), and (23). A maximally simple deterministic algorithm licensing binary metrical constituents will incorporate only one of the two directional subrules of (28). We thus have two maximally simple deterministic procedures for binary constituents, the Left-to-Right Algorithm consisting of conventions (22), (23), (28a), and (21), and the Right-to-Left Algorithm consisting of conventions (22), (23), (28b), and (21). The former gives rise to left-to-right alternating patterns, and the latter to right-to-left patterns. Thus, a left-to-right pattern is simply a product of the left-to-right organization of the chain of dependencies generated by conventions (23) and (28a) applying from an initial intrinsic boundary. Symmetrically, a right-to-left pattern reflects the right-to-left organization of the chain of dependencies generated by conventions (23) and (28b) applying from an initial intrinsic boundary.

It turns out, then, that the result obtained for structures with unbounded constituents can be partially extended to structures with binary constituents. As in the case of unbounded constituents, the Faithfulness Condition for binary constituents ultimately follows from the formal definition of the notion "constituent" adopted here, which states that the projection of the head of a given bracketed domain onto a higher line *is* the constituent that dominates that domain. The obligatory line 1 positions in an input representation are then analyzed as precursors of metrical constituents and induce boundaries on the side corresponding to the direction of headedness.

As for the Exhaustivity Condition, it again derives from the fact that the procedure for constructing natural constituents is a maximally simple deterministic procedure. More specifically, the Exhaustivity Condition follows from the deterministic application of convention (23) and of the Binariness Rule: as a consequence of determinism, both rules will apply obligatorily and will thus erect a continuous sequence of constituents over the input string. We have demonstrated the existence of two maximally simple and deterministic algorithms: the algorithm that includes the left-to-right subrule but not the right-to-left subrule and the algorithm that includes the right-to-left subrule but not the left-to-right subrule. The first algorithm generates left-to-right patterns and the second right-to-left patterns. We thus derive the Directionality Condition illustrated in (5) from the requirements of determinism and maximal simplicity.

The Maximality Condition, on the other hand, apparently cannot be derived from these primitive principles in the case of binary constituents. This is not surprising, though, for the notion of maximality in the case of binary constituents will have to be defined in terms of explicit representations of the relevant strings. It is the *SPE* notion of disjunctive ordering that applies here, as originally assumed by Chomsky and Halle.[3]

---

3. Kiparsky (1973 and elsewhere) has suggested that the *SPE* parenthesis notation and the notation for unbounded domains should be subsumed under a more general principle, the *Elsewhere Condition*. The results of this section suggest otherwise. In fact, one should expect on formal grounds that it would be impossible to collapse the two notations, since one case involves a notation that derivatively implies a count of positions and the other a notation without count. Common principles do exist at the origin of the structures described by the two notations, namely, the principles of determinism and of maximal simplicity discussed in this section. However, these principles are more abstract than the one assumed by Kiparsky and could not lead by themselves to collapsing the two notations. The principle of disjunctive ordering might be viewed as a particular consequence of the principle of Full Interpretation of Chomsky (1986), assuming a general interpretation of the latter principle. Specifically, one could postulate that the principle of Full Interpretation applies to all aspects of the "assembly language" that

4.4 Ternary Constituents

As shown in section 1.1, ternary constituents are characterized as constituents in which a governed element must be adjacent to the head, with no particular restriction on the direction of government. Thus, ternary constituents differ both from unbounded constituents and from binary constituents: from the former in that governed elements must be adjacent to the head, and from the latter in that the direction of government is undefined. The same considerations that were applied to binary constituents would show that a deterministic characterization of ternariness must involve two directional construction schemata, a left-to-right schema that introduces a right metrical bracket under the control of a left natural bracket at most three positions away, and a symmetric right-to-left schema.

(47)
a. *Left-to-Right Ternariness Principle*
  $[* (_b * (_a * {}_a)_b) \rightarrow [* (_b * (_a * {}_a)_b))$
b. *Right-to-Left Ternariness Principle*
  $*(_b * (_a * {}_a)_b)] \rightarrow (* (_b * (_a * {}_a)_b)]$

As in the case of binary constituents, the Directionality Condition and the Exhaustivity Condition will follow from the requirement that the construction algorithm be both deterministic and maximally simple, and the Maximality Condition will follow from the *SPE* convention governing the parenthesis notation.

We observed in section 1.1 that ternary structures may not in general include constituents with fewer than two positions. For example, words in Cayuvava bear stress on every third mora counting from the end, except that in words where the number of moras is $3n+2$, the first mora is not stressed (see (48c) in chapter 1). We assumed that Cayuvava constituents are ternary and are constructed from right to left, and we postulated that the last mora in each word is marked extrametrical. These hypotheses immediately account for the stress pattern of words with $3n$ moras and $3n+1$ moras. We pointed out that the surprising fact that there is no stress on the initial syllable in words with $3n+2$ moras follows from the Recoverability Condition ((19) of section 1.1). This condition relates three variables:

---

describes the mental computations at the lowest level. Thus, in the same way that this principle will require that every element of PF (Phonetic Form) and LF (Logical Form) receive an appropriate interpretation, it will require that every rule in the program governing the mental computations be actualized.

the direction of government, the location of the heads, and the location of the constituent boundaries. Given a setting of any two of these three variables, the Recoverability Condition requires that the setting of the third be uniquely determined. In particular, it states that, if the specification of the parameter [HT] and the direction of government are known, it must be possible in general to reconstruct the complete constituent structure solely from the location of the heads or solely from the location of the boundaries. Consider in this light the following input form in Cayuvava.

(48) [* * * *]
     1 2 3 4

The right-to-left construction rule (47b) applies to this form, ultimately producing the structure (49).

(49) (*)(* * *)
     1 2 3 4

Head Location now assigns a line 1 asterisk to position 3. It will not assign a line 1 asterisk to position 1, though, for such an assignment would result in the conjugate structure (50), which violates the Recoverability Condition.

(50) * . * .
     * * * *
     1 2 3 4

Given the setting of the parameter [− HT], it is not possible to unambiguously reconstruct (49) from (50), because (50) is also compatible with the structure (51).

(51) (* *)(* *)
     1 2 3 4

In other words, the fact that the direction of government is left unspecified in Cayuvava entails that it is not possible to ascertain whether position 2 in a representation like (50) is governed by position 1 or by position 3. It is ultimately this indeterminacy that blocks marking element 1 as a head. Since Head Location cannot apply to position 1, the brackets around that position will be erased and the structure (52) will be produced.

(52) . . * .
     * (* * *)
     1 2 3 4

The Recoverability Condition entails the following general property.

(53) Two consecutive constructed heads in a ternary metrical structure are
      separated by at least two intervening positions.

The exclusion of the pattern in (50) is a particular instance of (53). In the
case of a degenerate ternary constituent with two positions, property (53)
means that headedness will be assigned to the position within the constituent that is the farther away from the preceding head in the direction of
constituent construction. This implication is correct, as the example of
Cayuvava shows. In this language the pattern in (54a) is excluded and the
Right-to-Left Ternariness Principle will associate the structure (54b) to a
string of five positions.

(54)

a. . * . * .
    (* *)(* * *)
    1 2 3 4 5

b. * . . * .
    (* *)(* * *)
    1 2 3 4 5

In this case the Recoverability Condition eliminates the ambiguity arising
from the fact that the grammar leaves the direction of government undefined. We shall show in section 5.4 that, given the proper formulation of the
boundedness principles, the result concerning the placement of the head in
a degenerate ternary constituent with two positions independently follows
from the Maximality Condition (that is, in this case, from the principle of
disjunctive ordering).[4]

It is clear that the Faithfulness Condition will not give rise to the same
conventions in the case of ternary constituents as in the case of unbounded
or binary constituents. Thus, convention (22b) will not apply in ternary
structures, and it must be replaced by the principles in (55) (see the
formalization in chapter 5).

(55)

a. Licensing by an accent in a left-to-right pattern

    *   *
    * ($_a$ * $_a$) → * ($_a$ * $_a$))

---

4. The property in (53) will also determine the direction of the stress shift when the
head of a complete ternary constituent is deleted. Moreover, the deletion of the
head of a degenerate ternary constituent should lead to the disappearance of the
constituent. Unfortunately, we have no evidence bearing on these two predictions.

b. Licensing by an accent in a right-to-left pattern

$$\ast \qquad\qquad \ast$$
$$(_a \ast {}_a) \ast \; \rightarrow \; ((_a \ast {}_a) \ast$$

A column with two asterisks in the structural descriptions of these rules represents an accented element, whereas a column with only one asterisk represents an unaccented position.[5]

To conclude, we have observed that ternary constituents have rather marked properties, ultimately due to the ambiguity created by the indeterminate character of the direction of government. As we shall show in chapter 5, this marked behavior is reflected at another level, at which constituent structure is analyzed as a coding of the concatenation of positions. At this more abstract level ternary constituents differ again from both unbounded and binary constituents by the indeterminacy to which they give rise.

4.5 The Domino Condition

Finally, we examine the Domino Condition, illustrated in chapter 1 with the case of Winnebago. Consider the initial input in (56a) and the associated metrical pattern in (56b).

(56)
```
a. .   .   .   .   .   .   .   .   .
   *   *   *   *   *   *   *   *   *
   1   2   3   4   5   6   7   8   9
b. .   .   *   .   *   .   *   .   *   *
   *   *   *   *   *   *   *   *   *
   1   2   3   4   5   6   7   8   9
```

The pattern in (56b) is the surface manifestation of the left-to-right construction of a sequence of binary right-headed constituents. The metrical constituent structure corresponding to (56a,b) is displayed in (57).

(57)
```
      .   .   .   .   .   .   .   .   .
   (* *)(* *)(* *)(* *)(*)
    1   2   3   4   5   6   7   8   9
```

---

5. The rules in (55) may have to be invoked when the recoverability of the constituent structure from the representation of the heads is assessed for a string in which some accented element is separated by only one position from another head.

The grammar generating this structure will include the left-to-right option (28a) of the Binariness Rule. The intrinsic natural brackets in the input to the iterative algorithm are those indicated in (58).

(58) .   .   .   .
      [* * * * * * * * *]
       1 2 3 4 5 6 7 8 9

There are only two intrinsic brackets in the structure in (57), the leftmost left bracket and the rightmost right bracket. All the other brackets are dependent brackets. The right bracket after position 2 is licensed by the left bracket before position 1, by the Left-to-Right Binariness Rule (28a). This right bracket in turn licenses the left bracket before position 3, via convention (23). This left bracket in turn licenses the right bracket after position 4, again by (28a). And so on.

   The left-to-right chain of dependencies just described sets the stage for the discussion of the domino effect. Suppose that a new position, call it q, is inserted by some phonological rule between the original positions 3 and 4. As the grammar now stands, the metrical constituent structure will be as follows after the insertion of q.

(59) .   .   .   .
      (* *)(* * *)(* *)(* *)(*)
       1 2 3 q 4 5 6 7 8 9

However, as we know from the study of the Winnebago alternating pattern, the structure in (59) is not the correct metrical structure for the string augmented by q. In fact, the binariness restriction on the constituents is "persistent" and continues to hold even after the insertion of the new position q. We can formalize this observation as follows.

(60) Binariness is projected across levels: at all levels, a right (resp. left) bracket in a left-to-right (resp. right-to-left) binary structure must be licensed by (28a) (resp. (28b)).

This principle immediately entails that the bracketing in (57) cannot be preserved after the insertion of q into the string, since the right bracket that follows position 4 will not be licensed by the Binariness Rule in the output of the insertion rule. Then the right bracket after position 4 in this output is "delicensed"—that is, deleted. Consequently, the structural description in (23) for the licensing of the left bracket before position 5 is no longer met, and the latter bracket in turn is delicensed. The delicensing of the left bracket before position 5 then entails that of the paired right bracket after position 6—which in turn triggers the delicensing of the left bracket before position 7. Step by step, the delicensing procedure will eventually affect all the dependent brackets to the right of position 4, up to the next intrinsic natural bracket, which, in this case, is the right bracket at the right limit of the string. Assuming principle (60) and the delicensing it entails, then, the bracketing present in the output of the insertion rule is in fact as shown in (61), not (59).

(61) . . . .
    (* *)[* * * * * * * *]
    1 2 3 q 4 5 6 7 8 9

The left bracket before position 3 and the right bracket at the right extremity of the string show up as natural brackets, and not as metrical brackets, because they are licensed neither by (28a) nor by (21). The abnormal structure in (59) will be repaired by means of a new application of the conventions (23) and (28a). The resulting output will be the bracketing in (62).

(62) . . . .
    (* *)[* *)[* *)[* *)[* *)
    1 2 3 q 4 5 6 7 8 9

The application of the interpretive rule (21) to (62) yields the metrical constituent structure in (63).

(63) . . . .
    (* *)(* *)(* *)(* *)(* *)
    1 2 3 q 4 5 6 7 8 9

The surface pattern corresponding to (63) is displayed in (64).

(64) . * . * . * . * . *
    * * * * * * * * * *
    1 2 3 q 4 5 6 7 8 9

The formal structure of the stress shift produced by the domino effect and the subsequent reconstruction of the constituents, exemplified by Winnebago, may be characterized as follows.

(65)

a. Given a substring u that is analyzed as a bounded constituent $C(u)$, the analysis $C(u)$ is destroyed if some element is inserted inside u.

b. The brackets that are dependents of the brackets of a destroyed constituent are delicensed, and the corresponding constituents in turn are destroyed. And so on.

c. The metrical rules reapply to the last bracket in each maximal sequence of dependent brackets in the output of (b).

A fundamental property underlying this procedure is that once a metrical constituent structure has been constructed, the rules generating that structure reapply whenever their structural description is met. They are "persistent" rules, whose behavior crucially differs from that of ordinary phonological rules and which are not linearly ordered with respect to these ordinary rules. This special behavior follows from the fact that rules that erect constituent boundaries are to be considered an integral part of the phonological representation, on a par with the constituent structure they generate (see chapter 5). They can be viewed as a "genetic code" for this constituent structure, which is activated whenever necessity arises. The stress shift triggered by the deletion of the head of a constituent also reflects the persistent nature of the rule that identifies the position of the head within the constituent. When the head of a constituent is deleted, the rule that specifies the parameter setting for the direction of government reapplies automatically to the output of the deletion rule.

The description in (65) implies that the insertion of a new position between two consecutive constituents will not trigger any reconstruction of the constituent structure. For example, the insertion of a new position q between positions 4 and 5 in (57) leads to the structure shown in (66a), which gives rise to the surface pattern in (66b).

(66)

a. .   .   .   .

   (* *)(* *) * (* *)(* *)(*)

   1 2 3 4 q 5 6 7 8 9

b. . * . * . . * . * *

   * * * * * * * * * *

   1 2 3 4 q 5 6 7 8 9

It is because the cases of internal and external epenthesis behave differently that the metrical structure must be established in two steps. If external epenthesis were to shift the stress pattern in the same way as internal epenthesis, then the forms could be accounted for simply by ordering the construction of the metrical structure after the application of epenthesis. Note that an epenthetic position inserted externally between two consecutive constituents may be restructured if it is preceded in the left-to-right pattern by another epenthetic position internal to a constituent. Suppose, for example, that two positions were to be inserted into the structure (57), one between positions 3 and 4 and one between positions 6 and 7, yielding the truncated structure in (67).

(67)   .   .   .   .
       (∗ ∗)[∗ ∗ ∗ ∗ ∗ ∗ ∗ ∗ ∗]
        1 2 3 q 4 5 6 r 7 8 9

Then the form will be restructured as in (68a) and the pattern in (68b) will emerge.

(68)
a.   .   .   .   .
     (∗ ∗)(∗ ∗)(∗ ∗)(∗ ∗)(∗ ∗)(∗)
      1 2 3 q 4 5 6 r 7 8 9

b.   . ∗ . ∗ . ∗ . ∗ . ∗ ∗
     ∗ ∗ ∗ ∗ ∗ ∗ ∗ ∗ ∗ ∗ ∗
     1 2 3 q 4 5 6 r 7 8 9

The model just developed thus adequately accounts for the behavior of alternating patterns under insertion, exemplified by Winnebago. The restructuring procedure formalized above makes the interesting prediction that an intrinsic boundary will check the spreading of delicensing. Such a boundary is by definition not dependent on any other boundary and thus will not be deleted by the domino effect. To illustrate, consider an input with an intrinsic head, such as the one in (69).

(69)   .   .   .   .   .   ∗   .   .   .
       ∗ ∗ ∗ ∗ ∗ ∗ ∗ ∗ ∗
       1 2 3 4 5 6 7 8 9

As in the cases discussed above, let us assume a left-to-right structure of binary right-headed constituents. The intrinsic natural boundaries inserted into (69) are as follows.

(70)   .   .   .   .   .   ∗   .   .   .
       [∗ ∗ ∗ ∗ ∗ ∗) ∗ ∗ ∗]
        1 2 3 4 5 6 7 8 9

This intrinsic bracketing gives rise to the metrical structure in (71).

(71) . . . . . . * . . .
    (* *)(* *)(* *)(* *)(*)
    1 2 3 4 5 6 7 8 9

Suppose now that a new position is inserted between positions 3 and 4. This epenthesis will give rise to the structure in (72), in which all the brackets to the right of position 4, up to the intrinsic bracket following position 6, have been delicensed.

(72) . . . . . . * . . .
    (* *)[* * * * *)(* *)(*)
    1 2 3 q 4 5 6 7 8 9

The metrical right bracket after position 6 is not deleted, because it is licensed at all levels, by (22b). Consequently, the brackets that follow it in the structure remain intact. The restructuring of the form in (72) yields the metrical structure in (73a), which corresponds to the pattern in (73b).

(73)
a. . . . . . . * . . .
    (* *)(* *)(* *)(*)(* *)(*)
    1 2 3 q 4 5 6 7 8 9
b. . * . * . * * . * *
    * * * * * * * * * *
    1 2 3 q 4 5 6 7 8 9

If our formalization is empirically correct, it then means that the brackets associated with intrinsic heads should remain *distinguishable* from the dependent brackets throughout the process of metrical construction and it confirms that the nonintrinsic heads have a subordinate status within the metrical representation. Unfortunately, we have no empirical evidence bearing on the prediction of the formalism in this specific instance.

    To summarize, the Domino Condition follows from the directional character of the dependencies established by the construction of the bounded constituents and from the convention in (65a). Given these principles, the insertion of a position within a constituent triggers a chain reaction leading to the delicensing of a maximal continuous sequence of dependent brackets. This delicensing is followed by reconstruction of a sequence of bounded constituents, owing to the persistent character of the metrical rules. The licensing and delicensing procedures operate as indicated in (65). By contrast, the insertion of a new position outside constituents does not trigger delicensing. The fact that the domino effect is checked by an intrinsic natural bracket implies that nonintrinsic asterisks on line 1 are not on a par with intrinsic asterisks.

To conclude: The Exhaustivity Condition, the Maximality Condition, the Faithfulness Condition, the Directionality Condition, and the Domino Condition all ultimately follow from the formalization of the objects and the relations developed here. The Faithfulness Condition follows from the definition of the notion of constituent presented in chapter 1. The other conditions can be traced back to the fact that the procedure for constructing metrical constituent structure is a minimal deterministic procedure. Specifically, the observation in (24) concerning unbounded constituent structures can be extended to the case of bounded structures. We then revise (24) to (74).

(74) The procedure for constructing the metrical constituent structure is the simplest possible deterministic procedure. The constituent demarcations are those licensed by the extremities of the input string, by the intrinsic heads, and, in the case of bounded constituents, by the iterative application of the construction rule, and only those.

Of course, in order for this result to have significance, the requirement of determinism should be more than merely an ad hoc condition invoked for the formalization of metrical structure, whose effects would not extend beyond that special case. And in fact determinism appears to play a role at other levels of the grammar as well. An important result of Berwick and Weinberg (1984) is that some central properties of grammatical theory can be deduced from the requirement that parsing should be deterministic. For example, Berwick and Weinberg (1984) show that Subjacency, a constraint governing a certain class of syntactic relations, is in fact an effect of the deterministic character of language processing. In this section we have assumed that the requirement of determinism can be extended to other levels of grammatical description. In particular, we have assumed that determinism constrains not only the "on-line" mapping performed by the grammatical parser but also the relations between the various "wired-in" modules and principles that embody grammatical competence. We shall point out in chapter 5 that this extension of Berwick and Weinberg's idea has interesting consequences for other parts of our model. Essentially, we shall show that the fact that the head of a constituent is necessarily located at the (right or left) extremity of the constituent in the unmarked case also follows from the requirement of determinism.

Chapter 5
The Formal Theory of Metrical Constituent Construction

5.1 The Notion of Metrical Constituent Structure

The notion of constituent used in metrical theory is the same as the standard syntactic notion. Moreover, constituents are to be analyzed as complex objects made up of more elementary components: specifically, within a metrical representation the pure representation of the heads of the constituents, with no indication of the constituent boundaries, and the pure representation of the boundaries, with no indication of the heads, function as independent entities. These two components of the metrical representation are related to each other in a deterministic fashion. Given the specification of the parameters [HT] and [left/right], the complete constituent structure can be reconstructed either from the location of the heads or from the location of the boundaries, by the Recoverability Condition (19) of chapter 1. To illustrate, a representation such as the one in (1a) will be characterized as the combination of the two more elementary representations (1b) and (1c). Representation (1b) displays the constituent boundaries but not the heads; (1c), the heads but not the constituent boundaries.

(1)

a.   * . . . * . *
  (* * * *)(* *)(*)
   1 2 3 4 5 6 7

b. (* * * *)(* *)(*)
   1 2 3 4 5 6 7

c.   * . . . * . *
  * * * * * * *
  1 2 3 4 5 6 7

The grammar that generates (1a) contains the following rule (see chapter 1).

(2) Line 0 parameter settings are [+HT, −BND, left].

Given this rule, the representations in (1b) and (1c) are equivalent to each other, as well as to (1a), and hence can be termed *conjugate* representations. Informally speaking, given the statement that government is to the right, each of these representations contains as much information as the other, and as (1a).

The division of metrical constituent structure into distinct components is supported by the facts of stress shift discussed in section 1.1. To account for these facts, it is necessary to characterize the location of heads as a derived property of the pure representation of constituent boundaries. Further empirical evidence of the independence of the two components of metrical constituent structure is provided by such languages as Yidin^y, in which the placement of the heads, but not that of the boundaries, is influenced by rules of the phonological component that lengthen or shorten the stress-bearing units. The division of metrical constituent structure into more elementary subcomponents is then directly reflected in the grammar. Specifically, the construction of metrical constituents is effected in two stages, by means of two independent rules. First the constituent boundaries are erected; then the heads of the constituents are placed. For a constituent to be erected, both rules must apply.

The standard geometrical notation illustrated in (1) is obviously inadequate for formalizing the Recoverability Condition. Moreover, it is incapable of representing the dependency relations that hold between consecutive constituents within a bounded metrical structure (see the discussion of the Domino Condition in chapter 4). In this chapter we will argue that the geometrical notation in fact is a high-level notation that merely describes special aspects of the metrical structure and that, underlying this abstract notation, there exists another mode of description that in particular is capable of representing the relation between conjugate metrical components.

5.2 Metrical Representations as Logical Structures

The mode of description underlying the more abstract geometrical representation will be taken to be analogous to that used in declarative programming languages such as Prolog (see, for example, Clocksin and Mellish 1981). Specifically, we shall assume that a metrical constituent structure is represented as a set of logical formulae at the underlying level. For example, the component (1b) of the structure (1a) will be formalized as in (3a), where $C(u)$ is a predicate with the interpretation given in (3b) and where ˆ is the symbol for concatenation.

(3)

a. $C(1ˆ2ˆ3ˆ4)$, $C(5ˆ6)$, $C(7)$

b. $C(u)$, u some string $=_{\text{def}}$ "u is a bracketed domain"

Similarly, the component (1c) will be represented as in (4a), where $H(p)$ is a predicate with the interpretation given in (4b).

(4)

a. $H(1)$, $H(5)$, $H(7)$

b. $H(p)$, p some position $=_{\text{def}}$ "p is projected up onto the higher line"

The representation of the metrical constituent structure will also include the statement that the positions 1, 2, 3, 4, 5, 6, and 7 constitute a string. This statement is formalized in (5).

(5) $1ˆ2ˆ3ˆ4ˆ5ˆ6ˆ7$

In the formalization just sketched, the sign ˆ is construed as an operator in (3a) but as a predicate in (5). Throughout this discussion we shall assume that this sign may consistently have one interpretation or the other, depending on the context. The two competing definitions of ˆ are made explicit in (6).

(6)

a. $uˆv$, u and v some strings $=_{\text{def}}$ "the result of concatenating u and v in that order"

b. $uˆv$, u and v some strings $=_{\text{def}}$ "u and v are adjacent substrings arranged in that order within a larger string"

The motivation for adopting the formalization (3)–(5) should be clear. Assuming representations of the form in (3a), it is possible to describe the relations that hold between particular substructures by means of logical operators. Thus, the structure with the geometrical description in (1a) is now described as the conjunction of the set of formulae in (3a), corresponding to the geometrical description in (1b), and the set in (4a), corresponding to the geometrical description in (1c), and the relation between these two conjugate substructures will be represented by means of implications holding between the predicates $C(u)$ and $H(p)$:

(7) $C(p^\frown u) \leftrightarrow H(p)$

> p a position and u a maximal substring such that H does not hold of any position in u

Within the formalism just sketched, the formula in (7) will be taken to characterize the property of left-headedness in a grammar in which heads are terminal.

In order to provide an explicit formalization of the relation between (3a) and (4a), the representation underlying the geometrical notation will have to include other formulae besides those in (3), (5), and (7); the latter formulae must be viewed as embedded within a more comprehensive formal system, which we shall denote by M. The system M will incorporate features from logical programming. It will contain two main categories of expressions, *terms* (those objects that are arguments of the predicates of the system) and *formulae* (those expressions that are interpreted as making assertions). In the case of M, the terms will be strings of phonological units or variables standing for such strings.

There is a fundamental difference between a formal system like M, which is developed for empirical purposes, and a formal theory in the sense of logic. The construction of a formal theory in the sense of logic aims at characterizing the formulae whose validity is independent of the interpretation of the variables.[1] By contrast, a formal system such as M, like a program in Prolog, aims at characterizing the terms that are arguments of certain designated predicates.

We shall assume that the relation that holds between the underlying logical notation in (3a) and (4a) and the higher-level geometrical notation in (1a) is of the same nature as the relation that holds between a logical theory and an *interpretation* or a *model* of that theory (Lyndon 1966; Mendelson 1979). We postulate that the mapping between these two levels of notation has the property of "extensional completeness" defined in (8) (where $\sim$ is the sign for negation).

(8) *Axiom of Extensional Completeness*

> Let $P(u)$ be a predicate of the underlying logical system and let $p(u)$ be the geometrical interpretation of $P(u)$ at the higher geometrical level. If

---

1. A formal theory in the sense of logic is a class of formulae constructed from propositional connectives, punctuation marks, variables, predictates, functions, and constants, and derived from an initial set of logical and nonlogical (proper) axioms by applying the rules of *modus ponens* and generalization; see Mendelson (1979).

the underlying logical system does not include $P(w)$, w some constant string, then $\sim p(w)$ holds at the higher level.

The reason for introducing this axiom is that it allows for "underspecified" logical representations—logical representations such that, for some predicate $P(u)$ and for some substring w, it may be the case that neither $P(w)$ nor $\sim P(w)$ holds. For example, the logical representation in (3a) is underspecified in this sense. This representation is nevertheless sufficient to derive the geometrical representation in (1a) when the Axiom of Extensional Completeness is assumed. Without this axiom, the logical formulae in (3a) would have to be supplemented by the set of formulae of the form $\sim C(w)$, where w is any substring distinct from $1^{\wedge}2^{\wedge}3^{\wedge}4$, from $5^{\wedge}6$, and from 7; similarly, the formulae in (4a) would have to be supplemented by the set of formulae of the form $\sim H(s)$, where s is any position distinct from 1, from 5, and from 7. We shall demonstrate that, in fact, the underspecified character of the underlying logical representation plays a crucial role in the formalization of such phenomena as stress shift under deletion. To formalize underspecification, we shall use the connective $\neg$, defined as follows.

(9) Let T be a formal system and let $P(u)$ be a predicate of T and w be a constant term of T. The relation "$\neg$" holds between the formal system T, the predicate $P(u)$, and the constant string w iff T does not contain the formula $P(w)$, that is, iff T contains neither the formula $P(w)$ nor the formula $\sim P(w)$, or T only contains the formula $\sim P(w)$.

Thus, the connective $\neg$ in effect denotes a three-place metarelation among formal systems, predicates, and constant terms. When the formal system is held constant in this relation, we obtain a two-place relation. If there is no ambiguity with regard to the identity of the formal system concerned, we shall omit it from the formulation of the relation $\neg$, by convention. Thus, we shall use formulae like $\neg P(w)$, $P(u)$ some predicate and w some constant term, with the following interpretation.

(10) $\neg P(w) =_{\text{def}}$ "$P(w)$ does not hold within the formal system under consideration"

Note that $\neg P(u)$, where $P(u)$ is a predicate of some formal system T, *is not* a predicate of the system T.

One crucial stage in the construction of the logical system M that will underlie the geometrical representation in (1a) will consist in providing a purely formal "syntactic" characterization of the predicate $C(u)$ defined in (3b). Following the analysis put forth in chapter 4, we shall assume that the predicate $C(u)$ is a compound predicate of the form $L(u)$ *and* $R(u)$, where the more elementary predicates $L(u)$ and $R(u)$ have the interpretation in (11).

(11)

a. $L(u)$, u some string $=_{\text{def}}$ "u is adjacent to a left metrical bracket and, if v is a substring of u that is adjacent to a left metrical bracket, then $u = v\char94 w$ for some w"

b. $R(u)$, u some string $=_{\text{def}}$ "u is adjacent to a right metrical bracket and, if v is a substring of u that is adjacent to a right metrical bracket, then $u = w\char94 v$ for some w"

These definitions may be formalized as follows.

(12)

a. $L(u)$ and $\neg L(v) \leftrightarrow L(u\char94 v)$,
   for every pair of strings u, v

b. $R(u)$ and $\neg R(v) \leftrightarrow R(v\char94 u)$,
   for every pair of strings u, v

The characterization in (12) ensures that the predicates $L(u)$ and $R(u)$ give rise to well-formed bracketings. For example, in the case of structure (1a) the formulae in (13a) are true, whereas those in (13b) are false.

(13)

a. $L(1\char94 2\char94 3)$, $L(1\char94 2)$, $L(1)$, $L(5)$

b. $L(1\char94 2\char94 3\char94 4\char94 5)$, $L(5\char94 6\char94 7)$

We shall denote the compound predicate $L(u)$ *and* $R(u)$ by $LR(u)$. Thus, we have the definition in (14).

(14) $C(u) \leftrightarrow LR(u)$, for every string u

The complete description of a metrical constituent structure will involve the notion of "natural boundary." To formalize this notion, we shall introduce the two predicates $l(u)$ and $r(u)$, with the interpretation in (15).

(15)

a. $l(u)$, u some string $=_{\text{def}}$ "u is adjacent to a left natural bracket and, if v is a substring of u that is adjacent to a left natural bracket, then $u = v\char94 w$ for some w"

b. $r(u)$, u some string $=_{\text{def}}$ "u is adjacent to a right natural bracket and, if v is a substring of u that is adjacent to a right natural bracket, then $u = w\char94 v$ for some w"

Quite clearly, $l(u)$ and $r(u)$ will be characterized syntactically in a way analogous to $L(u)$ and $R(u)$. Specifically, they will verify the following formal axioms.

(16)

a. l(u) and $\neg$l(v) $\leftrightarrow$ l(u^v),
   for every pair of strings u, v

b. r(u) and $\neg$r(v) $\leftrightarrow$ r(v^u),
   for every pair of strings u, v

The notion of metrical boundary is subsumed under the more general notion of natural boundary. Thus, Universal Grammar includes the formulae in (17).

(17)

a. L(u) $\rightarrow$ l(u), for every string u

b. R(u) $\rightarrow$ r(u), for every string u

The rule of metrical constituent boundary construction (12) of chapter 4, repeated here as (18), will be formalized as in (19).

(18) [...] $\rightarrow$ (...)

(19)

a. l(u) $\rightarrow$ L(u), for every string u

b. r(u) $\rightarrow$ R(u), for every string u

In a grammar that lacks the construction rule (19) the metrical bracketing will be induced by the accented positions and by rule (21) of chapter 4, repeated here as (20).

(20) A left (resp. right) bracket that is paired with a right (resp. left) metrical bracket is interpreted as a metrical bracket.

This rule will be formalized as the following axiom of Universal Grammar.

(21)

a. L(u) and r(u) $\rightarrow$ R(u), for every string u

b. l(u) and R(u) $\rightarrow$ L(u), for every string u

We shall take the Maximality Condition (rule (17) in chapter 4) to be a basic axiom of the formal system M. For the purpose of formalizing this condition, it will be useful to introduce the notion of "free string."

(22) Given a formal system T whose constant terms are strings over some alphabet, we shall say that a constant term w *is free in* T iff every predicate of T that holds of a substring of w holds of w.

In effect, within the formal systems we are considering, the free strings will be those substrings that do not cross constituent boundaries. We shall assume that M obeys the following condition.

(23) Only free strings or variables are terms.

Condition (23) means that the set of arguments of each predicate of M is included within the set of substrings that do not cross constituent boundaries. In section 5.7 we shall propose an explanation for this condition. Note that (23) is in fact a recursive constraint. The notion "free" is defined with respect to the output of the permissible logical derivations. Yet logical derivations are permissible only if they obey the constraint that only free strings are substituted for variables in the axioms of the system. In fact, it appears that the architectures of the grammars of natural languages are such that (22) and (23) never give rise to any circularity (for illustration of this property, see section 5.3). An effect of adding (23) to the system is that it permits a simple and maximally general formulation of many conditions. In particular, it allows us to give the following formulation of the Maximality Condition.

(24) $u^\smallfrown v \rightarrow (l(v) \leftrightarrow r(u))$,
for every pair of strings u, v

To complete the construction of M, we shall extend the predicate $H(p)$ of (4b) to strings.

(25) $H(u)$, u some string $=_{def}$ "u contains one and only one position that is projected up onto the higher line"

The predicate $H(u)$ will be formally characterized as in (26).

(26) $H(u^\smallfrown v) \leftrightarrow (H(u)$ and $\neg H(v))$ or $(\neg H(u)$ and $H(v))$.
for every pair of strings u, v such that $u^\smallfrown v$ is free

The axiom (26) means in particular that, for every partition of a headed string $u^\smallfrown v$ into two substrings u and v, one and only one of the two substrings u and v contains a head. In other words, a headed string contains one and only one head. To formalize the constraint that the placement of heads is restricted to metrical domains, we shall postulate the following axioms.

(27)

a. H(u) and l(u) → L(u), for every string u

b. H(u) and r(u) → R(u), for every string u

We shall express left-headedness by the formula in (28).

(28) L(u) ↔ H(u), for every string u

We are now in a position to make explicit the relation between the representations in (3a) (= (1b)) and (4a) (= (1c)). Specifically, given the formal axioms in (12), (14), (16), (21), (24), and (28), (4a) is a logical consequence of (3a), and conversely. Consider for example the first formula in each of (3a) and (4a). By (14), the formula $C(1^{\wedge}2^{\wedge}3^{\wedge}4)$ implies the formula $L(1^{\wedge}2^{\wedge}3^{\wedge}4)$. By (12a), $L(1^{\wedge}2^{\wedge}3^{\wedge}4)$ implies $L(1)$. By axiom (28), the latter formula in turn implies $H(1)$. Thus, $H(1)$ follows from the representation in (3a). Conversely, by (28), the formula $H(1)$ implies $L(1)$. By (4a) and (12a), $L(1)$ implies $L(1^{\wedge}2^{\wedge}3^{\wedge}4)$. By (28) and (24), $H(5)$ in (4a) implies $r(4)$, which implies $R(1^{\wedge}2^{\wedge}3^{\wedge}4)$ by (4a), (16b), and (21). Thus, $LR(1^{\wedge}2^{\wedge}3^{\wedge}4)$ follows from the representation in (4a).

To summarize: The conjugate components of a metrical grid representation such as (1a) may be associated in a one-to-one fashion with sets of formulae within a formal system M. The complete metrical constituent structure corresponds to the union of the conjugate sets of formulae. In addition, each one of the two conjugate sets implies the other within M. The proper axioms of M (the axioms of M that are not purely logical axioms, in the sense used in the description of logical theories; see Mendelson 1979) are the following formulae.

(29) (12): The axiom that characterizes the predicates $L(u)$ and $R(u)$

(14): The formal definition of the predicate $C(u)$

(16): The axiom that characterizes the predicates $l(u)$ and $r(u)$

(17): The axiom that subsumes $L(u)$ under $l(u)$ and $R(u)$ under $r(u)$

(21): The axiom that defines a natural boundary that is paired with a metrical boundary as a metrical boundary

(24): The Maximality Condition

(26): The axiom that characterizes the predicate $H(u)$

(27): The condition that restricts the placement of heads to metrical domains

(28): The formula defining the direction of government

(19): The formula formalizing metrical construction

The system M will include the formula (28) or its symmetric counterpart only in case the grammar has the property [+HT]. It will include the formula in (19) only if the grammar includes a rule of metrical boundary construction. The axioms in (12), (14), (16), (17), (21), (24), (26), and (27) formalize principles of Universal Grammar. The axioms in (19) and (28) formalize language-specific rules, namely, the rule of metrical construction (assuming that it is present in the grammar) and the rule that stipulates the direction of headedness. The formal system is subject to the condition in (23), which restricts constant terms to free strings and is construed in accordance with the definition in (9), which formalizes underspecification. The interpretation of M is governed by the Axiom of Extensional Completeness in (8).

5.3 The Notions "Level of Representation" and "Rule of Grammar"

At this point we must explore the grammatical status of the formal system M. If this system is to be characterized as a grammatical object, there are two—and only two—possibilities: either M is a phonological representation or M is a set of phonological rules. It has traditionally been assumed that these two types of objects are completely segregated. The analysis of the preceding section then seems to lead to a puzzle. On the one hand, we have argued that the standard geometrical representation of the metrical structure should be defined as the interpretation of a subset of formulae of M, which implies that M should be characterized as a phonological representation. On the other hand, M includes principles like the one that specifies the direction of government, and such principles have been formalized as rules in chapter 1.

The answer to this puzzle lies with the special notion of persistent rule introduced in chapter 4. Within generative grammar the notion of rule was originally intended as a tool for formalizing the mappings between the various levels of representation. At the same time, however, it was recognized that the formalism of rules could also be used to describe generalizations about representations within a given level. For example, the redundancy and linking rules of *SPE* are rules of the second type.[2] This

---

2. This is not to imply that every redundancy rule is to be characterized as a rule of the second type. Some researchers are currently trying to develop theories in which redundancy rules ("default rules" and "complement rules") are treated on a par with phonological rules of the first type and, in particular, are linearly ordered with respect to such rules; see Archangeli (1984), Steriade (1986).

second notion of rule is conceptually very different from the original one. A rule of the second type does not derive a new grammatical representation from the input form; instead, it states a general property of the representation and may therefore be considered an integral part of that representation. We shall call rules of the first type *external rules* or *e-rules* and rules of the second type *internal rules* or *i-rules*. In a parallel fashion, we shall distinguish between *e-derivations* and *i-derivations*: an e-derivation formalizes a mapping between distinct levels of representation, whereas an i-derivation is a derivation internal to some given level. We observed in chapter 4 that rules like the one that specifies the parameter settings for a given line or the one that constructs constituent boundaries on a given line behave differently from the regular e-rules of the phonological component. Specifically, such rules, which we have called *persistent rules*, are not linearly ordered with respect to the regular e-rules but apply whenever their structural description is met. In this respect, they behave like the redundancy rules or linking rules of *SPE*, and we can characterize them as i-rules.

These definitions will allow us to maintain the characterization of the formal system M as a phonological representation. To illustrate the organization of the phonological component that is implied by these assumptions, let us consider again the structure in (1a). For the sake of illustration, we shall assume that the accented positions in this metrical constituent structure are those indicated in (30), that is, positions 5 and 7.

(30) . . . . * . *
     * * * * * * *
     1 2 3 4 5 6 7

The formal system M associated with the metrical constituent structure in (1a) is then characterized as follows.

(31)
a. M includes the universal axioms (12), (14), (16), (17), (21), (24), (26), and (27).

b. M includes the language-particular axioms (19) and (28).

c. M includes the following morpheme-particular axioms:
   i. $1 \char`^ 2 \char`^ 3 \char`^ 4 \char`^ 5 \char`^ 6 \char`^ 7$, l(1), r(7)
   ii. H(5), H(7)

The particular axioms in (31ci) state that the string is obtained by concatenating the positions 1, 2, 3, 4, 5, 6, and 7, in that order, and that it is enclosed within natural brackets. (Note that the formal object ˆ must be construed here as a predicate.) The axioms in (31cii) identify the accented positions. It is easy to check that the characterization in (31) is sufficient to describe the structure in (1a). Specifically, within a formal system that includes the axioms in (31), the formulae in (3a) and (4a), which formalize the structure (1a), are theorems. To put it differently, a formal system that includes the axioms in (31) automatically includes the formulae in (3a) and (4a).

The formal relation between the metrical constituent structure in (1a) (= (3a) and (4a)) and the boundary lexical conditions in (31) is to be characterized not as a grammatical e-derivation but as a logical i-derivation. The sets of formulae in (31c) and in (3a) and (4a) are not representations at distinct levels; instead, they are different sets of properties of the same level of representation. At the same time a logical ordering obtains between these two sets of properties. The formulae in (31c) are logically prior to those in (3a) and (4a) and function as boundary conditions within the level of representation formalized as M. We state this result in (32), where it is assumed that the level formalized as M is in fact the underlying level of phonological representation.

(32) The formulae representing the metrical constituent structure are theorems within the formal system that characterizes the initial level of representation. This formal system includes as its proper axioms

    a.   the universal principles in (12), (14), (16), (17), (21), (24), (26), and (27),

    b.   the language-particular axioms that state whether there is a rule of metrical construction and characterize the properties of government, and

    c.   the morpheme-particular axioms that describe the string of positions over which the metrical constituent structure is erected and, in particular, identify the accented elements.

We have thus constructed a formal system within which the metrical constituent structure is embedded and that permits us to state precisely the relation holding between the components of the metrical structure, as well as the relation holding between the whole structure and the various rules and principles discussed in chapters 1 through 4. At the same time, though, the metrical constituent structure—the complete list of formulae of the form $LR(u)$, u some string, and of the form $H(p)$, p some position—must be described as a theoretically independent entity, which is not on a par

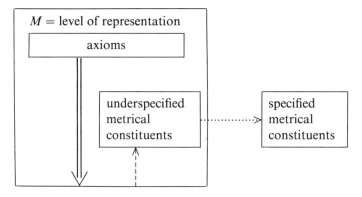

Figure 5.1

with the other formulae of the formal system within which it is embedded. In other words, the metrical structure must be characterized as a mode of representation by itself. The relation between this mode of representation and the original formal system is not derivational and contrasts with the standard relation between levels established by the e-rules of the phonological component. The relevant notion here is that of "projection" in the sense of Halle and Vergnaud (1978). A subset of some level L may be identified as an independent mode of description if it has a special interpretation or function with respect to some other cognitive representation, linguistic or otherwise. The special interpretation associated with the projected level of metrical constituent structure will be characterized in section 5.4. The notion of projection contrasts with that of derivation: a projected level is a subpart of its source level, whereas a derivation from one level to another involves the application of phonological rules. However, the relation between a level and a projection of it, although not derivational, is by definition an e-relation. The diagram in figure 5.1 represents the structure of each phonological level of representation as it emerges from the preceding construction. In this diagram an arrow linking the edge of a box A to the edge of a box B indicates that the set of formulae in B is related to the set of formulae in A in the way defined by the arrow. A double arrow ($\Rightarrow$) represents an implicational i-relation (internal to a given level of representation). The diagram "$A \dashrightarrow B$" represents the projection of B from A. A dotted arrow ($\cdots\rightarrow$) represents the relation between a set of formulae and their geometrical interpretation.

It remains to describe the manner in which e-rules apply to systems like this one. For the sake of illustration, we shall again consider the structure in (1a), and we shall suppose that a phonological rule applies to delete position 5 in that structure. This rule takes as input the formal system M and yields as output a new formal system M'. We shall postulate the following principle.

(33) The null string is not a term.

Application of the deletion rule will then merely result in the disappearance of the formula $H(5)$, which will not be included in the derived system M'. We cannot assume that the proper axioms of M' are those of M modified by the deletion rule. This would incorrectly entail that the output of the deletion rule is the metrical constituent structure in (34).

(34) * . . . . *
     (* * * * *)(*)
      1 2 3 4 6 7

It appears that the stock of axioms of the derived formal system M' should be assumed to include all the formulae in M. With this assumption, and with the assumption that a deletion rule such as the one hypothesized above will apply to all occurrences of the concerned position in the formal system, the correct constituent structure will be derived. In particular, the formulae $LR(5\hat{\ }6)$ and $H(5\hat{\ }6)$ of M will be replaced by the formulae $LR(6)$ and $H(6)$, respectively. Position 6 will be identified as the head of the new constituent within the output of the deletion rule. Thus, the stress shift effect follows from the proposed formalization. Note that the underspecified character of the representation plays a crucial role in this account: if the initial system M were to include the formula $\sim H(6)$, the system produced by the application of the deletion rule would be contradictory.

The central aspects of the structure of the phonological component that emerge from this discussion may be represented by means of figure 5.2. The graphic conventions in this figure are the same as in figure 5.1, with the addition that a standard arrow ($\rightarrow$) represents an e-derivational relation.

The implicational relation that holds between the axioms of a given level of representation and the complete level is to be contrasted with the relation between levels established by phonological e-rules. The implicational relations internal to a level are formalized by means of i-rules, which have the property of "persistence." The persistent i-rules are not linearly ordered with respect to e-rules but apply whenever their structural description is met. Thus, when present in a given grammar, the rule that characterizes constituents as bounded will apply at each stage of the derivation (see the discussion of the Domino Condition in chapter 4 and the next section).

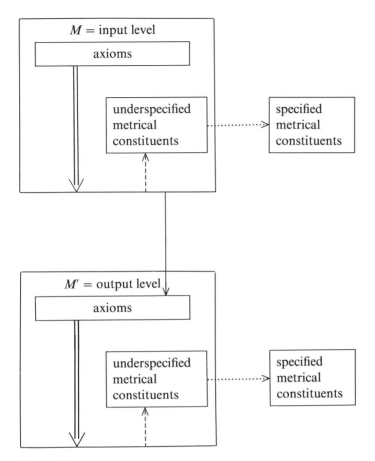

Figure 5.2

5.4 The Formalization of Boundedness and Directionality

Metrical i-rules are formalized as logical implications at the underlying logical level. For example, the rule of metrical construction is formalized as follows at that level ($=$ (19)).

(35) *Rule of metrical construction*
  $l(u) \rightarrow L(u)$, for every string u
  $r(u) \rightarrow R(u)$, for every string u

Similarly, the rule that specifies the direction of government is formalized as one of the logical implications in (36) (see (28)).

(36)
a. *Left-headed constituent structure*
  $H(u) \leftrightarrow L(u)$, for every string u
b. *Right-headed constituent structure*
  $H(u) \leftrightarrow R(u)$, for every string u

The property of boundedness has not been formalized yet. The most general formulation would be the following.

(37)
a. $u\hat{\ }v$ and $\neg H(u) \rightarrow (l(u\hat{\ }v) \leftrightarrow H(v))$,
  for every pair u, v such that $u\hat{\ }v$ is free
b. $u\hat{\ }v$ and $\neg H(v) \rightarrow (r(u\hat{\ }v) \leftrightarrow H(u))$,
  for every pair u, v such that $u\hat{\ }v$ is free

The formulae in (37) state that an arbitrary parenthesis-free substring without any head which abuts a constituent boundary is necessarily adjacent within the same constituent to a substring that contains a head, and that conversely an arbitrary substring that contains a head is necessarily adjacent to a free substring abutting a constituent boundary. It is easy to show that the constituents that are generated by a grammar that includes (37) will contain at most three positions. Suppose that a grammar with the condition in (37) generates at least one constituent of length strictly greater than 3, and let this constituent be as follows.

(38) $(1 \ 2 \ . \ . \ . \ n-1 \ n)$, $n > 3$

If the head of the constituent in (38) is to the right of position *2*, then, by (37a), there will be a left bracket located between position *1* and position $n-1$. And if the head is to the left of position $n-1$, then, by (37b), there will be a right bracket between position *1* and position *n*. In both cases a contradiction results. Q.E.D. In effect, this result means that in a derivation that involves the axioms (37a,b) the constant strings that are substituted for the variables u or v in these axioms may not contain more than one position. (Constant strings with more than three positions are not free.)

There is a problem, though, with the specific formalization in (37). Namely, it gives rise to nondeterministic grammars. This is due to the recursive character of the condition in (23) (which requires constant terms to be free strings). As an example, consider a grammar that includes (37) and is specified $[-HT]$; that is, it includes neither of the rules in (36). Suppose that the metrical rules apply to a string of four positions, formalized as the set of axioms in (39).

(39) $1\hat{}2\hat{}3\hat{}4$, $l(1)$, $r(4)$

There are three possible logical i-derivations from the axioms in (39), which are incompatible with each other. These three derivations are displayed in (40a), (40b), and (40c) and give rise to the geometrical representations (41a), (41b), and (41c), respectively.

(40)

a. From (39) and from (16), derive the formula $l(1\hat{}2)$. From the latter and from (37a), derive the formula $H(2)$ (by taking u equal to 1 and v equal to 2 in (37a)). From the latter formula and from (37b), derive the formula $r(2\hat{}3)$ (by taking u equal to 2 and v equal to 3 in (37b)). From the preceding formulae, derive the formulae $l(1\hat{}2\hat{}3)$ and $r(1\hat{}2\hat{}3)$. From the latter, from $H(2)$, and from the axioms (26) and (27), derive the formulae $L(1\hat{}2\hat{}3)$ and $R(1\hat{}2\hat{}3)$.[3]

b. From (39) and from (16), derive $l(1\hat{}2)$ and $r(3\hat{}4)$. From $l(1\hat{}2)$ and from (37a), derive $H(2)$. From $r(3\hat{}4)$ and from (37b), derive $H(3)$. From $H(2)$ and from (37b), derive $r(2)$ (taking u equal to 2 and v equal to the empty string in (37b)). From $H(3)$ and from (37a), derive $l(3)$ (taking u equal to the empty string and v equal to 3 in (37a)). Derive $lr(1\hat{}2)$ and $lr(3\hat{}4)$. Then, from the latter formulae and from the axioms (26) and (27), derive $LR(1\hat{}2)$ and $LR(3\hat{}4)$.

c. From (39) and from (16), derive the formula $r(3\hat{}4)$. From the latter and from (37b), derive the formula $H(3)$. From the latter and from (37a), derive the formula $l(2\hat{}3)$. From the preceding formulae, derive

---

3. Here and in (40c) below the derivation must stop at this point for reasons of recoverability; see chapter 1.

the formulae $l(2\hat{\ }3\hat{\ }4)$ and $r(2\hat{\ }3\hat{\ }4)$. From the latter, from $H(3)$, and from the axioms (26) and (27), derive the formulae $L(2\hat{\ }3\hat{\ }4)$ and $R(2\hat{\ }3\hat{\ }4)$.

(41)

a.   . * .   .
    (* * *) *

b.   . * * .
    (* *)(* *)

c.   .   . * .
    * (* * *)

The three derivations in (40) are incompatible with each other because each one involves constant terms that are not free with respect to the logical systems defined by the others. Thus, the argument $1\hat{\ }2$ in (40a) and (40b) is not a free string with respect to the logical system derived in (40c), the argument $2\hat{\ }3$ in (40a) and (40c) is not free with respect to the logical system derived in (40b), and the argument $3\hat{\ }4$ in (40b) and (40c) is not free with respect to the logical system derived in (40a).

It appears, then, that boundedness cannot be formalized as in (37) within a theory that requires determinism. Specifically, for the boundedness principle to apply in a deterministic fashion, it is necessary that the formula on the right of the arrow in (37a) or (37b) be an "if ... then" condition, not a biconditional. Assuming determinism, we are then led to postulate two independent symmetrical formal principles for the characterization of boundedness, those in (42a) and (42b). In effect, the formulae in (42a) formalize the rules licensing right metrical brackets in (28a) and (47a) of chapter 4, and those in (42b) formalize the rules licensing left metrical brackets in (28b) and (47b) of chapter 4. Accordingly, we shall call the set of formulae in (42a) the *Left-to-Right Boundedness Principle* and the set in (42b), the *Right-to-Left Boundedness Principle*.

(42)

a. *Left-to-Right Boundedness Principle*
   i. $u\hat{\ }v$ and $\neg H(u) \rightarrow (l(u\hat{\ }v) \rightarrow H(v))$,
      for every pair u, v such that $u\hat{\ }v$ is free
   ii. $u\hat{\ }v$ and $\neg H(v) \rightarrow (H(u) \rightarrow r(u\hat{\ }v))$,
      for every pair u, v such that $u\hat{\ }v$ is free

b. *Right-to-Left Boundedness Principle*
   i. $u\hat{\ }v$ and $\neg H(v) \rightarrow (r(u\hat{\ }v) \rightarrow H(u))$,
      for every pair u, v such that $u\hat{\ }v$ is free

ii. u^v and ¬H(u) → (H(v) → l(u^v)),
     for every pair *u*, *v* such that *u*^*v* is free

As shown in chapter 4, the simplest deterministic theory will be the one in which only one of the two principles in (42) will apply in any given grammar with bounded structures. To illustrate the workings of the formalization in (42), let us consider the case of a grammar that includes the Left-to-Right Boundedness Principle (42a) and is specified [+HT] and [right-headed]; that is, it includes the axiom in (36b). Suppose that the metrical rules apply to a string of seven positions without accent formalized as follows.

(43) 1^2^3^4^5^6^7, l(1), r(7)

The following formulae will be involved in the derivation of the metrical structure associated with (43).

(44) (12):   The axiom that characterizes the predicates $L(u)$ and $R(u)$

      (14):   The formal definition of the predicate $C(u)$

      (16):   The axiom that characterizes the predicates $l(u)$ and $r(u)$

      (17):   The axiom that subsumes $l(u)$ under $l(u)$ and $R(u)$ under $r(u)$

      (21):   The axiom that defines a natural boundary that is paired with a metrical boundary as a metrical boundary

      (24):   The Maximality Condition

      (26):   The axiom that characterizes the predicate $H(u)$

      (27):   The condition that restricts the placement of heads to metrical domains

      (42a): The Left-to-Right Boundedness Principle

      (36b): The formula for right-headedness

The derivation proceeds as follows:

(45) Start with the axiom *l(1)* in (43). From this axiom, the characterization of $l(u)$ (see (16)), and the first axiom of the Left-to-Right Boundedness Principle in (42ai), derive the formula $H(2)$. From the formula $H(2)$ and the axiom for right-headedness in (36b), derive the formula $R(2)$. Note that this formula can also be derived from the second axiom of the Left-to-Right Boundedness Principle in (42aii) and from condition (27) by setting the variables *u* and *v* in (42aii) to be equal to *2* and to the empty string, respectively. From the characterization of $R(u)$ in (12), from axioms (26) and (27), or from axiom (21), derive the formulae $L(1^2)$ and $R(1^2)$. From the latter formula and

from the Maximality Condition (24), derive the formula $l(3\,\hat{}\,4)$. From $l(3\,\hat{}\,4)$ and from the first axiom of the Left-to-Right Boundedness Principle in (42ai), derive the formula $H(4)$. And so on. When the derivation reaches the last position 7 in the string (43), the first axiom of the Left-to-Right Boundedness Principle will have to be applied with u set equal to the null string.

We see that the Left-to-Right Boundedness Principle gives rise to a left-to-right pattern. This result is, of course, independent of the direction of government: it has been established under the assumption of right-headedness, but it would also be true under the symmetric assumption of left-headedness. In the case of a left-headed structure the first axiom of the Left-to-Right Boundedness Principle will always apply with the value of u set equal to the null string, because a string of the form $u\,\hat{}\,v$ such that $H(v)$ holds cannot be a free string in a grammar specified [left], unless u is null.

In the present elaboration of the formalization in sections 4.3 and 4.4, as well as in this initial formalization, the *SPE* convention of disjunctive ordering plays a crucial role in the derivation of bounded structures. In the case of the present formalism this convention will restrict the range of a variable in a formula in which the assignment of different overlapping values may lead to contradictions. In that case only maximal free substrings belong to the range of the variable. The formalization in (42), in conjunction with the principle of disjunctive ordering, will ensure that in a degenerate ternary constituent with two positions the head is placed in a way consistent with the Recoverability Condition of chapter 1 (see section 4.4).

A fundamental aspect of the formalization illustrated in (45) is that the order in which the positions are scanned in the process of metrical construction exactly reflects the logical order of the derivation of the formulae. In fact, that logical order may be taken to represent the chain of dependencies that links consecutive constituents in a directional bounded structure and that is revealed by the Domino Condition (see sections 4.3 and 4.5). In other terms, if we assume that the set of formulae that represents a metrical structure at the underlying level (the set M defined in section 5.2) is not an unorganized set but is structured as a partially ordered set by the implication relation, we shall have an account of the dependencies described in sections 4.3 and 4.5. For example, we may adopt the format used in natural deduction techniques (see Thomason 1970) and represent a given metrical structure as a set of lists of formulae, such that within each list the formulae are in the order in which they appear in the derivation. To illustrate, the logical system underlying the metrical structure associated with the input string in (43) will be represented as in (46) (see (45)).

(46)
a. l(1)
b. Axiom (16) (definition of $l(u)$)
c. l(1 ˆ 2)
d. Axiom (42ai) (left-to-right boundedness)
e. H(2)
f. Axiom (36b) (right-headedness)
g. R(2)
h. Axiom (26) (definition of $H(u)$)
i. H(1 ˆ 2)
j. Axiom (27) (restriction of head placement to metrical domains)
k. L(1 ˆ 2)
l. Axiom (12) (definition of $R(u)$)
m. R(1 ˆ 2)
n. Maximality Condition (24)
o. l(3 ˆ 4)
p. Axiom (42ai) (left-to-right boundedness)
q. H(4)
Etc.

The formalization illustrated in (46) allows us to give a simple formulation of the Domino Condition.

(47) *Domino Condition*
   a.   If an insertion rule affects a string w that is an argument of some predicate in a list representing a logical i-derivation, erase the first formula in the list that involves the constant string w and erase all the formulae that follow it in the list (in particular, erase all the formulae that follow *from* it).
   b.   Start the derivation again from the last remaining formula in the list with a constant argument.

It appears, then, that the domino effect is a consequence of the implicational relations that hold between the successive constituents in a bounded structure. Let us consider the two clauses of (47) in turn. Clause (47a) describes the way in which formulae with constant arguments are transformed by derivational rules. We showed in section 5.3 that when a position is deleted from a string, it is deleted in all the formulae where it occurs, and the persistent rules apply to the resulting system. Obviously, the matter cannot be so simple in the case of epenthesis. Within a theory in which rules like the Boundedness Principles in (42) are persistent, a string that is free in the input to an epenthesis rule will not necessarily give rise to a free string in the output of that rule. As an example, consider the structure formalized in (46), and suppose that an epenthesis rule applies that inserts a position q between positions 3 and 4. The free string $3\char94 4$ is transformed by the epenthesis rule into the string $3\char94 q\char94 4$, which is not a free string in the system under consideration. Then the formula $l(3\char94 q\char94 4)$ cannot be substituted for the formula $l(3\char94 4)$ in (46o). On the other hand, the expression $l(3\char94 4)$ is ill formed after the application of the insertion rule, since $3\char94 4$ is no longer a string in the output of that rule and hence is no longer a possible term. The formula $l(3\char94 4)$ will then be erased, and as a result all the formulae that follow from it in the input representation will be erased.

Part (a) of the Domino Condition (47) is therefore an instance of the general behavior of formulae under epenthesis. This behavior follows from the constraint that constant arguments must be free strings and from the implicational nature of the relations that link the formulae in a bounded metrical structure. An epenthesis applying between constituents will not trigger the deletion of any formula, since it will not affect any of the arguments that show up in the list of formulae (although it will break the chain of implications that link consecutive formulae in the structure). We thus obtain a principled account of the difference in behavior between external and internal epenthesis (see section 4.5).

Turning now to clause (b) of (47), we observe that it implies a revision of the organization postulated in figure 5.2. Specifically, it appears that it is not the case that all the formulae with constant strings in the transformed level of representation will initiate new logical derivations. Only those formulae that are at the ends of logical lists of the form in (46) will combine with the persistent rules of the system to yield new formulae. It is as if the remnants of former derivations were immune from any alteration, even though they may no longer be actual logical derivations (as will be the case, for example, if an epenthesis rule applies in a site between two constituents not affected by the domino effect). We thus have a *Principle of Structure Preservation*.

(48) *Principle of Structure Preservation*
The lists in the output of a derivational rule may not be broken up by the persistent rules of the system. In figure 5.2 the set of axioms includes the persistent rules and only those of the rules with constant arguments that are at the end of the derived lists.

To summarize, the most general formalization of boundedness is that given in (37). For reasons of determinism, such a formalization is not grammatically legitimate and must be split into the two independent directional principles (42a) and (42b). The principle in (42a) gives rise to left-to-right patterns and the one in (42b) gives rise to right-to-left patterns. Each pattern reflects the chain of logical implications that hold between the successive formulae that represent the constituent structure, whence the domino effect. Assuming the format used in natural deduction techniques for the representation of metrical structure, the Domino Condition reads as in (47). The first part of it follows from the structure of the logical representation postulated in this chapter. The second part reflects the Principle of Structure Preservation (48), which constrains the application of the principles illustrated in figure 5.2.

5.5 The Nature of Metrical Constituent Structure

Within the theory presented in this chapter the metrical constituent structure is an independent mode of representation projected from the underlying logical level M. Like any other level, then, metrical structure must be characterized as having some special interpretation or some special function with respect to some other (possibly linguistic) cognitive representation or computation. We shall argue in this section that metrical constituent structure in fact describes the way positions in the string are concatenated.

As noted in chapter 1, metrical trees reflect the fact that strings of syllables are perceived not as unanalyzed sequences of elements but as structurally organized patterns. Formally speaking, positing a metrical constituent structure in the grammatical description of a string of syllables means that the concatenation of syllables that gives rise to the string is done in an orderly, deterministic fashion: first, the syllables are gathered into the substrings corresponding to the domains of the lowest metrical constituents, then these substrings are gathered into larger substrings corresponding to the next line of constituents, and so on. As an example, consider the metrically organized string in (49) and compare it to a string without metrical structure, such as the one in (50).

(49) .   *

    (* .   * .)

    (* *)(* *)

    1 2 3 4

(50) * * * *

    1 2 3 4

The constituent structure in (49) will be interpreted as follows: first the syllables *1* and *2*, on the one hand, and the syllables *3* and *4*, on the other, are concatenated to form the substrings *1^2* and *3^4*, respectively. Then the complete string *1^2^3^4* is assembled by concatenating the latter two strings. The sequence of concatenations leading to (49) can be represented by means of the parenthesized form in (51) or, equivalently, by means of the tree structure in (52).

(51) ((1,2),(3,4))

(52)

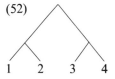

  1   2   3   4

Such concatenation contrasts with that leading to an unanalyzed string like the one in (50). The latter string is assembled from the initial elements *1, 2, 3,* and *4* in a totally nondeterministic fashion, implying that there are five grammatically indistinguishable parenthesizations (equivalently, five tree structures) corresponding to that string, namely, (53a–e).

(53)

a. (((1,2),3),4)

b. (1,(2,(3,4)))

c. ((1,(2,3)),4)

d. (1,((2,3),4))

e. ((1,2),(3,4))

The fact that the structures in (53) are grammatically equivalent is tantamount to saying that, as far as the grammar is concerned, the concatenation operator at work in a representation like (50) has the property of being *associative*.[4] The notion "associative computation" is equivalent in this context to those of "nondeterministic computation" and "unconstrained computation." In the case of (49), on the contrary, the sequence of operations leading to the final string $1^2^3^4$ is constrained: the constraint is reflected by the existence of a supplementary level of linguistic representation at which the string $1^2^3^4$ is analyzed as a sequence of constituents.

A representation such as (52), or the equivalent representation in (51), we shall call an *applicative tree*. The set of applicative trees associated with a given string we shall call the *applicative form* of the string. For example, (53) is the applicative form of the bare string in (50), and (51) (= (52)) is the applicative form of the metrical configuration in (49). Given these definitions, constructing a metrical structure over a string is equivalent to imposing a constraint on the form of the applicative trees that may be associated with the string. We have the following characterization.

(54) The metrical constituent structure is a representation of the part that is common to all the trees in the applicative form. This common part may be empty, as in the case of the string in (50), which has no metrical structure associated to it.

Within that description, a substring is characterized as a metrical constituent just in case it is a factor shared by all the trees in the applicative form. The fact that words in most languages have a main stress can be explained naturally within the formal interpretation developed here: this fact merely reflects the tendency for the computations to be completely deterministic.

An assumption implicit in this account is that there is only one primitive concatenation operator, which is binary. Every multiple concatenation can be obtained by iterative applications of this primitive operator. Of course, this assumption is not logically necessary. One could perfectly well conceive of an algebraically consistent model that would include nonbinary operators in addition to the binary one. For example, one could postulate the existence of a ternary concatenation operator. The special role played by the binary concatenation is due to the fact that this operation merely is the other facet of the notion of adjacency, which plays a fundamental role in linguistic theory. As we have shown, the fact that binary, ternary, and unbounded are the only options allowed for the size of metrical con-

---

4. A binary operation (a,b) is associative iff the following relation holds:

(i) $((a,b),c) = (a,(b,c))$,
    for every triplet a, b, c

stituents can be derived from the hypothesis that "adjacency" is the sole primitive positional predicate in the theory. More generally, all the positional predicates actually found in natural languages turn out to be reducible to that primitive notion. Accordingly, we shall postulate that the theory admits only one primitive concatenation operator, the binary one.

To summarize so far, we have introduced the notions of applicative tree and applicative form. An applicative tree for a string represents a sequence of binary concatenations generating the string. Grammatical concatenation is taken to be binary, as a matter of necessity. This property reflects the fact that all positional predicates found in natural languages are reducible to the primitive notion of adjacency. It constitutes a particular instance of a more general constraint that excludes counting predicates, in the sense of Crespi-Reghizzi, Guida, and Mandrioli (1978). We have hypothesized that a metrical structure for a string is a representation of the "deterministic" component of the set of concatenations that leads to the string: this deterministic component is the maximal common subpart of the trees contained in the applicative form for the string; see (54).

We note, however, that the analysis developed up to this point is incomplete, since, in the most general case, it will not account for unbounded metrical structures. Thus, although a structure like the one in (55a) can be straightforwardly interpreted in terms of (54), the existence of structures such as the one in (55b) remains a puzzle in the same context: what could be the use of such a structure, since, given what we have said up to now, it does not appear to impose any particular restriction on the applicative form of the dominated string?

(55)
a. * . . * . *
   (* * *)(* *)(*)
    1 2 3 4 5 6
b. * . . . . .
   (* * * * * *)
    1 2 3 4 5 6

The problem posed by unbounded constituents may be stated as follows. A given sequence of metrical constituents imposes a constraint on the form of the applicative trees associated with the dominated string by virtue of defining a partition of that string. When the metrical constituents involved are binary, this partition is sufficient to completely specify the initial concatenation operations in each applicative tree. However, when the constituent structure is unbounded, the question arises whether it defines any constraint at all on the concatenation of the positions included within each individual constituent and, if so, how. We shall argue that every metrical constituent actually determines a unique applicative structure for the substring it dominates. Specifically, we shall sharpen the thesis in (54), and we shall assume that the metrical constituent structure acts as a program for computing the common *initial* subpart of the applicative trees associated with a given string. For example, the metrical constituent structure in (55a) will be shown to completely determine the set of concatenations for each of the substrings delimited by the constituent boundaries, and the structure in (55b) will be shown to give rise to a unique applicative structure for the dominated string.

To derive this interpretation of metrical constituent structure, we postulate that the property of headedness that characterizes the notion of constituent reflects the way concatenations are carried out. We assume that the description of a set of concatenations crucially involves a cancellation operation: each substring that is a factor in a concatenation is not represented as such but is denoted by means of one particular position selected from the set of positions it contains. Thus, suppose that two positions x and y are combined by the concatenation operator to form the string $x\hat{\ }y$. In the description of subsequent concatenations, the value of (x,y) will be identified not as $x\hat{\ }y$ but as x or as y. In other words, for the purpose of characterizing the applicative structure of a string, the product of a concatenation is carried forward not as such, but in a reduced form, with one of the two factors x or y canceled. For example, consider the applicative tree in (52) again. Within the formalization just sketched, this tree will be represented either as the ordered pair ((56a), (56b)) below or as the ordered pair ((57a), (57b)) (where (56a) = (57a) is itself a pair of unconnected applicative subtrees, but not an applicative tree structure).

(56)

a. (1,2),(3,4)

b. (1,3)

(57)

a. (1,2),(3,4)

b. (2,4)

In a description like (56) the positions are treated as right-identities for the concatenation operator, that is, as elements satisfying the equation $(x,y) = x$, for every x. Thus, in (56) we have the equivalences $(1,2) = 1$ and $(3,4) = 3$, and the two forms $(1,2)$ and $(3,4)$ are substituted for by their left-hand factors 1 and 3, respectively, in the description of the next concatenation. In (57) the positions are treated as left-identities for the concatenation operator, that is, as elements satisfying the equation $(y,x) = x$, for every x. Thus, we have the equivalences $(1,2) = 2$ and $(3,4) = 4$, and the two forms $(1,2)$ and $(3,4)$ are substituted for by their right-hand factors 2 and 4 in the description of the next concatenation.

The mode of representation for applicative structures illustrated above gives rise to a simple interpretation of metrical constituent structure: a metrical constituent structure is a higher-level representation of some partial applicative tree. The mapping between the metrical structure and the corresponding applicative tree is defined by means of the equivalences in (58).

(58)
a. y is a right-dependent of x $\leftrightarrow$ $(x,y) = x$
b. y is a left-dependent of x $\leftrightarrow$ $(y,x) = x$

The identification in (58) means in particular that an applicative tree may include no concatenation of the form (u,v) unless u or v is a head in the associated metrical structure (since nonheads do not have dependents). The well-formed character of the metrical bracketing implies that, in a rooted applicative tree compiled from a metrical constituent, all the positions except one will be (right- or left-) identities. In other words, the same position will always be carried forward at all the stages in the applicative tree. This position, which is common to all the pairs in the description of the tree, is the head of the associated metrical constituent. It corresponds to one of the two most deeply embedded nodes in the applicative tree (see the example in (60) and (61) below).

We illustrate the above characterization by considering the representations in (56) and (57). The descriptions in (56) and (57) are associated with the metrical constituent structures in (59a) and (59b), respectively.

(59)
a. (∗ . ∗ .)
   (∗ ∗)(∗ ∗)
    1 2 3 4

b. (. * . *)
   (* *)(* *)
    1 2   3 4

Since concatenation is a binary operation, the applicative structure of the string will be known once it is known which elements are left- or right-identities at any given stage. The function of the metrical representation then appears to be that of fixing the form of the deterministic part of the applicative structure by designating the positions that are (left- or right-) identities in the representation of that deterministic component. This designation is done by identifying right- (resp. left-) identities with right- (resp. left-) dependents. This is exemplified further in (60)–(61). In a grammar that is [−HT] (a grammar that generates ternary constituents) the dependent positions will be identified as identities, with no reference to any particular direction of concatenation. We come back to that case later.

The interpretation just developed allows us to solve the problem raised by unbounded structures such as the one in (55b). That form does in fact represent a unique applicative structure, namely, the one depicted by the following tree diagram.

(60)

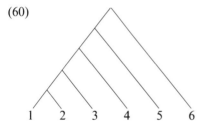

The uniqueness of the applicative tree associated with a constituent like (55b) can be shown as follows. Suppose that there were more than one applicative structure associated with the metrical constituent in (55b). Then in one of these applicative structures there would be a concatenation of the form (i, j), where i is different from 1. But then one of the two positions i or j should be a metrical head. Which is not the case. Q.E.D. The representation in (60) is equivalent to the ordered set of pairs in (61).

(61) $(1,2),(1,3),(1,4),(1,5),(1,6)$

Our characterization of metrical structure implies that in a string that is reduced to one position, that unique position is necessarily a head (a position is a dependent only if there is another position with which it is collapsed in the intermediate representation of the applicative tree).

The preceding considerations give some insight into the nature of the marked character of ternary constituent structures. In a [+HT] constituent structure the sequence of concatenation operations is identified unambiguously within each constituent. This is trivially true in the case of a bounded [+HT] structure, since at most one concatenation operation is involved in each constituent. We have just noted that an unbounded [+HT] constituent also gives rise to a unique applicative tree. Ternary constituent structures contrast with [+HT] structures in that in their case the succession of concatenation operations cannot be derived unambiguously from the sole internal structure of the metrical constituents. Consider for example the ternary structure in (62).

(62)   *
        (* * *)
         1 2 3

In the absence of any other principle, the form in (62) will give rise to two distinct applicative subtrees, namely, (63a) and (63b).

(63)
a.

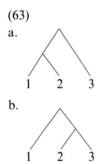

    1   2   3

b.

    1   2   3

Thus, the representation in (62) does not identify any unique applicative tree by itself. The ambiguity will be eliminated, though, if we postulate that the set of concatenation operations obeys the same directionality condition as the construction of metrical boundaries. Specifically, we assume that in a bounded structure, concatenation is in part governed by the higher-level grammatical principle of directionality: concatenation will apply first between the head and its left-hand neighbor in a left-to-right structure and, symmetrically, it will apply first between the head and its right-hand neighbor in a right-to-left structure. Given these assumptions, then, ternary structures are marked to the extent to which they require supplementary principles in order to generate unique applicative structures.

It appears that the requirement that a metrical constituent give rise to a unique applicative structure goes a long way toward explaining the restrictions on the shapes of constituents. As matters now stand, however, some constituent structures are consistent with the requirement of uniqueness, although they are not actually encountered in natural languages and are, in fact, excluded by the Recoverability Condition. For example, consider the structure in (64), in which constituents are bounded on the left but unbounded on the right.

(64)   *   *
      (* * * * *)(* * * *)
      1 2 3 4 5 6 7 8 9

A constituent structure such as this would arise in a grammar that would permit the specification of [BND] to depend on the direction of government. Assuming that a structure like (64) involves the application of the Directionality Condition (with the left-to-right setting), then a unique applicative structure will be derived from each one of the metrical constituents.

Thus, the univocity constraint on the correspondence between applicative trees and metrical constituents is not sufficient as it stands to predict the range of actually occurring constituent shapes. On the other hand, a structure like the one in (64) will be excluded by the Recoverability Condition. Taking note of this fact, we formulate the uniqueness condition on the derivation of applicative structures and postulate that the applicative structure associated with a given constituent should be completely determined once the head and the dependents, but not necessarily the constituent boundaries, are identified and the parameter settings of the grammar are known. It is easy to see that, with this elaboration, the range of possible constituent shapes will be predicted, as well as their relative degrees of markedness. Assuming this version of the uniqueness condition, the Recoverability Condition is merely a higher-level translation of it.

To summarize, we have assumed that a metrical structure over some string acts as a program that directs an initial subpart of the set of concatenations that leads to the string. To compile the computation associated with the metrical constituent structure, we have postulated a representation of the applicative tree in which the result of the concatenation of two factors x and y is carried forward in a reduced form, with one of the two factors x or y canceled and the other taken as a representative of the string $x \char"5E y$. This means that an applicative structure will be pictured as a partially ordered set of concatenations of the form (u, v), where each factor u or v is an individual position that may be a new element in the computation or is a factor in an immediately preceding concatenation. Under this formalization, the applicative tree is completely identified by determining at each stage which elements act as right- or left-identities in the procedure. The function of the metrical structure is then to designate these elements for some initial part of the computation. This is done via the correspondence in (58). We have noted that the Recoverability Condition can be viewed as the high-level expression of a constraint requiring that an applicative structure be uniquely determined once the heads and the dependents are identified and the parameter settings are known. This constraint predicts the range of possible constituent structures and their relative degrees of markedness. Thus, ternary structures are more marked than [+HT] structures, because supplementary principles must be invoked in their case to ensure uniqueness of compilation.

5.6 The Formalization of the Grammar of Stress

The logical formalism presented in sections 5.2–5.5 constitutes the content of the grammatical descriptions put forth in chapters 1, 2, 3, 6, and 7. In this section we shall examine the way in which the latter grammatical descriptions actually translate into the underlying formalism. As a first step, let us consider the four fundamental parameters of metrical theory: the features [HT] ("[head-terminal]"), [left/right] ("[left-/right-headed]"), [BND] ("[bounded]"), and [left-to-right/right-to-left]. The setting [+HT] means that the grammar includes one of the two rules in (65) (= (36)).

(65)

a. *Left-headed constituent structure*
   $H(u) \leftrightarrow L(u)$, for every string u

b. *Right-headed constituent structure*
   $H(u) \leftrightarrow R(u)$, for every string u

A [+HT] constituent structure must be further specified [left] or [right]: it is specified [left] if the grammar includes rule (65a), and it is specified [right] if the grammar includes rule (65b).

The setting [+BND] means that the grammar includes one of the two rules in (66) (= (42)).

(66)

a. *Left-to-Right Boundedness Principle*
   i. $u\,\hat{}\,v$ and $\neg H(u) \rightarrow (l(u\,\hat{}\,v) \rightarrow H(v))$,
       for every pair u, v such that $u\,\hat{}\,v$ is free

    ii. u ˆ v and ¬H(v) → (H(u) → r(u ˆ v)),
        for every pair u, v such that u ˆ v is free

b. *Right-to-Left Boundedness Principle*
    i. u ˆ v and ¬H(v) → (r(u ˆ v) → H(u)),
       for every pair u, v such that u ˆ v is free
    ii. u ˆ v and ¬H(u) → (H(v) → l(u ˆ v)),
       for every pair u, v such that u ˆ v is free

A [+ BND] constituent structure is further specified [left to right] or [right to left]: it has the setting [left-to-right] when the grammar includes rule (66a) and the setting [right-to-left] when the grammar includes rule (66b). A rule like (66a) or (66b) will apply obligatorily, by the general principle of deterministic application (see chapter 4). A grammar that includes (66a) or (66b), then, necessarily includes a rule of metrical boundary construction.

An important property of the formalization of directional construction in (66) is that in the case of binary (that is, [+ HT]) bounded constituents, the formulae are equivalent to formulae that do not involve the predicate $H(u)$. To illustrate this, let us consider the axioms in (66a) in some detail. The first axiom, (66ai), means that, given a position that is adjacent to a left bracket, the head of the constituent that includes the position is separated by no more than one position from that left bracket. The second axiom, (66aii), means that, given the head of a constituent, the right bracket is separated by no more than one position from that head. In the absence of any statement specifying the directionality of government, in a [− HT] constituent structure, these two axioms will define a ternary structure constructed from left to right. Suppose now that the constituent structure is specified [+ HT]. Then the axioms in (66a) can be reduced to the statement that the right bracket is at most one position away from the position adjacent to the left bracket, because under the specification [left] for the direction of headedness, the set of two axioms in (66a) reduces to the axiom (66aii), which states that the right bracket is at most one position away from the head, and symmetrically under the specification [right] for the direction of government. In other words, in a [+ HT] structure, the axioms for boundedness can bypass any mention of the predicate $H(u)$. (The preceding argument has been made on the assumption of left-to-right construction; but obviously it would hold under the symmetric assumption or right-to-left construction.)

The fact that in the case of binary constituent construction the axioms for boundedness can bypass mention of the predicate $H(u)$ is what allows cases where the direction of headedness is not determined until after metrical boundaries have been constructed. We note that such cases will not allow for accenting, since the metrical boundary induced by an accented element cannot be constructed until the direction of headedness is specified. We note that the bypassing of the predicate $H(u)$ is possible only in the case of binary constituents, but not in that of ternary or unbounded constituents. We have found no actual example illustrating such bypassing.

A constituent structure is specified $[-\text{BND}]$ when the corresponding grammar does not include either of the rules (66a) or (66b). Such a grammar has the option of including or not including a rule of metrical boundary construction. Such a rule has the form in (67) ($= (19)$ and (35)).

(67) *Rule of Metrical Construction*
   l(u) $\rightarrow$ L(u), for every string u
   r(u) $\rightarrow$ R(u), for every string u

The rule of Head Location will be formalized as a component of the projection mapping between the underlying logical level M and the (underspecified) metrical constituent structure (see figure 5.1).

(68) *Head Location*
   Project the predicates $H(p)$, p some position.

An important function of the projection mapping that relates the underlying logical level and the metrical structure proper is to filter out incomplete structures: an assemblage of formulae will be projected only if it represents a constituent structure in the sense of section 1.1. In particular, the formulae representing a bracketed domain will be projected only if there is also a head associated to that domain that is projected. The notion of constituent relevant to metrical theory is then characterized in particular by the following condition.

(69) $LR(u)$ belongs to the projected level if and only if $H(u)$ belongs to the projected level.

We shall assume that the Recoverability Condition acts as a constraint on rule (68): (68) will apply only if the affected formula $H(p)$, p some position, does not violate the Recoverability Condition when combined with logically prior formulae. In this way, we can account for the behavior of ternary constituent structures described in section 1.1 and in chapter 4. In particular, maximally degenerate ternary constituents that include only one position will not be projected.

Another case where the filtering role of the projection mapping is crucial is that of conflation. Before analyzing this particular grammatical rule, though, we must describe the formalization of structures that involve more than one line of metrical constituents. For the sake of concreteness, we shall consider the elementary case of a structure with two lines above line 0. Such a structure will involve two sets of predicates.

(70)

a. $l(u)$, $r(u)$, $L(u)$, $R(u)$, $H(u)$, corresponding to the bottom line (line 0), and

b. $l'(u)$, $r'(u)$, $L'(u)$, $R'(u)$, $H'(u)$, corresponding to line 1

In a compound structure with three lines, the positions on line 1 will be identified as images (in the set-theoretic sense) of the line 0 strings to which they are associated by the constituent structure. Accordingly, we introduce the mapping $h(u)$ defined as follows.

(71) If u is projected up onto the higher line as the position p, then $h(u) = p$. Otherwise, $h(u)$ is the empty string on the higher line.

We shall use the following notation.

(72) $(h(u) = *) =_{\text{def}}$ "$h(u)$ is some nonnull position on the higher line"

We have then the equivalence in (73).

(73) $H(u) \leftrightarrow (h(u) = *)$

The embedding of constituent structure is expressed by means of the following formulae, where $H'(u)$ formalizes the property of headedness on line 1 and $L'R'(u)$, the property of being bracketed on line 1 (see (70b)) and where t, h, and v are strings on line 0 or line 1.

(74)

a. $LR(u) \rightarrow (H'(t\,\hat{}\,h(u)\,\hat{}\,v) \leftrightarrow H'(t\,\hat{}\,u\,\hat{}\,v))$

b. $LR(u) \rightarrow (L'R'(t\,\hat{}\,h(u)\,\hat{}\,v) \leftrightarrow L'R'(t\,\hat{}\,u\,\hat{}\,v))$

These axioms state that a bracketed string on line 0 and its projection on line 1 (which *is* the constituent that dominates the string) can be substituted for each other in all relevant line 1 formulae. These axioms express the nature of hierarchically organized constituent structure as it is described and illustrated in the text surrounding (7)–(12) in chapter 1.

To illustrate the above definitions, consider the following grammar.

(75)

a. Line 0 parameter settings are [+HT, +BND, left, left to right].

b. Construct constituent boundaries on line 0.

c. Locate the heads of the line 0 constituents on line 1.

d. Line 1 parameter settings are [+HT, −BND, right].

e. Construct constituent boundaries on line 1.

f. Locate the heads of the line 1 constituents on line 2.

Now consider the input string in (76a). The application of the rules in (75) to that string will yield the constituent structure in (76b) (the numbers identify the positions on line 0, and the uppercase letters identify the positions on line 1).

(76)

a. * * * * * * * *
    1 2 3 4 5 6 7 8

b. .   .   .   *
    (* . * . * . * .)
    A   B   C   D
    (* *)(* *)(* *)(* *)
    1 2 3 4 5 6 7 8

The formulae representing this structure are those in (77).

(77)

a. First line

    i. $1\hat{\ }2\hat{\ }3\hat{\ }4\hat{\ }5\hat{\ }6\hat{\ }7\hat{\ }8$

    ii. LR($1\hat{\ }2$), LR($3\hat{\ }4$), LR($5\hat{\ }6$), LR($7\hat{\ }8$)

    iii. H(1), H(3), H(5), H(7)

b. Second line

    i. $A\hat{\ }B\hat{\ }C\hat{\ }D$, $A = h(1\hat{\ }2) = h(1)$, $B = h(3\hat{\ }4) = h(3)$, $C = h(5\hat{\ }6) = h(5)$, $D = h(7\hat{\ }8) = h(7)$

    ii. the set of formulae of the form $L'R'(X\hat{\ }Y\hat{\ }Z\hat{\ }W)$, where X is either A or $1\hat{\ }2$; Y, either B or $3\hat{\ }4$; Z, either C or $5\hat{\ }6$; and W, either D or $7\hat{\ }8$

    iii. $H'(D)$, $H'(7\hat{\ }8)$

In a grammar that includes a rule of conflation, the projected set of metrical formulae will be a strict subset of the underlying set of formulae of the form $LR(u)$ and of the form $H(u)$. The rule of conflation will be formalized as the following restriction on the projection mapping in (68).

(78) *Principle of Conflation*
    $H(p)$ is projected, p some position on the bottom line, iff $H'(h(p))$
    holds.

The equivalence in (73) holds at all levels, by definition. Hence, in a
grammar where rule (78) applies, the only nonnull position on line 1 in the
projected representation is the head of the line 1 metrical constituent
structure. As an example, consider a grammar identical to that in (75) in
all respects, except that it includes the rule of conflation in (79).

(79) Conflate lines 1 and 2.

Such a grammar will be formalized as including the constraint in (78).
Suppose that the rules of that grammar apply to the input string in (76a).
The logical level generated by the grammar in conjunction with that input
will include the formulae in (77). By the Principle of Conflation (78), only
$H(7)$ among the formulae of (77aiii) will be projected. By (69), only
$LR(7\hat{\,}8)$ among the formulae of (77aii) will then be projected. By (73), the
only nonnull position on line 1 in the projected metrical structure will then
be $D = h(7\hat{\,}8) = h(7)$. The metrical structure constructed over the string
(76a) by the grammar that comprises the rules in (75) and the Principle of
Conflation (78) will then be the list of formulae in (80).

(80)
a. First line
    i. $1\hat{\,}2\hat{\,}3\hat{\,}4\hat{\,}5\hat{\,}6\hat{\,}7\hat{\,}8$
    ii. $LR(7\hat{\,}8)$
    iii. $H(7)$

b. Second line
    i. $D, D = h(7\hat{\,}8) = h(7)$
    ii. $L'R'(1\hat{\,}2\hat{\,}3\hat{\,}4\hat{\,}5\hat{\,}6\hat{\,}D), L'R'(1\hat{\,}2\hat{\,}3\hat{\,}4\hat{\,}5\hat{\,}6\hat{\,}7\hat{\,}8)$
    iii. $H'(D), H'(7\hat{\,}8)$

The geometrical interpretation of this list of formulae is the structure
in (81).

(81) .   .   *
     (. . . . . . * .)
             D
   * * * * * *(* *)
   1 2 3 4 5 6 7 8

The formalization just proposed makes specific predictions concerning the consequences for a conflated structure of inserting a new position within the dominated string. Since a conflated structure like the one in (80)–(81) is analyzed as the reduction by projection of an underlying structure in which line 0 positions are covered by a complete sequence of bounded constituents, we expect to observe some effects of the Domino Condition. Thus, suppose that a new position is inserted between positions *3* and *4* in the string dominated by the structure in (81). This epenthesis will destroy the constituent *3 ˆ 4* in the underlying structure in (77) (= (76b)) and will trigger a domino process, with the ultimate effect that main stress will shift to the right onto the final syllable. If, on the other hand, the new position is inserted between positions *2* and *3* in the string dominated by the structure in (81), the location of the main stress will not be affected: it will remain on the original syllable, *7*. This is because, in that case, the epenthetic position would be outside all line 0 constituents in the underlying structure (77) (= (76b)). At present we do not know of any data that would verify or falsify this prediction.

To conclude this section, let us briefly consider the issue of the organization of the phonological component in connection with the notion of persistent i-rule. Specifically, we must address the following question: given that persistent i-rules are, by definition, part of phonological representations, what does it mean to assign such rules to one or the other of the phonological strata? To be able to answer this question, we must formalize the notions "cyclic" and "noncyclic" more precisely. Within the formalization developed in this chapter, a metrical plane consists of a set of formulae together with a statement to the effect that this set of formulae constitutes a certain morpheme. We shall formalize such a statement by means of an indexed bracketing, where the index denotes the morpheme involved. We illustrate this notation in (82) with the case of English stress. The numbers denote the various metrical i-rules as they are presented in this section; for example, (66b) refers to the Right-to-Left Boundedness Principle. A reference without a prime represents a formula belonging to the constituent structure of line 0. A reference with a prime represents a formula belonging to the constituent structure of line 1. The index m refers to the morpheme m in which the various formulae displayed are contained. In (82) we mention only the language-particular and morpheme-particular formulae.

(82) $(1 ˆ 2 ˆ 3 ˆ 4 ˆ 5)_m$
    $((65a))_m, ((66b))_m$
    $((65b)')_m, ((67)')_m$

The formulae in (82) generate the complete plane that underlies the metrical description of the string $1\hat{}2\hat{}3\hat{}4\hat{}5$. Conflation will apply to this underlying plane and reduce the line 0 constituent structure to a single constituent in the projected representation. To say that a certain persistent i-rule is cyclic is to say that this rule belongs to the representation of a morpheme if and only if this morpheme is cyclic. To say that a certain persistent rule is noncyclic is to say that this rule belongs to the representation of a morpheme if and only if this morpheme is a word. We postulate that affixation of a morpheme m' to a morpheme m consists in adding the representations of the two morphemes to each other and in replacing the base string of m' in the resulting plane by the concatenation of the base strings of m and of m' and by indexing the resulting string by m'. Thus, suppose that the cyclic suffix represented in (83) is added to the stem in (82). The resulting form will be the set of formulae in (84).

(83) $(6\hat{}7)_{m'}$
    $((65a))_{m'}, ((66b))_{m'}$
    $((65b)')_{m'}, ((67)')_{m'}$

(84) $(1\hat{}2\hat{}3\hat{}4\hat{}5)_m, (1\hat{}2\hat{}3\hat{}4\hat{}5\hat{}6\hat{}7)_{m'}$
    $((65a))_m, ((65a))_{m'}, ((66b))_m, ((66b))_{m'}$
    $((65b)')_m, ((65b)')_{m'}, ((67)')_m, ((67)')_{m'}$

A characteristic property of cyclic suffixes is that they trigger the erasure of the rules that bear the index of the stem. Once this has taken place, the morpheme $m + m'$ will have the following representation.

(85) $(1\hat{}2\hat{}3\hat{}4\hat{}5)_m, (1\hat{}2\hat{}3\hat{}4\hat{}5\hat{}6\hat{}7)_{m'}$
    $((65a))_{m'}, ((66b))_{m'}$
    $((65b)')_{m'}, ((67)')_{m'}$

Suppose now that we append to the stem in (82) the noncyclic suffix in (86) (since the suffix is noncyclic, it does not contain the rules for primary stress assignment).

(86) $(6\hat{}7)_{m'}$

The resulting form will be (87).

(87) $(1\hat{}2\hat{}3\hat{}4\hat{}5)_m, (1\hat{}2\hat{}3\hat{}4\hat{}5\hat{}6\hat{}7)_{m'}$
    $((65a))_m, ((66b))_m$
    $((65b)')_m, ((67)')_m$

If the morpheme $m + m'$ in (85) or (86) is also a word, then the Alternator formulae will have to be added to their representations, with the index m'.

Finally, when each of the morphemes m and m' is a cyclic domain, their combination does not result in any reduction of the set of formulae and the complex morpheme has the structure in (88) (assuming that the morpheme m' is the morphological head).

(88) $(1\,\hat{}\,2\,\hat{}\,3\,\hat{}\,4\,\hat{}\,5)_m$, $(6\,\hat{}\,7)_{m'}$, $(1\,\hat{}\,2\,\hat{}\,3\,\hat{}\,4\,\hat{}\,5\,\hat{}\,6\,\hat{}\,7)_{m'}$
       $((65a))_m$, $((65a))_{m'}$, $((66b))_m$, $((66b))_{m'}$
       $((65b)')_m$, $((65b)')_{m'}$, $((67)')_m$, $((67)')_{m'}$

5.7 Conclusion

An important feature of the model that has been developed here is that it involves a more extensive and more intricate system of levels than the models that are currently assumed. This is because it goes much further than all other models in making precise and explicit the functioning of the phonological component and its articulation with low-level cognitive components (such as the module responsible for the concatenation of elements, for example). One should expect that a correctly executed theory of the language capacity will in fact involve a vast array of levels of representation with complex interactions. In certain cases it might not be possible to study a higher level without taking into account its interaction with lower levels. For example, it should be obvious from the descriptions found in this book that a correct understanding of alternating patterns requires that all the relevant levels of description be investigated.

The study of stress patterns has led us to sharpen the notion of rule and to distinguish between external rules and internal or "persistent" rules. In connection with this distinction, we note that the domino phenomenon provides strong evidence for the existence of derivations in phonology: the only possible way to characterize the surface pattern of Winnebago words is as transforms of alternating patterns constructed before the application of Dorsey's Law. This of course does not imply that nonderivational models will not be required in other components of phonology. What we have shown is that at least one aspect of phonological theory necessarily involves derivations. In that respect, the phonological component appears to parallel the syntactic component, at least as it emerges from recent descriptions.

The notion of persistent rule plays a crucial role in the characterization of metrical patterns. Persistent rules, like the linking rules of *SPE*, are not linearly ordered with respect to the derivational rules of the phonological component. They act as a "genetic code" for the representation and come into play each time the constituent structure is affected in one of its essential aspects by a deletion or epenthesis rule.

The logical formalization put forth in the preceding sections has some standard features as well as more special "boundary" characteristics, which reflect the specificity of the object that is being computed. Thus, an important formal notion within the formalization is that of free string, which allows us to give a simple formulation of the axioms of the logical level and also plays a central role in the account of the Domino Condition. It seems to us that this notion should be viewed as expressing a fundamental property of grammars of natural languages, namely, the property that grammars never involve counting predicates. It is a fact that a grammar where constant terms must be free strings will not involve counting predicates. Conversely, a noncounting grammar will obey the condition that constant terms are free strings. It is an interesting fact that standard constituent structure appears to be one of the simplest formal constructs that conform to the property of being string-free.

Another special characteristic of this model is the relevance of the algebraic notion of identity, which plays a role in the compilation of applicative trees from metrical constituents. That it should be so should not be surprising, however, for the algebraic notion of identity will arise naturally in a system like the one we propose. To see this, consider constituent structures like the ones in (89).

(89)
a. $*$. $*$.
    $(*\ *)(*\ *)$
    1 2 3 4

b. $*$ . . . . .
    $(*\ *\ *\ *\ *\ *)$
    1 2 3 4 5 6

These structures are [+HT] and [left]. Clearly, such structures may be characterized as structures in which line 0 positions are projected as line 1 identities iff they are to the right of another position within the same constituent. We shall posit the equivalence relation in (90), where $h(x)$ is defined as in section 5.6.

(90) $u \equiv v$ iff $h(u) = h(v)$

By (90), every dependent in a structure like (89a) or (89b) is equivalent to the identity element on line 0. The internal structure of a left-headed constituent is then formalized as follows.

(91) $u\hat{\ }v \equiv u$, for every pair of strings u, v

Symmetrically, the structure of a right-headed constituent will be formalized as follows.

(92) $v\hat{\ }u \equiv u$, for every pair of strings u, v

Dependent elements in ternary structures will be characterized as nondirectional identities. This algebraic definition of government exactly mirrors the structure of the intermediate representation of the applicative tree that arises in the course of the compilation (see (58)).

PART III
Applications

Chapter 6

Case Studies

6.1 The Stress Pattern of Odawa

6.1.1 Subsidiary Stress in Odawa

The studies by Kaye (1973) and Piggott (1980, 1983) of the phonology of the Odawa dialect of the Algonquian language Ojibwa have provided the material and some of the major leads for the treatment below. The stress pattern of Odawa shows a remarkable resemblance to that of Aklan, as can readily be seen by comparing the Odawa facts listed in (1) with those of Aklan given in section 1.1.

(1)

a. Long vowels are always stressed.

b. Short vowels are stressed in even-numbered syllables counting from the beginning of a word or from the immediately preceding long vowel.

c. The word-final syllable is always stressed.

d. The short vowel in the first syllable of bisyllabic stems of the form CVNCV (N = nasal C) is stressed.

e. Main stress is on the antepenultimate stressed vowel, or on the penultimate or only stressed vowel in shorter words.

Examples of relevant forms will be found in (3), (5), and (9).

Except for main stress assignment, the facts in (1) can be captured with the simple rules in (2).

(2)

a. Stressable elements are the head vowels of syllables.

b. Assign a line 1 asterisk to the head of syllables with long vowels and the first syllable of bisyllabic stems of the form CVNCV.

c. Line 0 parameter settings are [+ HT, + BND, right, left to right].

d. Construct constituent boundaries on line 0.

e. Locate the heads of line 0 constituents on line 1.

Odawa words are subject to two processes of deletion and reduction. The first process

> may delete an unstressed vowel entirely or simply reduce it to a schwa-like quality. Several Ojibwa dialects show the reduction process, but it appears to be an outstanding feature of Odawa that it carries reduction to the point of deleting some of these unstressed vowels. The conditions under which deletion or reduction results from this process cannot be precisely stated at present, but there can be no doubt that they both occur. (Piggott 1980, 81)

The second process deletes a word-final short vowel (3a), shortens a word-final long vowel (3b), and deletes a word-final glide (3c).[1]

(3)

a. ni-nágamò-mìn   'we sing'
    ni-nágàm   'I sing'
    ni-wí:ndigò:wi-mìn   'we are monsters'
    ni-wí:ndigò:w   'I'm a monster'

b. ni-bímosè:-mìn   'we walk'
    ni-bímosè   'I walk'
    ni-níbà:-mìn   'we sleep'
    ni-níbà   'I sleep'

c. nagámò   'he sings' (from *nagamo-w*)
    bimósè: 'he walks' (from *bimose:-w*)

This process differs from vowel reduction in that it never results in the replacement of a full vowel with schwa but invariably shortens the word by one segment. This fact seems to us just one of several reasons for not attempting to combine final deletion and vowel reduction into one rule, as proposed by Piggott (1983). Speaking informally, we believe that the resemblances between the two processes are accidental and that no formal account should be given for them in a grammar of the language, especially since the attempt to coalesce the two processes into a single rule significantly complicates the description. Following Piggott (1980), then, we shall capture these processes with the help of two rules.

Word-final deletion is effected by rule (4), which is modeled on Piggott's rule 218 (1980, 306) and follows it in assuming that Odawa /h/ is not a

---

1. Following Piggott, we represent long vowels with a colon (:) after the vowel letter. We also assume that tense vowels are underlyingly long (that is, dominate a branching rime) and that tenseness is assigned to them by a late rule.

sonorant and hence not subject to the rule. It eliminates a word-final timing slot that is dominated by a [−cons, +son] segment (that is, by a vowel or a glide).[2]

(4) *Word-Final Deletion*

$$[+son, -cons]$$
$$|$$
$$X \rightarrow \emptyset \; / \; \underline{\quad} \; \#$$

The coalescence of the deletion of word-final glides and short vowels with word-final shortening of long vowels is possible only in an account in which word-final deletion is treated as separate from Vowel Reduction. This fact seems to us yet another reason for keeping these two rules separate.

We follow Piggott (1980, 306–311) in dealing with exceptions to Word-Final Deletion (4), all of which occur in bisyllabic stems, by treating these as lexically marked exceptions to (4). These vowels appear not to undergo Vowel Reduction either. Special attention should be paid to Piggott's important observation that the exceptions include forms both with final vowels and with final glides. It is worth noting that exceptionally accented bisyllabic stems are also exceptions to Word-Final Deletion (Piggott 1983, 41). Moreover, Word-Final Deletion precedes the rules of stress placement of Odawa, whereas Vowel Reduction must obviously follow the stress rules. Since the context in which Vowel Reduction results in actual deletion of the reduced vowel has at present not been ascertained, we shall not include the latter effect in our formal account.

To sum up, the stress rules (2) and Word-Final Deletion (4) together account for all major phenomena of interest here. We illustrate this in (5) (where UR signifies "underlying representation").

(5)		a.	b.
UR		ni-namadabi	ni-gi:-namadabi
(4)		ni-namadab	ni-gi:-namadab
	line 1	. . . .	. * . . .
	line 0	* * * *	* * * * *
(2b)		ni-namadab	ni-gi:-namadab
	line 1	. * . *	. * . * *
	line 0	(* *)(* *)	(* *) (* *)(*)
(2c,d)		ni-namadab	ni-gi:-nama dab

---

2. Kaye (1973) does not show the shortening of word-final tense vowels in his transcriptions. To describe the dialect represented in Kaye's transcriptions, it would be necessary to limit (4) to nonbranching segments.

Other rules	ni-námadàp	ni-gí:-namàdàp
	'I sit'	'I sat'

	c.	d.
UR	ni-gi:-namadabi-min	ni-bimibato:
(4)	not applicable	ni-bimibato
line 1	. *	. . . . .
line 0	* * * * * * *	* * * * *
(2b)	ni-gi:-namadabi-min	ni-bimibato
line 1	. * . * . * *	. * . * *
line 0	(* *)(* *)(* *) (*)	(* *)(* *)(*)
(2c,d)	ni-gi:-nama dabi-min	ni-bi miba to
Other rules	ni-gì:-namádabì-mìn	ni-bímibàtò
	'we sat'	'I run'

	e.	f.	g.
UR	bimibato:w	biziw	ninda
(4)	bimibato:	not applicable	not applicable
line 1	. . . *	. .	* *
line 0	* * * *	* *	* *
(2b)	bimibato:	biziw	ninda
line 1	. * . *	. *	* *
line 0	(* *)(* *)	(* *)	(*) (*)
(2c,d)	bimi bato:	biziw	ninda
Other rules	bimíbatò:	bizíw	níndà
	'he runs'	'lynx'	'these' (inan.)

The derivations in (5) are basically self-explanatory. Perhaps the only matters worth noting here are these: As shown in (5d,e), Word-Final Deletion (4) affects only the last timing slot in the word. It therefore shortens the last vowel in (5d) but preserves vowel length intact in (5e).

More important is the fact that the Odawa examples cited above provide crucial evidence in favor of the manner in which rules of metrical constituent construction take account of previously assigned asterisks (accented elements). As noted in section 1.1 in our discussion of the examples (40)–(42), there are at least two plausible alternatives. We might assume that the constituents governed by a previously assigned asterisk are constructed first and that only subsequently are the constituents erected over the remaining elements. On this account, the input to the Odawa constituent construction rule (2d) would be of a form such as (6).[3]

(6) .   .   *   line 1
    * (* *) line 0

When (2d) is applied to (6) the result is the grid in (7).

(7) * . *   line 1
    (*)(* *) line 0

The other alternative is to follow the procedure employed throughout this study and construct constituents so as to respect previously assigned asterisks. This procedure will yield the output in (8).

(8) . * *   line 1
    (* *)(*) line 0

The fact that in the forms in (9) stress surfaces on adjacent syllables shows that (8) rather than (7) is the current procedure.

(9) bimósè: 'he walks'
    niníbà:mìn   'we sleep'

6.1.2 Main Stress in Odawa

Main stress in Odawa falls on the third stressed vowel counting from the end of the word. If there are fewer than three stressed vowels in the word, main stress falls on the penultimate, or on the only stressed vowel in the word. In addition to those in (3), (5), and (9) we cite the following examples.

(10) kit-ò:tà:wé:-wikàmikò-m   'your store'
     ni-wì:-pimí-takkònà:n   'I'll carry it along'

We shall assume that the regular rules of Odawa locate main stress on the last stressed syllable and then retract it from there by the boundary metathesis rule (11), which in many respects resembles the Aklan stress retraction rule (92) of section 1.3.

(11) line 1 $\{*\}$ *) →){*} * / * ____ #
     where $\{*\}$ represents an optional element
            # represents the word boundary

The essential difference between the Aklan rule and the Odawa rule is that

---

3. This alternative is explored by Prince (1985).

in Aklan the metathesis affects a boundary and an asterisk that directly adjoin, whereas in Odawa the boundary may metathesize across a sequence of two asterisks. This implies that in applying phonological rules there is the possibility of counting, and counting is a type of expressive power that no other rules appear to need. There is therefore reason to consider the following alternative to rule (11).

We could obtain the Odawa retraction facts if we postulated that the third stressed syllable counting from the end had more stress than the second. To obtain this kind of stress distribution, we would have to assume that in Odawa right-headed binary constituents are constructed from right to left on line 1 and their heads are located on line 2. Next a right-headed unbounded constituent is constructed on line 2 and its head marked on line 3. The retraction rule can then be formulated as in (12), without recourse to the extra expressive power required in rule (11).

(12) line 2   *) →) * / ____ #

Rule (12) applies in two distinct cases: (a) when there are more than one asterisk on line 2, and (b) when there is precisely one asterisk on line 1. The rule has the following effect in these two cases.

(13)

a.	*	.	.		b.	*	.		line 3
	*)	.	*#			.)	*#		line 2
	)(	*)				*	*)		line 1

Case (13a) needs no additional explanation. To understand (13b), it is necessary to recall condition (42) of section 2.4, which states that when a grid line contains no asterisk, the head is placed over the rightmost (resp. leftmost) asterisk on the next lower line in the grid. This procedure would yield the correct results except that it would imply that there are differences among the subsidiary stresses in the word, for which the published data provide no evidence. We can readily eliminate these stress differences from the grid by postulating after stress retraction a rule conflating lines 2 and 3.

If the account just sketched is adopted, the rules in (2) will have to be supplemented by those in (14).

(14)

a. Line 1 parameter settings are [+HT, +BND, right, right to left].

b. Construct constituent boundaries on line 1.

c. Locate the heads of line 1 constituents on line 2.

d. Line 2 parameter settings are [+ HT, − BND, right].

e. Construct constituent boundaries on line 2.

f. Locate the head of the line 2 constituent on line 3.

g. (12)

h. Conflate lines 2 and 3.

If the earlier account is adopted, the rules in (2) will have to be supplemented by those in (15).

(15)

a. Line 1 parameter settings are [+ HT, − BND, right].

b. Construct constituent boundaries on line 1.

c. Locate the head of the line 1 constituent on line 2.

d. (11)

In (16) we illustrate the application of the rules in (2) and (14) to *kitò:tà:wé:wikàmikòm*.

```
(16)   .  *  *  *      .  .  .  .      line 1
       *  *  *  *      *  *  *  *      line 0  ⟶(2a−d)
       kit-o:ta:we:- wikamikom

       .  *  *  *      .  *  .  *      line 1
       (*  *)(*) (*)   (* *)(* *)       line 0  ⟶(14a−f)
       kit- o:ta:we:- wikamikom

       .  .  .  .      .  .  .  *      line 3
       (.  *  .  *      .  .  .  *)      line 2
       (.  *)(*  *)    (.  *  .  *)      line 1
       (*  *)(*).(*)   (* *)(* *)       line 0  ⟶(14g)(=(12))
       kit- o:ta:we:- wikamikom

       .  .  .  *      .  .  .  .      line 3
       (.  *  .  *)    .  .  .  *      line 2
       (.  *)(*  *)    (.  *  .  *)      line 1  ⟶(14h)
       (*  *)(*) (*)   (* *)(* *)       line 0
       kit- o:ta:we:- wikamikom

       .  .  .  *      .  .  .  .      line 3
       (.  .  .  *)    .  .  .  .      line 2
       .  * (*  *)    .  *  .  *      line 1
       (*  *)(*) (*)   (* *)(* *)       line 0
       kit- o:ta:we:- wikamikom
```

6.2 Stress and Intonation in Lithuanian

6.2.1 The Central Core

In modern literary Lithuanian as described by Senn (1966) each word has exactly one stressed syllable. Intonationally, the language has one kind of unstressed syllable and three kinds of stressed syllable.

(17) Short   piktas 'evil'   pile   'fortress'
     Long acute   výras   'man'   Výslas 'Vistula'
     Long circumflex   vỹnas   'wine'   vỹksmas 'course'[4]

In phonetic descriptions of Lithuanian it is commonly said that long circumflex syllables are pronounced with a rising intonation whereas long acute syllables are pronounced with a falling intonation. In order to capture these facts, we shall assume that long vowels occupy two consecutive nucleus slots and that only one of these is stress-bearing: the head vowel of the nucleus or a following tautosyllabic sonorant. We shall further assume that in Lithuanian words a High tone is linked to the nucleus slot bearing the word stress, whereas all other rime slots dominated by sonorants in the word are linked to Low tones. If the word stress is on the rime-final slot, the intonation is *circumflex* ("rising"); if word stress is on a prefinal slot, it is *acute* ("falling"). We illustrate this in (18), where the asterisk indicates the location of the word stress.

(18) L H L   H L L
      | | | | | |
    v i i n a s = vỹnas   v i i r a s = výras
      | | | |
      * .   * .   line 2

Since, in addition to vowels, sonorant consonants that follow the head vowel in a rime are tone-bearing in Lithuanian, we should expect similar intonational contrasts in syllables with vowel + sonorant rimes but not in syllables where the head vowel is the only element capable of bearing tone. These expectations are borne out by the facts of the language. As illustrated in the top line of (17), no intonational contrasts are found in short stressed syllables; as illustrated in (19), however, such contrasts *are* found in stressed syllables with vowel + sonorant rimes.

---

4. The letter *y* represents long /i/ in the Lithuanian orthography. V́ represents a long stressed vowel with acute intonation; Ṽ, a long stressed vowel with circumflex intonation; and V̆, a short stressed vowel.

(19) pìlnas   'full'
     rìmtas   'serious'
     pil̃vas   'belly'
     šim̃tas   'hundred'

By postulating that in Lithuanian only and all rime sonorants bearing the word stress are linked to a High tone whereas all other tone-bearing phonemes in the word are linked to Low tones, we have simultaneously captured as well the fact that syllables that do not have word stress exhibit no intonational contrasts. Thus, the tonal contour of a Lithuanian word can readily be determined once the word stress has been located.

The basic idiosyncrasy of Lithuanian prosody, which differentiates it from all other languages examined to this point, is that the stress-bearing element of a syllable need not be the head. We have already encountered languages like Southern Paiute, where not only the head of the rime but also other elements of the syllables nucleus bear stress. This is true of Lithuanian as well; but Lithuanian, like many other languages and unlike Southern Paiute, imposes the further restriction that there must be exactly one stress-bearing element per syllable. The stress-bearing elements in Lithuanian therefore constitute a subset of those that are capable of bearing tone. We illustrate this in (20), where the stress-bearing timing slots dominated by the rime are supplied with a line 0 asterisk.

(20)

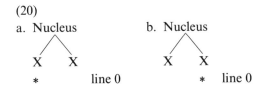

In Lithuanian the timing slots X dominated by the Nucleus must be sonorants, that is, vowels, liquids, or nasals. Since syllable nuclei are left-headed constituents, the left X is the head in both (20a) and (20b), but it is stress-bearing (supplied with a line 0 asterisk) only in (20a) (acute), and not in (20b) (circumflex).

Leskien (1919, 128) observed that this contrast between acute and circumflex must be stipulated in the underlying representation of each syllable with a branching nucleus even though the contrast is phonetically actualized only when certain conditions are met. An example of this is provided by the verb forms in (21).

(21) *Infinitive*   *3 sg.pres.*

im̃ti	ìma	'take'
mir̃ti	mìra	'die'
gìnti	gìna	'defend'
vìrti	vìra	'cook'

As shown in (21), the contrast between acute and circumflex that surfaces in the infinitive is neutralized in the 3sg. present tense forms. The contrast is neutralized in these forms because the stem-final sonorant is no longer part of the syllable nucleus, and elements that are not part of the nucleus can bear neither stress nor tone. Since every syllable must have exactly one stress-bearing element, we shall assume that Lithuanian has a default rule that assigns this function (a line 0 asterisk in the metrical grid) to the head of the nucleus. The default rule will not apply in cases where a line 0 asterisk has been assigned in the lexical representation. Since the default rule will render the head of the syllable nucleus capable of bearing stress—that is, generate a syllable whose potential intonation is acute—it is not necessary to mark such syllables in their underlying representation. The only syllables that need to be assigned a line 0 asterisk in their underlying representations are those whose potential intonation is circumflex; these syllables automatically block the default rule. When a morpheme with a circumflex nucleus is followed by a vowel-initial morpheme and as a result its marked stress-bearing sonorant becomes the onset of the following syllable, the sonorant loses its capacity to bear stress because elements in syllable onsets are universally not stress-bearing. Formally this will be reflected by eliminating line 0 asterisks from elements in syllable onsets. Since the syllable now contains no line 0 asterisk, it becomes subject to the default rule that supplies a line 0 asterisk to the rime head. (For additional discussion of these contrasts, see section 6.2.2.)

Underlying intonational contrasts are also neutralized when a syllable appears without surface stress. The interaction of stress and intonation is illustrated in (22), which reproduces part of the declensional paradigm of masculine nouns.

(22)

	I	II	III	IV
	'greyhound'	'finger'	'morning'	'wolf'
nom.sg.	kùrt-as	pir̃št-as	rýt-as	vil̃k-as
loc.pl.	kùrt-uose	pir̃št-uose	ryt-uosè	vilk-uosè
loc.sg.	kùrt-e	piršt-ė̃	ryt-ė̃	vilk-ė̃
acc.pl.	kùrt-us	piršt-ùs	rýt-us	vilk-ùs

We follow the traditional description and classify noun stems into four accentual classes, each designated by a Roman numeral. We assume that the stem syllables in classes II and IV are marked "circumflex" (a nonhead element is assigned a line 0 asterisk), whereas the stem syllables in classes I and III are "acute" (their heads are assigned a line 0 asterisk by the default rule). Moreover, the noun stems in classes I and II are underlyingly accented (assigned a line 1 asterisk in their underlying representation), whereas those in classes III and IV are not. We also assume that the nom.sg. and the acc.pl. case suffixes are unaccented, whereas those of the loc.pl. and loc.sg. are accented. The placement of word stress in Lithuanian is governed by the Basic Accentuation Principle of Indo-European (see section 3.1), which in Lithuanian is implemented by the rules in (23).

(23)

a. Stressable elements are as follows: in marked syllables, the element following the head of the syllable nucleus; elsewhere, the head of the nucleus.

b. Line 0 parameter settings are [+ HT, − BND, left].

c. Line 1 parameter settings are [+ HT, − BND, left].

d. Construct constituent boundaries on line 1.

e. Locate the head of the line 1 constituent on line 2.

f. Conflate lines 1 and 2.

   In (24) we illustrate the operation of (23) with the derivation of a few of the forms cited in (22).

(24)

a.
	kurte		kurte		kùrte
	| |				| |
line 2	. .		* .		* .
line 1	* *	(23b−e)	(* *)	(23f)	(* .)
line 0	* *		(*)(*)		(*) *

b.
	vilkas		vil̃kas
	| |		| |
line 2	. .		* .
line 1	. .	(23b−f)	(* .)
line 0	* *		* *

c.
	vilkuose		vilkuosè
	| | |		| | |
line 2	. . .		. . *
line 1	. . *	(23b−f)	. . (*)
line 0	* * *		* * (*)

Given the assumption made above concerning the inherent accentual properties of the stem and the case suffixes, the stress rules in (23) will generate the correct stress contours in all forms of the paradigms of the acute stems *kurt* and *ryt*. They will not work as well in the paradigms of the two circumflex stems *piršt* and *vilk*. In particular, we are not yet in a position to account for the stress shift from the stem to the suffix in forms such as the loc.sg. and the acc.pl.

The exceptional stressing of these forms was explained in a famous essay by Saussure (1896). Saussure proposed that word stress in Lithuanian is advanced from a syllable that is short, or long and circumflex, to the next syllable if it is long and acute. In the notation of (20) the context for Saussure's Law would be represented as in (25), where the symbol = indicates that the element in question is nucleus-final.[5] Since we assume that Saussure's Law applies after the stress rules in (23), any lexically marked stress (line 1 asterisk) on the second syllable will have been eliminated by Stress Conflation (23f) and can therefore play no role at this state. The structural change effected by Saussure's Law is to make the stressed nucleus incapable of bearing stress (which we express formally by deleting the line 0 asterisk).

(25) *Saussure's Law*

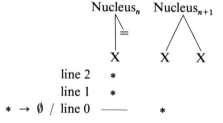

As explained in section 1.1, when a head in a constituent becomes incapable of bearing stress by being deleted or for some other reason, the next element in the constituent becomes head. Since constituents in Lithuanian are left-headed, the effect of rule (25) is to shift the stress to the next stress-bearing element on the right.

As formulated in (25), Saussure's Law will not be capable of applying to any of the forms in (22) since none of the case endings has a branching nucleus whose head is capable of bearing stress (that is, has a line 0 asterisk). For example, as written, the rule will apply to neither *piršte* nor

---

5. The condition on Saussure's Law is tantamount to requiring that the affected line 0 positions be consecutive stress-bearing elements.

pirštus because the case endings do not have a branching nucleus whose head is capable of bearing stress. What enables it to apply in these cases is that polysyllabic words are subject to a rule, generally known as Leskien's Law, which shortens a vowel in a final syllable if it is acute (see Senn 1966, I, 84ff.). We formulate Leskien's Law as follows.

(26) *Leskien's Law*

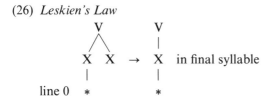

Since Leskien's Law is part of the synchronic phonology of modern Lithuanian, we can represent both the loc.sg. suffix -*e* and the acc.pl. suffix -*us* as having a long vowel underlyingly.[6] By ordering Leskien's Law after Saussure's Law, we ensure that the former does not prevent the latter from advancing the stress from the stem to the case suffix in the forms under discussion. Leskien's Law applies to long vowels in final acute syllables regardless of whether or not these are subject to Saussure's Law; thus, Leskien's Law applies regardless of the accentual properties of the stem, whereas this is not true of Saussure's Law.

According to (23b) Lithuanian has left-headed constituents on line 0. Although the headedness of line 0 constituents has no effect on the placement of stress by the rules in (23) (see section 1.3), the effect of headedness becomes apparent in the operation of Saussure's Law. Thus, it is because of (23b) that Saussure's Law causes rightward stress shift in words such as *darbininkùs* 'workmen' (acc.pl.) or *dainininkùs* 'singers' (acc.pl.). After the application of the rules in (23), words of this type will appear in the form (27).

(27) . . * .   line 2
      (. . *) .   line 1
       * *(* *)   line 0
      darbininkuus

Saussure's Law will then yield (28).

---

6. Saussure's Law does not apply to the verb forms in (21) since their endings are underlyingly short.

(28) .` . * .   line 2
   (. . *).   line 1
   * *(. *)   line 0
   darbininkuus

The deletion of the line 0 asterisk by Saussure's Law results in a transfer of headship to the syllable on the right because this syllable is now leftmost in the line 0 constituent. This in turn results in the transfer of the line 2 asterisk to the same syllable since that syllable now bears the leftmost asterisk on line 1. Subsequent application of Leskien's Law yields the correct output (29).

(29) . . . *   line 2
   (. . . *)   line 1
   * *. (*)   line 0
   darbininkuus

Had there been no constituent on line 0, the deletion of the line 0 asterisk would not have produced the correct results. In particular, a metrical grid such as (28) without constituents on line 0 would have to be interpreted as transferring headship to the leftmost asterisk on line 0 (see convention (43) in chapter 2), and this contradicts the facts.

It might be proposed that Saussure's Law should be formulated as a rule moving the line 2 asterisk to the next stress-bearing element on the right, rather than as a rule deleting a line 0 asterisk, as in (25). This proposal is inferior to the solution we have adopted: when the line 2 asterisk is shifted, the line 1 asterisk will remain, implying contrary to fact that a degree of stress persists as a trace of the former main stress. To overcome this inadequacy, a rule deleting secondary stresses would have to be added to the account. As there are no arguments in favor of such a rule, our alternative (25) is to be preferred.

6.2.2 Cyclic Stress Effects in Lithuanian

Like the derivational suffixes of Sanskrit and English, the derivational suffixes of Lithuanian are either cyclic or noncyclic, and, as in Sanskrit, this fact is reflected in the accentual properties of the derived word. In the case of cyclic suffixes the inherent accentual properties of the stem play no role in determining the stress of the derived word, whereas in the case of noncyclic suffixes the location of the word stress is determined by the inherent accentual properties of the stem. The role of suffixes in the determination of word stress was discussed in some detail by Kiparsky and Halle (1977). In that study—much as in Halle and Mohanan's (1985) treatment of Vedic stress—cyclic suffixes were assumed to trigger a rule of stress and accent deletion. We review here the facts adduced by Kiparsky and Halle (1977) so as to show that they can be properly accounted for without postulating a stress deletion rule.

We have already illustrated the way in which stress is determined in simple underived words with (noncyclic) desinences. We now inquire what our theory should lead us to expect if a noncyclic derivational suffix is inserted between the root and the desinence.

In (30) we illustrate all the relevant cases in schematic form. On the left are the input forms, and on the right the result of applying to these forms the Lithuanian stress rules (23a–f). The letters R, S, and D stand for *root*, *suffix*, and *desinence*, respectively. In the left-hand column an asterisk above a morpheme indicates that the morpheme is underlyingly accented. In the right-hand column the asterisk indicates the location of the word stress. The eight sequences in (30) exhaust the logically possible cases. We disregard here the distinction between acute and circumflex syllable nuclei as well as the possible effects of Saussure's Law.

(30)

a. * * *   *   e.   * *   *
   R S D → R S D   R S D → R S D

b. * *   *   f.   *   *
   R S D → R S D   R S D → R S D

c. *   *   *   g.   *   *
   R S D → R S D   R S D → R S D

d. *   *   h.   *
   R S D → R S D   R S D → R S D

Since Lithuanian stress is governed by the rules of (23), it is to be expected that when the suffix is added to an underlyingly accented root—that is, to one belonging to the traditional accentual class I or II—the word stress will be fixed on the root throughout the paradigm, regardless of the accentual properties of the morphemes that follow (see (30a–d)). The only exceptions to this are words to which Saussure's Law applies and where stress is shifted to the following syllable. If, on the other hand, the suffix is added to a root that is not underlyingly accented—that is, one belonging to accentual class III or IV—location of the word stress will be determined by the accentual properties of the suffix. If the suffix is not underlyingly accented, the stress will fall on the desinence if *it* is underlyingly accented and on the root if it is not (see (30g,h)). If the suffix is underlyingly accented, however, then the word stress will fall on the suffix (see (30e,f)), except, again, in cases where Saussure's Law applies and where stress is therefore shifted to the desinence.

When these matters are treated in standard descriptions of Lithuanian prosody, they are usually considered from the standpoint of the derivational suffix, and the facts are given under two main headings: (a) when the suffix is underlyingly accented and (b) when the suffix is unaccented.

Examples of noncyclic suffixes are not particularly common in the language. Dudas (1972) cites only one suffix—the agentive -*inink*-—which is underlyingly accented. We expect here the result in (30a,b,e,f); that is when the root belongs to class I or II, the stress of the derived word falls on the root, but when the root belongs to class III or IV, the word stress falls on the suffix. This is precisely the case, as shown in (31), except that since the last syllable of the suffix is circumflex, the words are subject to Saussure's Law. Standard treatises on Lithuanian state that with roots of class I or II this suffix generates words belonging to class I, whereas with roots of class III or IV it generates words belonging to class II.

(31) áuks-inink-as   (I)   'goldsmith' (from *áuks-as* (I) 'gold')
     vargõn-inink-as (I)   'organist' (from *vargõn-ai* (II) 'organ')
     darb-iniñk-as   (II)   'workman' (from *dárb-as* (III) 'work')
     dain-iniñk-as   (II)   'singer' (from *dain-à* (IV) 'song')

If the noncyclic suffix is not underlyingly accented, we expect the results in (30c,d,g,h). Such a suffix is apparently unattested in the modern language, though one was found in the dialect of the sixteenth-century writer Daukšas studied by Skardžius (1935): namely, the adjective-forming suffix -*isk*-, which when attached to roots of class I or II forms stems of accentual class I and when attached to stems of class III or IV forms words of class III (that is, words that have stress on the desinence when the latter is underlyingly accented and root stress when it is not). We cite a few examples in (32).

(32) výr-isk-as   (I)   'manly' (from *výr-as* (I) 'man')
     dvãš-isk-as   (I)   'spiritual' (from *dvas-ià* (II) 'spirit')
     kùning-isk-as (III)   'priestly' (from *kùning-as* (III) 'priest')
     diẽv-isk-as   (III)   'divine' (from *diẽv-as* (IV) 'go')

In contrast to the noncyclic derivational suffixes, the cyclic derivational suffixes are abundantly attested in the language. Since cyclic suffixation has the effect of eliminating any accentual information about the root, the only cases that could possibly arise are those in (30e–h). From the viewpoint of the effects of the suffixation process, there will be only two results. If the suffix is underlyingly accented, the derived word will be of class I or II with stress on the suffix except where Saussure's Law applies and the stress is shifted to the desinence. If the suffix is not underlyingly accented, the derived word will be of class III with stress alternating between underlyingly accented desinences and the root. Examples of the former type are given in (33a) and (33b) and examples of the latter type in (33c). Dudas (1972, 112) observes that the former type, "which is by far the largest . . . , includes nearly all the nominalizing suffixes of the language."

(33)

a. eln-íen-a   (I)   'venison' (from *éln-ias* (I) 'stag')
    kišk-íen-a   (I)   'rabbit meat' (from *kìšk-is* (II) 'rabbit')
    ož-íen-a   (I)   'goat meat' (from *õž-ys* (III) 'goat')
    vilk-íen-a   (I)   'wolf meat' (from *vil̃k-as* (IV) 'wolf')

b. puod-ė̃l-is   (II)   'little pot' (from *púod-as* (I) 'pot')
    kišk-ė̃l-is   (II)   'little rabbit' (see (33a))
    ož-k-ė̃l-is   (II)   'little goat' (see (33a))
    vilk-ė̃l-is   (II)   'little wolf' (see (33a))

c. eln-en-à   (III)   'deer skin' (see (33a))   éln-en-ai   (dat.sg.)
    kišk-en-à   (III)   'rabbit skin' (see (33a))   kìšk-en-ai   (dat.sg.)
    ož-en-à   (III)   'goat skin' (see (33a))   óž-en-ai   (dat.sg.)
    vilk-en-à   (III)   'wolf skin' (see (33a))   vil̃k-en-ai   (dat.sg.)

It is essential to note that in order for these stress patterns to be generated, the stress rules in (23) must be applied to the entire word including the desinences. As discussed in chapter 3, Lithuanian thus differs from Vedic in that in Lithuanian the stress rules in (23) are assigned not to the cyclic and noncyclic strata alike but to the noncyclic stratum alone. The two languages therefore differ in their treatment of words with cyclic suffixes that have no inherent accent. In Vedic such words surface with stress on the initial syllable, which shows that the stress rules must have applied immediately after the last cyclic suffix was added. In Lithuanian, by contrast, such words surface with initial stress only when the desinence is also without inherent accent; see (33c). The two languages thus merge metrical planes in accordance with the same general principle: when noncyclic suffixes are added, the stem stress remains intact, whereas when a cyclic suffix is added, the metrical grid of the stem above line 0 is erased.

6.2.3 Other Stress-Related Phenomena in Lithuanian

As discussed by Kenstowicz (1972, 4–8), nonhigh vowels are lengthened in nonfinal syllables when bearing the word stress. The vowels subject to this lengthening process are represented with the diacritic for circumflex in open syllables and with the diacritic for acute in closed syllables.[7]

(34) balà   'swamp' (nom.sg.)   bãlai   'swamp' (dat.sg.)
     galvà   'head' (nom.sg.)   gálvai   'head' (dat.sg.)

To account for these facts, we postulate the lengthening rule (35) that inserts a slot to the left of the head vowel of the syllable nucleus.

(35)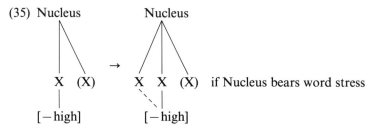

If we assume that the inserted element automatically becomes head of the syllable nucleus, we should expect the insertion rule (35) to change all affected syllables into circumflex—that is, into syllables whose (nucleus) head is not stress-bearing—because it does not supply a line 0 asterisk to the inserted element and it must follow the rules of stress assignment in (23). As pointed out to us by P. Kiparsky, in the standard orthography of Lithuanian the circumflex diacritic is assigned to a syllable with branching nucleus when its final element is stressed, rather than when stress falls on an element other than the head. This orthographic convention accounts for the representation of *gálvai* in (34) with the acute diacritic, as well as for the fact that in dialects where the nom.sg. suffix -*as* undergoes vowel deletion and becomes nonsyllabic this special deletion is accompanied by a change in notated intonations in the case of stems ending with a sonorant. We illustrate this process in (36).

(36)   *   *   *   line 2
     dvaras $\xrightarrow{(35)}$ dvaaras $\xrightarrow{-as \to -s}$ dvaars
                     dvãras   dvárs

---

7. The stem syllables in (34) are underlyingly unaccented and short. Therefore, when they are in position before the unaccented dat.sg. suffix -*ai*, they surface with stress themselves, but when they are in position before the underlyingly accented nom.sg. suffix -*a*, the suffix bears the stress.

It is instructive to compare the preceding with the results of another lengthening process of the language. This process is due to a morphologically governed rule that lengthens certain verb stems in the preterit and, in a special subclass of verbs, in the infinitive as well (see Senn 1966, 276–277). Unlike lengthening rule (35), this rule is not restricted to nonhigh vowels. Moreover, again unlike (35), this rule feeds a raising and rounding rule that turns lengthened [a] into [o] and [æ] into [e], represented in Lithuanian spelling by *ė*. We give the two rules in (37).

(37)

a. Lengthen the stem vowel in the preterit (and infinitive) of certain verbs.

b. $\begin{bmatrix} \alpha\,\text{back} \\ -\text{high} \end{bmatrix} \rightarrow \begin{bmatrix} \alpha\,\text{round} \\ -\text{low} \end{bmatrix}$ in long vowels

Examples of this process are given in (38).

(38)

a. gìnti (inf.)   gìna (3pres.)   gýnė (3pret.)   'defend'

b. iñti   ìma   ё̃mė   'take'

c. reñti   rẽmia   rẽmė   'support'

d. lémti   lẽmia   lěmė   'predict'

e. kárti   kãria   kórė   'hang'

We see the process most clearly in (38a). The lengthened vowel has acute intonation, because (37a) inserts an element to the right of the nucleus head. This suggests that the lengthening rule (37a) should be ordered before line 0 asterisk assignment by (23a). This ordering is supported by the remaining forms in (38). The infinitive *reñti* shows that this stem is marked so that (23a) assigns a line 0 asterisk to the final rime sonorant. In the preterit the rime ends in a long vowel, which again is assigned an asterisk by rule (23a). Notice that the stem vowel in the preterit is nonlow (orthographic *ė*) as a result of the application of rule (37b). In the present tense, however, the stem vowel is low (orthographic *e*), which shows that it was lengthened not by (37a) but by (35).

The preceding account is further supported by the verbs in (38d,e). These verbs have stems with short vowels in their underlying representation. The long surface vowels in the infinitive and present tense are due to nonhigh vowel lengthening (35), and the difference in intonation markings arises from the above-mentioned conventions of the Lithuanian

orthography. By contrast, the long vowel in the preterit form is due to
rule (37a), as shown by the fact that in the preterit the vowels are
nonlow (and rounded in the case of *kórė*) as a result of the subsequent
application of (37b). The acute intonation reflects the basic stem intonation. We illustrate the derivation of a few forms in (39) (omitting the
various steps connected with the construction of the metrical trees and
grids).[8]

(39)

a. karti $\xrightarrow{(23a)}$ k$\overset{*\ *}{\text{arti}}$ $\xrightarrow{(35)}$ k$\overset{*\ *}{\text{aarti}}$ = kárti

b. karia $\xrightarrow{(23a)}$ k$\overset{*\ *}{\text{aria}}$ $\xrightarrow{(35)}$ k$\overset{*\ *}{\text{aaria}}$ = kãria

c. karee $\xrightarrow{(37a)}$ kaaree $\xrightarrow{(37b)}$ koorėė $\xrightarrow{(23a)}$ k$\overset{*\ \ *}{\text{oorėė}}$ = kórė

d. remti $\xrightarrow{(23a)}$ r$\overset{*\ *}{\text{emti}}$ = rem̃ti

e. remia $\xrightarrow{(23a)}$ r$\overset{*\ *}{\text{emia}}$ $\xrightarrow{(35)}$ r$\overset{*\ *}{\text{eemia}}$ = rẽmia

f. remee $\xrightarrow{(37a)}$ reemee $\xrightarrow{(37b)}$ rėėmėė $\xrightarrow{(23a)}$ r$\overset{*\ \ *}{\text{ėėmėė}}$ = rẽmė

The stem *rem* is marked to take the first option in (23a), and the line 0
asterisk is therefore placed on the slot following the head. This is not the
case with the unmarked stem *kar*, where (23a) supplies a line 0 asterisk to
the syllable head.

Rule (37a) is not the only rule that must be ordered before line 0 asterisk
assignment (23a). The latter rule must also be preceded by the morphological rule referred to in the literature as *métatonie douce* (Stang 1966),
which has the effect of marking stem syllables as circumflex before certain
suffixes beginning with the glide /y/. Thus, the stem *kurp* 'shoe' is normally
acute, as shown by the fact that the noun *kùrpe* 'shoe' belongs to the
accentual class I. However, in the derivative *kur̃pius* 'shoemaker' the stem
has circumflex intonation, which is due to the application of *métatonie
douce*.

Finally, Lithuanian is subject to stress retraction. In the literary

---

8. The preterit suffix *ė* must be assumed to have circumflex intonation underlyingly,
for otherwise it would have been shortened by Leskien's Law (26).

language the retraction is rather similar to that produced by the Rhythm Rule in English in the following phrases.

(40) she was sìxtéen
    she had síxtèen books

Senn (1966, 76) writes, "When two accented words adjoin in a phrase, of which the first has stress on the last syllable and the second, on the first syllable, the stress in the first word may be retracted by one syllable. . . . The new main stress syllable does not change its quality as a result of this retraction. If it was originally long, it has invariably circumflex intonation under the new [retracted] stress." Compare (41a) and (41b).

(41)

a. šešiàs dẽšimtis → šẽšias dẽšimtis 'sixty'

b. naujàs kélnes → naũjas kélnes 'new trousers'

A very similar process is described by Senn (1966, 96) in his discussion of certain northern dialects that exhibit "stress restraction from a short final syllable to the penult, whereby the newly stressed syllable has circumflex intonation, respectively gravis (= high tone) in the case of short syllable." Senn illustrates the effects of this process with, among others, the nom.sg. forms of the nouns in (42). (The numerals in parentheses indicate the accentual class of the noun.)

(42) rankà 'hand' (II)   →   rañka
    galvà 'head' (III) →   gaĩva
    dienà 'day'   (IV)   →   diẽna

Although described by Senn as stress shifts, the processes under discussion are shifts in the placement of the high tone of the words in question. This is shown by the fact that the "landing site" of the shifted entity is always tone-bearing but not always stress-bearing and could therefore not receive stress. If we assume that the rule applies after the placement of the high tones but before the placement of the low tones, the rule can be characterized as shifting high tone to the preceding tone-bearing unit. We illustrate the process in (43).

(43) line 0   * *   * *   * *
         galva → galva → ga lva
          | | | | |
          H   H   L H L

6.3 Transderivational Relationships in Chamorro

Chamorro phonology has been discussed by Chung (1983), from whose paper almost all of our data and most of our major insights have been obtained. Chung analyzed the interaction of Chamorro stress with several phonological processes and was led to conclude that phonology should give up the widely held assumption that cyclic rule application accounts for all transderivational relationships between complex words and their parts. She justly characterized this as "a surprising conclusion" (p. 65), for it affects one of the most basic principles of generative phonology. The rule of Stress Copy whose operation has been illustrated and justified in the preceding sections has limited transderivational power, for it makes accessible to postcyclic rules information about stresses assigned on earlier passes through the cycle, information that is otherwise not available to such rules. In this section we shall attempt to show that this limited transderivational power of Stress Copy enables us to deal with the facts of Chamorro adduced by Chung, while maintaining the orthodox assumption that cyclic rule application accounts for all word-internal transderivational relationships.

The overwhelming majority of Chamorro words have main stress on one of the last three syllables.[9]

(44)

a. píkaru   'sly'
    kúnanaf   'to crawl'
    dáNkulu   'big'

b. bilimbínis   'star-apple'
    inéksa?   'cooked rice'
    paníti   'to strike'

c. lugát   'place'
    peskadót   'fisherman'
    kafé   'cafe'

Chung observes that "words formed with suffixes are stressed on the penultimate syllable, whatever the stress of the words from which they are derived" (p. 39). This suggests that the basic stress rule of Chamorro assigns stress to the penult and that stress on the antepenult and

---

9. We follow Chung's transcriptions except for replacing her *ä* and *ŋ* with *A* and *N*, respectively.

the ultima is due to special lexical properties of the words in question. Specifically, we shall assume that words such as those in (44a) are subject to a rule that marks their last syllable extrametrical. By contrast, end-stressed words of the type illustrated in (44c) have in their underlying representation a line 1 asterisk on the last syllable. The basic stress of Chamorro words will then be assigned by the complex of rules in (45).

(45)

a. Stressable elements are vowels.

b. Line 0 parameter settings are [+HT, +BND, left, right to left].

c. Construct constituent boundaries on line 0.

d. Locate the heads of line 0 constituents on line 1.

e. Line 1 parameter setting are [+HT, −BND, right].

f. Construct constituent boundaries on line 1.

g. Locate the heads of line 1 constituents on line 2.

h. Conflate lines 1 and 2.

Chamorro possesses a number of prefixes (for a list, see Chung 1983, 40, fn. 6) that attract the word stress.

(46) mímantìka   'abounding in fat'   (mantíka 'fat')
    Ápanìti   'to strike one another'   (paníti 'to strike')
    sénmàypi   'very hot'   (máypi 'hot')

If it is assumed that these prefixes are cyclic, they will cause stress assigned on an earlier cycle to be deleted. As a result, the words in (46) will appear without line 1 asterisks at the input to the second pass through the cyclic rules. Since in Chamorro line 0 constituents (feet) are binary, left-headed, and constructed from right to left, there will always be a line 1 asterisk on the initial syllable after the application of rule (45d). We illustrate this in (47) with the last two words in (46).

(47) *   . *.   *   *   .   line 1
   (*   *)(**)   (*)   (*   *) line 0
   A + pa niti   sen + maypi

To obtain the correct output with stress on the word-initial syllable, a left-headed unbounded constituent must be constructed on line 1. We implement this by adding a proviso to rule (45e) stating that in the case of the prefixes under discussion the last parameter is set *left* rather than *right*.[10]

To this point we have limited our attention to the placement of main stress and have systematically eliminated from consideration the fact that in addition to main stress, Chamorro words have secondary stresses. Chung reports (p. 42) that "syllables which bear secondary stress in complex words bear primary stress in the corresponding non-complex (or less complex) ones" and that "the syllable immediately before the primary stress never exhibits secondary stress." She proposes to account for these facts by the twin assumptions that stress assignment is cyclic and that "a later Destressing rule affects syllables immediately preceding a primary stress." To capture these insights, we shall assume that the main stress rules in (45) are part of a cyclic stratum. Since in the framework developed here each cyclic affix creates a stress plane of its own, stresses assigned on earlier passes through the cycle are not automatically carried over to later planes. Since in Chamorro, as in English (chapters 3 and 7), stresses assigned on earlier passes through the cycle appear on the surface, we assume that, like English, Chamorro is subject to the rule of Stress Copy (48).

(48) *Stress Copy*
Place a line 1 asterisk over an element that has stress on any metrical plane.

In addition, as Chung notes, the rule of Clash Deletion (49) is required.[11]

(49) *Clash Deletion*

$$(*) \quad \text{line 2}$$
$$* \rightarrow \emptyset \ / \ \underline{\quad} \ * \quad \text{line 1}$$

We then account easily for examples such as those in (50) and many others cited by Chung.

---

10. In Halle and Vergnaud (1987) we dealt with these examples by postulating that the prefixes are inherently accented and that Strict Cyclicity will prevent the stress rules from applying on the second cyclic pass through the rules. This was an error, for Strict Cyclicity limits the application of "structure-changing" rules only—that is, of rules that assign lexically distinctive features—and stress in Chamorro (unlike stress in Sanskrit or Lithuanian) is not distinctive. The Chamorro rules of stress assignment are therefore not constrained by Strict Cyclicity.

11. As stated in (49), the rule will delete secondary stress also if followed directly by a syllable with secondary stress. This extension is motivated below; see (53b).

(50)

a. inéNNulu?   'peeping'
   inèNNuló?ña   'his peeping'
   inèNNulu?níha   'their peeping'

b. kwentúsi   'to speak to'
   Ákwentùsi   'to speak to one another'

c. néNkanu?   'food'
   mínèNkanu?   'abounding in food'

As these examples show, stress assigned on earlier cycles is preserved both in the case of suffixation and when stress-attracting prefixes are adjoined.

In addition to stressed prefixes, Chamorro has unstressed prefixes. Chung remarks that words formed with such prefixes "are stressed on the same syllable as words from which they are derived" (p. 39); that is to say, in such words "the next-to-last layer determines the result" (p. 41). She illustrates this (p. 41) with the very important derivation (51).

(51)   túgi?   'to write' →
            tugí? + i   'to write to' →
            Á + tugi? + i   'to write to one another' →
            man + Á + tugi? + i 'to write to one another (pl.)'

This derivation shows that main stress remains on the stressed prefix to which it was assigned before the unstressed prefix was added.[12] Thus, unlike the adjunction of suffixes and stressable prefixes, the adjunction of unstressed prefixes does not trigger a reapplication of the main stress rules. These prefixes are therefore stress-neutral. We shall formally capture this fact by postulating that, like the stress-neutral suffixes of English and the recessive suffixes of Vedic and Lithuanian, the unstressed prefixes of Chamorro are noncyclic. Adding such a prefix to a word therefore does not create a new stress plane; rather, such prefixes are added on the preceding cyclic stress plane and have no effect on the placement of stress.

Chung remarks (p. 42) that "not all secondary stresses in Chamorro correspond transderivationally to the primary stress of some smaller word" and illustrates this with examples such as those in (52).

(52) magágu 'clothes'   màgagú-ña   'his clothes'
     kadúku 'crazy'   màn-kadúku   'crazy' (pl.)

---

12. The rules postulated here predict that the surface form will have a secondary stress on the penult. The form cited by Chung does not contain a secondary stress.

Chung suggests that secondary stress in these words is due to a special noncyclic stress rule. The situation in Chamorro is similar to the one encountered earlier in English. As in English, postcyclic alternating stress in Chamorro is assigned by a rule that constructs bounded left-headed constituents and thus resembles a part of the main stress rule (see (45b)). Chamorro differs from English in that the Chamorro noncyclic Alternator rule constructs line 0 constituents from left to right, whereas the cyclic rule (45b) has the parameter setting right to left. As pointed out to us by D. Steriade, the evidence showing that the Alternator rule in Chamorro must apply from left to right rather than from right to left is provided by the forms *pùtamunéda* 'wallet', which according to Chung has primary stress on the penult and secondary stress on the initial syllable, and *inèNNuluʔníha* 'their peeping', which has primary stress on the penult and secondary stress on the second syllable. If the Alternator rule applied right to left, the stress pattern of these words could not be generated. As *pùtamunéda* has no internal constituent structure, Stress Copy will not add stresses in addition to that assigned to the penult by the main stress rule. The Alternator rule (53c–e) will then assign line 1 asterisks to the initial and third syllables of the word, yielding *pùtamùnéda*. The stress on the third syllable, however, will subsequently be deleted by Clash Deletion (49). In *inèNNuluʔ-niha* 'their peeping' the cyclic stress rules and Stress Copy (48) will assign secondary stress to the second syllable and main stress to the penult. Assuming that the Alternator rule is ordered after Stress Copy, the application of the Alternator will result in stresses on the first syllable and on the antepenult. These stresses, however, will be eliminated by the subsequent application of the Clash Deletion rule (49). If the Alternator rule had applied from right to left, it would have placed stress on both the third and the first syllable of the word. Since Stress Copy (48) assigns stress to the second syllable, this would result in stresses on the first three syllables of the word. Clash Deletion (49) would subsequently delete stress on the first two syllables. Thus, if the Alternator were to apply from right to left, the incorrect stress contour *ineNNùluʔ-niha* would be generated.

In (53) we list the rules developed to this point in the order in which they are applied. The letters *c* and *n* indicate the stratum to which each rule is assigned.

(53)

a. c/n   Stressable elements are vowels.

b. n   Place a line 1 asterisk over an element that has stress on any metrical plane.

c. c/n   Line 0 parameter settings are [+ HT, + BND, left,
$\left\{ \begin{array}{l} \langle \text{right to left} \rangle_c \\ \langle \text{left to right} \rangle_n \end{array} \right\}$].

d. c/n   Construct constituent boundaries on line 0.

e. c/n   Locate the heads of line 0 constituents on line 1.

f. c   Line 1 parameter settings are [+ HT, − BND,
$\left. \begin{array}{l} \text{right]} \\ \text{left] in some prefixed words} \end{array} \right\}$.

g. c   Construct constituent boundaries on line 1.

h. c   Locate the head of the line 1 constituent on line 2.

i. c   Conflate lines 1 and 2.

j. c/n   Clash Deletion (= (49))

We now come to the most interesting part of Chamorro phonology: the interaction of the stress rules with four segmental rules. The first of these is the *gemination* rule that closes the syllable bearing main stress and is triggered by a small number of word-final suffixes listed by Chung in footnote 7, all of which are of the form CV in their underlying representation. Chung writes, "The conditions on Gemination are, first, that the word must contain a stressed closed syllable; and, second, that the syllable immediately preceding the suffix must be open. What the rule does is close this syllable by doubling the initial consonant of the suffix." We illustrate this with the words in (54). Note that the words in (54b) have no surface stress on the preceding closed syllable, although, as shown by the stress of the underlying stem, this syllable must have borne stress prior to the application of Clash Deletion (53j). In (54c) no gemination takes place, since there is no closed syllable preceding the penult. Of special interest are the forms in (54d) where no gemination takes place even though the target syllable is preceded by a closed syllable that bears stress. The difference between these forms and those in (54a,b) is that whereas in the latter the stress on the closed syllable is a reflex of the cyclically assigned main stress, in the former the stress on the closed syllable is due to the noncyclic Alternator (53c–e).

(54)

a. déddigu   'heel'
    dèddigómmu   'your heel'

b. maléffa   'forgetting'
    malèffámmu   'your forgetting'

c. hígadu   'liver'
   higadúña   'his liver'
d. cincúlu   'fishing net'
   cìnculúmu   'your fishing net'

These facts can readily be accounted for by assigning Gemination to the noncyclic stratum and ordering it after Stress Copy (53b) and before the Alternator (53c–e). Since the Alternator is ordered before Clash Deletion (53j), this order will also account for the facts in (54b). We state Gemination informally as follows.

(55) *Gemination*
     Geminate the initial consonant of certain word-final suffixes if the suffix adjoins a vowel-final stem and if the stem contains a stressed closed syllable.

Up to this point our treatment of the facts essentially parallels that of Chung. We deviate from her account only in certain details in the form and ordering of the rules that arise from basic differences between our theoretical framework and hers. It may be worth noting in this connection that Chung's treatment includes no rule of Stress Copy, for in her framework, as in the framework of *SPE*, stresses assigned on earlier cycles are automatically carried over to later cycles. Since we have given evidence in chapter 3 that stresses assigned on earlier cycles should not be carried over automatically to later cycles, our treatment requires the noncyclic rule of Stress Copy (53b). We shall now show that it is this difference that forces Chung to the radical conclusion that there exist transderivational relationships not accounted for by cyclic rule application.

A number of particles and affixes (including an infix) containing a front vowel trigger Umlaut—that is, fronting and unrounding of the vowel in the following syllable—as illustrated in (56).

(56)
a. gúma?   'house'
   i gíma?   'the house'

   sóNsuN   'village'
   i séNsuN   'the village'

   tulÁyka   'to exchange'
   t-ìn-ilÁyka   'to be exchanged, exchanging'
b. púgas   'uncooked rice'
   mí-pìgas *or*   'abounding in uncooked rice'
     mí-pùgas

gúma?   'house'
i gìma?-níha *or*   'their house'
  i gùma?-níha

As is clear from comparing (56a) and (56b), Umlaut is obligatory if the syllable bears main stress but optional if the syllable bears secondary stress.[13] If Umlaut is assigned to the noncyclic stratum and ordered before Stress Copy (53b), it will affect only vowels with main stress. On the other hand, if Umlaut is ordered after Stress Copy, it will affect vowels with main stress as well as vowels that had main stress on an earlier cycle. To account for the optionality of Umlaut, we assume that there is a local indeterminacy in the ordering of two noncyclic rules: in some cases the order is Umlaut— Stress Copy, in other cases the order is Stress Copy—Umlaut. Since in all cases Umlaut is ordered before the Alternator, it will never apply to syllables whose secondary stress is supplied by the Alternator. This is illustrated in (57).

(57)
a. pùtamunéda   'wallet'
  i pùtamunéda 'the wallet'

b. pulónnun   'trigger fish'
  i pùlulónNa   'his trigger fish'

Kiparsky (1986) has observed that Umlaut in syllables with main stress and with secondary stresses that derive from stress assigned on earlier cycles is obtained if Umlaut is assigned as the last rule in the cyclic stratum. On the other hand, as we have shown, if Umlaut is assigned as the first rule of the noncyclic stratum, it will apply only to the vowel with main stress. Kiparsky therefore proposes that the vacillation in Umlaut on syllables with secondary stress is due to the indeterminacy in ordering Umlaut as the last rule of the cyclic stratum or as the first rule of the noncyclic stratum.

This alternative is not readily available in our framework, for the following reasons. Rule order in our framework is governed by the proposal of Mohanan (1982) as updated and revised by Halle and Mohanan (1985), according to which the organization of the rule system is determined by two independent principles: the familiar linear ordering of rules put forth in *SPE*, and the assignment of individual rules to particular rule

---

13. Chung states that optional Umlaut is a feature of the Saipan dialect, "though there is some slight general preference for the nonfronted forms" (p.46, fn. 10).

strata. Since these two principles function independently, a rule R_1 ordered before a rule R_2 may consistently apply after R_2, if R_1 is assigned to the noncyclic stratum and R_2 is assigned exclusively to the cyclic stratum. Moreover, in this framework it is possible for a given rule to be assigned to two strata. For example, the Chamorro stress rules (53d,e) are assigned to both the cyclic and the noncyclic strata. If, following Kiparsky's proposal, we were to capture the Chamorro Umlaut vacillation by ordering Umlaut optionally as the last cyclic or as the first noncyclic rule, we would have to order Umlaut after all stress rules in the former case, whereas in the latter case we would have to order Umlaut before all stress rules. The indeterminacy invoked to account for the Umlaut vacillation would therefore involve two separate factors. First, there would be an indeterminacy regarding whether Umlaut is cyclic or noncyclic. Second, there would be an indeterminacy regarding whether Umlaut is to be ordered before or after the stress rules. We have adopted the account presented above because (as noted) it involves but a single indeterminacy: the ordering of Umlaut before or after Stress Copy.

Another phenomenon in Chamorro that shows a similar type of indeterminacy of rule ordering and therefore presents the same sort of challenge to the theory of phonology is Vowel Lowering. We believe that Chung's treatment of the facts of Vowel Lowering can be improved somewhat, and our exposition of this phenomenon will therefore deviate more markedly from hers.

The basic generalization to be captured here is characterized by Chung as follows: "Non-low vowels surface as mid in stressed closed syllables, and as high elsewhere" (p. 46). To capture this generalization formally, we follow Chung in postulating the rule (58).

(58) *Vowel Lowering*
Stressed vowels become [−high] in closed syllables.

We allow both high and mid vowels in underlying representations, but assume that mid vowels are marked whereas high vowels are unmarked. Mid vowels appear in underlying representations only in words where they could not be accounted for by rule (58)—that is, in words such as those in (59) where rule (58) is inapplicable.

(59) kósas   'things'
     néni   'baby'
     bóti   'boat'
     pakéti   'pack of cigarettes'

It is here that we deviate from Chung's analysis. Chung deals with these words by complicating her equivalent of rule (58) so that in lexically marked cases the rule will lower stressed vowels everywhere, not only in closed syllables. We shall assume that words such as those in (59) have mid vowels in their underlying representation, and we can therefore keep (58) intact. We also represent with mid vowels the stressed prefixes *sen* 'very', *gof* 'very', and *ke*^ʔ 'to try, be about to', for these prefixes never surface with a high vowel, even in open syllables.

We again follow Chung in the treatment of the handful of words with high vowels listed in her example (42), which exceptionally fail to undergo rule (58) despite meeting its structural conditions. Such words are marked as lexical exceptions to (58).

A potential problem with this approach is that it fails to account for the fact that nonlow vowels in some of the words in (59) do optionally alternate with high vowels. Thus, Chung cites both *ninihu* and *nenihu* as alternants for 'my baby'. We propose to deal with these cases by postulating an optional raising rule that is ordered after Clash Deletion (53j).

(60) *Raising*
    Nonlow vowels become [+high] immediately before main stress.

The need for this rule is independently motivated by the fact noted by Chung that /kupblin/ 'cash' shows height alternations when a monosyllabic suffix is adjoined but appears only with a nonhigh vowel when a bisyllabic suffix is added. Thus, Chung cites both *kobblékku* and *kubblékku* as admissible variants for 'my cash' but (p. 52) but specifically admits only *kòbblinmámi*, and not *kùbblinmámi*, for 'our (excl.) cash' (p. 55). On Chung's account Vowel Lowering "obligatorily affects vowels which bear secondary stress, and which would have primary stress if the word were decomposed into its parts" (p. 48). To deal with the forms under discussion, Chung proposes the special provision that Vowel Lowering applies optionally to "vowels which are destressed, because they occur to the immediate left of the primary stress, but which would bear primary stress if the word were decomposed into its parts" (p. 48). However, this optional case of height alternation differs from "true" instances of Vowel Lowering in that it applies to vowels in both open and closed syllables, whereas otherwise Vowel Lowering is restricted to closed syllables (and, on Chung's account, to lexically marked forms). Since rule (60) applies without reference to syllable structure, the forms under discussion are handled straightforwardly on the account proposed here.

A desirable by-product of the proposed account is that it simplifies markedly the treatment of the rest of the vowel lowering facts. We find now that Vowel Lowering applies obligatorily if the syllable bears main stress or secondary stress supplied by Stress Copy (53b); it applies optionally if the stress is supplied by the Alternator rule (53c–e). The optional alternation before main stress need not be considered here, since it is already dealt with by rule (60). The case of optional Vowel Lowering thus appears to parallel closely that of Umlaut, and it might seem that it should be dealt with by admitting alternative assignment of the rule to the cyclic and noncyclic strata, as proposed by Kiparsky (1986) for Umlaut. The main difference between the two cases would then reside in the fact that Umlaut is assigned optionally to the cyclic stratum and obligatorily to the noncyclic, whereas Vowel Lowering is assigned optionally to the noncyclic stratum and obligatorily to the cyclic. Moreover, Vowel Lowering would be ordered after Umlaut in the cyclic stratum and after the Alternator in the noncyclic stratum. A most important result, due to Chung, is that this solution is not viable.

The relevant data are provided by the phenomenon of cluster simplification. Chung observes that in Chamorro geminate consonants are optionally degeminated "when these are not immediately preceded by stress" (p. 55). All of her examples, however, are instances of degemination before main stress. We therefore propose that Chamorro is subject to the optional noncyclic rule of Cluster Simplification (61).

(61) *Cluster Simplification*
    Degeminate consonants before main stress.

The fact that Gemination (55) takes place both in *malèffámmu* 'your forgetting' and in its optional variant *màlifámmu* shows that Cluster Simplification must be ordered after Gemination, because Gemination requires a preceding closed syllable. If Cluster Simplification were ordered before Gemination, there would be no explanation for gemination in *màlifámmu*.

Chung observes further that "non-low vowels are always high in (unstressed) syllables open by Cluster Simplification" (p. 56). This fact can readily be captured by ordering Cluster Simplification, an optional rule, before Vowel Lowering. Since Vowel Lowering applies only to closed syllables and since Cluster Simplification opens closed syllables, this ordering will correctly ensure that Cluster Simplification always bleeds Vowel Lowering. In Chung's account it is necessary to assume either that Vowel Lowering (and Umlaut) apply cyclically in some derivations and noncyclically in others, or that Vowel Lowering (and Umlaut) include transderivational conditions. Chung shows that the former hypothesis is not compatible with the fully justified assumption that Cluster Simplification is a noncyclic rule. This result leads her to conclude that transderivational conditions must be allowed in phonological rules.

In the framework developed here the effect of the transderivational constraints is obtained by assigning Vowel Lowering to the noncyclic stratum and ordering it after Stress Copy. The optional application of Vowel Lowering to syllables stressed by the Alternator (53c–e) can be captured by stating that Vowel Lowering is freely ordered with respect to the Alternator rule.

With the modifications outlined above it has been possible for us to maintain the well-motivated constraint that cyclic rule application accounts for all transderivational relationships between complex words and their parts. We conclude this section by listing the rules of the noncyclic stratum of Chamorro as developed above.

(62)

a. c/n Stressable elements are vowels.

b. n   Umlaut

c. n   Place a line 1 asterisk over an element that has stress on any metrical plane. (48) ($=$(53b))

d. n   Gemination (55)

e. n   Cluster Simplification (61)—optional

f. n   Vowel Lowering (58)

g. c/n Line 0 parameter settings are [$+$HT, $+$BND, left, $\begin{Bmatrix} \langle \text{right to left} \rangle_c \\ \langle \text{left to right} \rangle_n \end{Bmatrix}$].

h. c/n Construct constituent boundaries on line 0.

i. c/n Locate the heads of line 0 constituent on line 1.

j. c   Line 1 parameter settings are [$+$HT, $-$BND, $\begin{Bmatrix} \text{right]} \\ \text{left] in some prefixed words} \end{Bmatrix}$.

k. c   Construct constituent boundaries on line 1.

l. c   Locate the head of the line 1 constituent on line 2.

m. c   Conflate lines 1 and 2.

n. n   Clash Deletion (49) ($=$ (53j))

o. n   Raising (60)—optional

As discussed earlier, there are two indeterminacies in the rule order, both involving adjacently ordered processes: Umlaut (62b) may be ordered after Stress Copy (62c), and Vowel Lowering (62f) may be ordered after the Alternator (62g–i).

6.4 Stress in Lenakel

As shown in section 3.5, in English the rules (40a–c) constructing right-headed binary constituents on line 0 are assigned both to the cyclic and to the noncyclic strata, but the rule of stress copy (42) is assigned only to the noncyclic stratum. The Austronesian language Lenakel differs from English in that it has a rule of stress copy that must be assigned both to the cyclic stratum and to the noncyclic stratum.[14]

In Lenakel, main stress is located on the penultimate syllable in the large majority of words and on the final syllable in a class of specially marked words. As in a great many other languages, in Lenakel the main word stress is preceded by a series of subsidiary stresses. In nouns these fall on every even-numbered syllable preceding the main stress; in verbs they fall on odd-numbered syllables preceding the main stress, except for the syllable immediately preceding main stress. Examples are given in (63).[15]

(63)
a. lÈdubɔ̀lugálUk   'lungs' (loc.)
   kayÈlawÉlaw   'kind of dance'

b. kɜ̀namargɔ́nim   'they have been pinching it'
   tìnagàmyasinɔ́vɨn   'you will be copying it'
   nàdyagàmEdwàdamnìmɔn   'why I am about to be shaking'

We have assumed that main stress is assigned by the set of rules in (64). As above, the letters *c* an *n* preceding each rule indicate whether it is assigned to the cyclic stratum, the noncyclic stratum, or both.

---

14. For more details on English stress, see chapter 7. The Lenakel data discussed here are taken from Hammond (1985), which in turn is based on Lynch (1974, 1978).

15. In the transcriptions of Lenakel words the capital letters represent lax variants of the vowels. Palatalized /d/ has been represented by the digraph *dy*. Additional diacritics in Lynch's transcriptions have been omitted. The omitted diacritics represent phonetic properties that are in no way involved in the phenomena of interest here.

(64)

a. c/n   Stressable elements are vowels.

b. c/n   Line 0 parameter settings are [+HT, +BND, left, right to left].

c. c/n   Construct constituent boundaries on line 0.

d. c/n   Locate the heads of line 0 constituents on line 1.

e. c   Line 1 parameter settings are [+HT, −BND, right].

f. c   Construct constituent boundaries on line 1.

g. c   Locate the heads of the line 1 constituent on line 2.

h. c   Conflate lines 1 and 2.

We shall assume further that the noncyclic Alternator rules for nouns in Lenakel are identical with (64b–d); in other words, as in English, the identical set of rules is assigned both to the cyclic stratum and to the noncyclic stratum. As Hammond (1985) notes, this proposal works perfectly in the case of words with an even number of syllables. In the case of words with an odd number of syllables the rules given above predict that the Alternator will place stress on both the first and the second syllable of the word as illustrated in (65).

(65)
```
        . . . . . * .                    . . . . . * .
      ( . . . . . *).              (* * . * . *).
      * * * * *(* *)   Alternator    (*)(* *)(* *)(* *)
        1 2 3 4 5 6 7                 1 2 3 4 5 6 7
```

To eliminate this unattested stress clash, we postulate, following Hammond, the rule of Clash Deletion (66).

(66) *Clash Deletion*
    Delete a line 1 asterisk if followed directly by a line 1 asterisk.

Examination of the verbal forms with an odd number of syllables, such as *kɔ̀namargɔ́nim* 'they have been pinching it' in (63b), shows that the suggested procedure will not work, for, as already noted, in verbs secondary stresses fall on odd-numbered syllables preceding the main stress except for the immediately pretonic syllable. The minimal change in the rules already postulated that will produce this result is to modify rule (64b) as in (67), where the parenthesized portion of the statement applies *only in the noncyclic stratum*—that is, when the rule functions as the Alternator.

(67) Line 0 parameter settings are [+HT, +BND, left, right to left (in nouns, and left to right in verbs)$_n$].

This new version of the Alternator will then assign line 1 asterisks to nouns as shown in (68a) and to verbs as shown in (68b).

(68) a.   . . . . . . * .   b. . . . . . . * .   line 2
          (* * . * . * .)   * . * . * * .   line 1
          (*)(* *)(* *)(* *)   * * * * * * *   line 0
           1 2 3 4 5 6 7   1 2 3 4 5 6 7

Clash Deletion (66) will apply to these representations and eliminate the left one of two adjacent asterisks (here, the line 1 asterisks above position 1 in (68a) and above position 5 in (68b)).

In addition to words with penultimate main stress Lenakel has a class of words with final stress, as shown in (69). The obvious way to deal with these words is to postulate that they contain accented morphemes, which, in their underlying representation, have a line 1 asterisk over their last (or only) syllable. The rules stated above will then apply in their normal fashion and place main stress on the final syllable.

(69) r-ɨs-gən-án   'he didn't eat it'
     r-ɨm-Edy-áw   'he arrived'
     r-ɨm-asOw-yáw   'he went north'

Hammond points out that when two such lexically marked morphemes occur next to each other, the second loses its stress and main stress surfaces on the penult, as shown in (70a). However, as shown in (70b), when the sequence contains three lexically marked morphemes, main stress is final and only the penultimate suffix surfaces without stress.

(70)
a. r-ɨs-Edyáw-an   'he didn't arrive'
   r-ɨm-Edyáw-yav   'he arrived in the north'
b. r-ɨs-Edyàw-yav-án   'he didn't arrive in the north'

We can obtain these results if we assume that, when suffixed to a stem with final main stress, a lexically supplied asterisk is deleted. To account for the fact that, in a sequence of three lexically supplied asterisks, only the penultimate is deleted, we must assume that the affixes are cyclic and that the rule deleting such asterisks applies cyclically. The cyclic rule of asterisk deletion required here is a different rule from the noncyclic Clash Deletion (66), for it deletes a following, rather than a preceding, asterisk. We formulate it as follows.

(71) Delete a word-final line 1 asterisk, if preceded directly by a line 1 asterisk.

The formulation in (71) raises a question about the procedure suggested above. We have stated that information about stress assigned on previous cycles is not in general available on subsequent cycles. It is obvious that this condition would prevent us from obtaining the correct results in the present instance because there would never be more than one stressed vowel on a cyclic stem plane. We must therefore circumvent this restriction in some way. We propose to do this by adding to the cyclic rules of Lenakel the asterisk copying rule (72), which is identical with the stress copying rule of English given as (42) in section 3.5.

(72) Copy line 1 asterisks assigned on preceding cycles.

Because Subjacency restricts the application of cyclic rules to the plane generated on the immediately preceding cycle, only a single asterisk will be copied on each pass through the cyclic rules; as in English, however, when assigned to a noncyclic stratum, the copying rule will copy all previously assigned asterisks, since noncyclic rules are not restricted by Subjacency. As we shall demonstrate, this result holds also for Lenakel.

According to Hammond, in Lenakel tense and lax vowels are in near complementary distribution: "High vowels are tense in open syllables and lax in closed ones. Mid vowels are lax before consonants and tense otherwise" (p. 7). To capture this fact formally, we assume that the language includes a vowel tensing rule that applies in open syllables subject to certain further conditions.

In addition to vowels with a predictable distribution of tenseness, Lenakel has tense vowels in contexts other than those subject to the tensing rule. Thus, the stressed vowels in (73a) are tense, although in closed syllables the tensing rule does not apply, as shown in (73b).

(73)

a. asís	'to swell up'	amnúm	'to drink'	
abgén	'to be jealous'	yElmów	'salt water eel'	
b. kÍn	'a kind of worm'	sÚk'	'spear'	
Élmas	'to frighten'	tigÓmgOm	'branches'	

To account for the examples in (73a), we shall assume that, in Lenakel, there are words that have tense vowels in their lexical representation.

A fact of special interest is that lexically tense vowels attract stress. For instance, as shown in (73a), words with lexically tense vowels in their last syllable have final stress, although normally Lenakel words have penultimate stress. To account for this, we postulate rule (74), which applies before the cyclic stress rules.

(74) Assign a line 1 asterisk to tense vowels.

Citing the examples in (75), Hammond observes that the vowels we have characterized here as lexically tense interrupt the alternating pattern of stresses.

(75) ni-gi-níl-ar   'their hearts'
     nì-man-si-níl-ar   'their bottoms'

The morphemes /gi/ and /si/ have lexically tense vowels, and we can account for their stress by assigning rule (74) to the noncyclic stratum (it is already assigned to the cyclic stratum in order to guarantee main stress on the final syllables in words like those in (73a)). These forms also show that (74) must be ordered before the rules that construct metrical constituent structure—namely, the Alternator (64b–d). Consequently, the two forms in (75) would appear after the application of the Alternator with the stress grids given in (76).

(76)   .   .   * .   .   .   .   * .
      (* * *).   (*   .   * * .)
      (*)(*)(* *)   (*   *) (*)(* *)
      ni-gi-nil-ar   ni-man-si-nil-ar

There is a problem with the forms in (76), however. These forms would undergo the noncyclic Clash Deletion rule (66) and would then surface with incorrect stress contours. In particular, the deletion rule would remove all line 1 asterisks in /niginilar/ and the asterisk over /si/ in /nimansinilar/. But, as noted already, lexically tense vowels are not subject to Clash Deletion (66). This rule must therefore be reformulated as follows.

(77) *Clash Deletion*
     Delete a line 1 asterisk if followed directly by a line 1 asterisk, provided that the asterisk to be deleted dominates a lax vowel.

If this rule is ordered before the rule tensing vowels in open syllables, the correct output is produced.

   We conclude this section by listing in the order of their application the Lenakel rules discussed above.

(78)
a. c/n   Stressable elements are vowels. (64a)

b. c   On each stress plane copy the line 1 asterisk assigned on preceding cycles. (72)

c. c/n   Assign a line 1 asterisk to tense vowels. (74)

d. c   Delete a word-final line 1 asterisk, if preceded directly by a line 1 asterisk. (71)

e. c/⟨n⟩   Line 0 parameter settings are [+HT, +BND, left, right to left ⟨in nouns, and left to right in verbs⟩].

f. c/n   Construct constituent boundaries on line 0. (64c)

g. c/n   Locate the heads of line 0 constituents on line 1. (64d)

h. c   Line 1 parameter settings are [+HT, −BND, right]. (64e)

i. c   Construct constituent boundaries on line 1. (64f)

j. c   Locate the heads of line 1 constituents on line 2. (64g)

k. c   Conflate lines 0 and 1. (64h)

l. n   Delete a line 1 asterisk if followed directly by a line 1 asterisk, provided that the asterisk to be deleted dominates a lax vowel. (77)

m. n   Tense nonlow ⟨nonhigh⟩$_a$ vowels in open ⟨nonfinal⟩$_b$ syllables. Condition: if a, then b.

6.5 The Interaction of Stress and Length in Yidin^y

Hayes (1980/1, 126) has succinctly formulated the basic facts of the Yidin^y stress pattern as follows.

(79) Stress falls on even-numbered syllables, if the word contains an even-numbered syllable with a long vowel; otherwise, stress falls on odd-numbered syllables.

In addition, Hayes notes (p. 132) that the final syllable in odd-syllabled words is never stressed. We proposed in section 1.1 that this stress pattern should be captured by the rules given in slightly modified form in (80).

(80)
a. Line 0 parameters are [+HT, +BND, left to right, $\left\{ \begin{matrix} \text{right} \\ \text{left} \end{matrix} \right\}$].

b. Construct constituent boundaries on line 0.

c. Locate the heads of the line 0 constituents on line 1.

d. Delete a line 1 asterisk if it is directly preceded by a stress-bearing element with a line 1 asterisk.

The Yidin^y stress pattern is significant because it provides a clear example where the setting of the parameter (in (80a)) is separate and distinct from the rules (80b,c) that construct the metrical grid in accordance with these parameter settings. To apply rule (80b) and place the line 0 constituent boundaries correctly, it is necessary to know the setting of the parameters [HT] and [BND], whereas to apply rule (80c) and locate the line 0 constituent heads on line 1, it is necessary to know the setting of the parameter [left/right]—which in turn presupposes information about the placement of the constituent boundaries by rule (80b). As proposed in section 1.1, we capture this fact by assuming that in Yidin^y, as in Tiberian Hebrew, the stress rules construct metrical grids on two planes simultaneously. On one plane—P1—the line 0 constituents are right-headed; on the other plane—P2—they are left-headed. A subsequent rule deletes P2 if on P1 there is a constituent head dominating a long vowel; otherwise the rule deletes P1.

In this section we examine additional facts from Yidin^y that provide further support for the proposed account and, by implication, for the theoretical framework on which it is based. Hayes notes that with the exception of 17 morphemes that contain long vowels, vowel length in Yidin^y is totally predictable. Vowels are lengthened in the following contexts:

(81)

a. before three verbal suffixes,

b. in the penultimate syllable of a word with an odd number of syllables, and

c. before /y/ in a word-final syllable.

Examples of the three lengthening processes are given in (82).

(82)

a. wáwa-l   'see' (inf.)   wawá:-d^{y}in-ú   (antipass.past)

b. gúdagá-gu 'dog' (purp.)   gudá:ga   (abs.)

c. galbí:(y) 'catfish' (abs.)   galbí:y # alá   (clit.)[16]

Among these rules, Penultimate Lengthening (81b) is of special interest. This rule applies only in words with an odd number of syllables. Whether a given syllable is odd- or even-numbered is established as a by-product of constructing binary constituents. Clearly, we must take advantage of this fact in formulating the rule of Penultimate Lengthening, which we therefore state as follows.

---

16. Syllable-final *y* is deleted by a special rule not discussed here.

(83) *Penultimate Lengthening*

Lengthen a vowel in the environment ____

where the parentheses represent metrical constituent boundaries

Since the rule makes crucial use of constituent boundaries, it must be ordered after the rule (80b) that first introduces the boundaries into the grid. Since two parallel metrical grids are constructed by the stress rules (80a–c) it is not necessary to order any of the lengthening rules before the stress rules. It is, however, essential that the rule deleting one of the two alternative metrical grids be ordered after the lengthening rules, in particular after Penultimate Lengthening. We know of no arguments for ordering the lengthening rules relative to one another.

In Yidin^y long vowels never occur on consecutive syllables. According to Dixon (1977a), in position next to a long vowel, a long vowel is shortened if it occurs in an odd-numbered syllable of an odd-syllabled word, by a process he terms *Illicit Length Elimination*. Since this process shortens an odd-numbered vowel when it is next to another long vowel, the process can only take place in words with even-numbered long vowels, that is, in words where in view of (79) all even-numbered syllables must be stressed. It follows, as already noted by Hayes, that the rule of Illicit Length Elimination can be simplified so as to affect only stressless vowels.

(84) *Illicit Length Elimination*

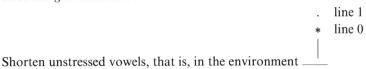

Shorten unstressed vowels, that is, in the environment ____

In order for this simplification to be implemented, however, it is necessary to apply rule (84) after all line 1 asterisks have been properly placed by rules (80c) and (80d).

In (85) we list the rules for Yidin^y in the order in which they apply. As noted above, we have no evidence for ordering the lengthening rules relative to one another.

(85)

a. Stress rules (80a–c)

b. Vowel lengthening before specified suffixes (81a)

c. Vowel lengthening before word-final /y/ (81c)

d. Penultimate Lengthening (83)

e. Alternative metrical plane deletion

f. Stress Clash Deletion (80d)

g. Illicit Length Elimination (84)

6.6 The Stress Pattern of Pirahã

Everett and Everett (1984) have drawn attention to the interesting case of stress placement in Pirahã, a Brazilian language, which is sensitive to the sonority of the syllable. Syllable sonority is determined first by the syllable nucleus—syllables with a branching nucleus are more sonorous than syllables with a nonbranching nucleus—and second by the onset— syllables with onsets are more sonorous than those without and, moreover, syllables whose onset is a voiceless consonant are more sonorous than syllables whose onset is a voiced consonant. Thus, the following sonority hierarchy obtains among Pirahã syllables:

(86) CVV > GVV > VV > CV > GV
    where C = voiceless consonant, G = voiced consonant.

Stress in Pirahã is placed on the most sonorous of the last three syllables of the word. However, if more than one token of this type occurs in the word, the one farthest to the right is stressed. The fact that stress falls on one of the last three syllables of the word has already been encountered in a number of languages above, including Polish and Cairene Arabic. It was captured formally by constructing binary constituents supplemented by recourse to extrametricality. What is novel in Pirahã is that syllable sonority as defined in (86), and syllable onset in particular, plays a determining role in the location of stress.

We propose to capture the stress distribution in Pirahã by the same device as was used in Yidin^y: we construct metrical grids on two planes simultaneously, one (P1) with a word-final extrametrical syllable and the other (P2) without it. The grids on these planes will consist of binary constituents on line 0 constructed from right to left and an unbounded right-headed constituent on line 1. The headedness of the line 0 constituents is determined by comparing the two syllables in the last constituent. In Pirahã the constituent is left-headed if the left syllable in the last constituent is more sonorous than the right syllable; otherwise the constituent is right-headed.

Formally the stress grids are constructed by the set of rules in (87), of which all but (87a) apply in the construction on both planes.

(87)

a. Mark the last syllable extrametrical. (P1 only.)

b. Line 0 parameters are [+HT, +BND, right to left] and [left] (left-headed) if the left syllable in the last constituent is more sonorous than the right syllable; otherwise, [right].

c. Construct constituent boundaries on line 0.

d. Locate the heads of line 0 constituents on line 1.

e. Line 1 parameters are [+HT, −BND, right].

f. Construct constituent boundaries on line 1.

g. Locate the heads of line 1 constituents on line 2.

h. Conflate lines 0 and 1.

These rules will generate two separate grids, each with a single stressed syllable. On P1 stress will be placed on either the penultimate or the antepenultimate syllable, whereas on P2 stress will be placed on either the penult or the ultima. Our remaining task is, therefore, to determine which of the two grids is to be used in any given case. As in Yidin^y, we shall implement the choice by deleting the inappropriate plane:

(88) If on P1 the stressed (head) syllable is of greater sonority than the last syllable of the word, delete P2; otherwise delete P1.

It is worth noting that in formulating the account above we have allowed reference only to elements that were terminal in a sequence, that is, directly adjacent to one of the two ends of a constituent. This restriction permitted us to place stress on the antepenultimate syllable but would make it impossible to place stress on a syllable farther from the end of the word. It therefore provides an explanation for the observation that in stress placement syllable counting above three is never necessary (or possible).

It might also be noted that the account presented above implies that in a word where the sonority of the penult exceeds that of the ultima but not that of the antepenult, the metrical constituent structure will be that of (89a) rather than that of (89b):

(89)

a. $(A - P)\langle -U\rangle$ b. $A - (P - U)$

Although both structures assign surface stress to the same syllable, they differ with respect to the effects resulting from a rule deleting or destressing the penultimate syllable. In the case of (89a) this process will result in a stress shift to the left, whereas in the case of (89b) the stress will be shifted to the right. While our extremely limited knowledge of Pirahã precludes us from subjecting these implications of our account to an empirical test, the fact that such a test can at least in principle be conducted is of some significance.

Chapter 7
English Stress

7.1 The Main Stress Rule

7.1.1 Main Stress in Nouns

A major empirical result of *SPE* was the discovery of the central role played in stress assignment by the contrast between "strong" and "weak" clusters —that is, between syllables with branching and nonbranching rimes.

(1) Cánada   agénda   marína   túna   hénna
     alúminum   conúndrum cerébrum   póssum   vénom

As illustrated in (1), in a large class of nouns main stress falls on the antepenult when the penult contains a nonbranching rime, and on the penult otherwise. To account for the fact that this class of words lacks word-final stress, we follow Hayes (1980/1) and postulate that these words are subject to a rule that marks their last asterisk on line 0 as extrametrical. A preliminary formulation of this rule is given in (2), where extrametricality of an entity is indicated by assigning it a dot rather than an asterisk on line 0.

(2) *Extrametricality*
     $* \rightarrow .\ /\ \underline{\qquad}$]   line 0   in nouns

Having thus rendered the word-final rime invisible to the constituent construction rules, we must now detail our procedure for locating the main stress in English words. Since stress placement is sensitive to the distinction between syllables with branching and nonbranching rimes, we postulate the Accent Rule (3), which formally marks this distinction.

(3) *Accent Rule*
     Assign a line 1 asterisk to a syllable with branching rime.

Hayes (1980/1) made the important discovery that in English this distinction in rime structure is crucial only for the assignment of main stress and plays no role (or only a marginal role) in the assignment of the subsidiary stresses in the word. Accordingly, Hayes distinguished between the "English Stress Rule," which locates the main stress and is sensitive to rime structure, and the rule of "Strong Retraction," which locates subsidiary stresses and is not sensitive to rime structure. Moreover, as Hayes also observed, the placement of subsidiary stresses depends crucially on the placement of the main stress. When main stress falls on the penult, the subsidiary stresses fall on even-numbered syllables counting from the end of the word (see (4a)); when main stress falls on the antepenult, subsidiary stresses fall on odd-numbered syllables counting from the end of the word (see (4b)).[1]

(4)

a. ònomàtopéia   Àpalàchicóla   arìstocrátic

b. sèrendípity   Càlifórnia   hàmamèlidánthemum

As noted in section 3.5, we deal with these observations in much the same way as we dealt with similar facts in our discussion of stress in Spanish and Lenakel (see sections 3.4.1 and 6.4). We assume that English stress is assigned by the rules in (5) and that (5a–c) are assigned to both the cyclic and the noncyclic strata of rules and (5d–g), (2), and (3) to the cyclic stratum alone.

(5)

a. c/n   Line 0 parameter settings are [+ HT, + BND, left, right to left].

b. c/n   Construct constituent boundaries on line 0.

c. c/n   Locate the heads of line 0 constituents on line 1.

d. c   Line 1 parameter settings are [+ HT, − BND, right].

e. c   Construct constituent boundaries on line 1.

f. c   Locate the head of the line 1 constituent on line 2.

g. c   Conflate lines 1 and 2.

When the rules in (2), (3), and (5) apply cyclically, they are the counterpart of Hayes's English Stress Rule; when (5a–c) apply in the noncyclic stratum, they are the counterpart of Hayes's Strong Retraction and we shall refer to them here also as the Alternator. We illustrate this in (6) in (7).

---

1. In this section different degrees of subsidiary stress are not distinguished in the representations; all subsidiary stresses are marked uniformly with a grave accent (`). These distinctions are systematically taken into account beginning with section 7.2.

```
                                            .  .  .  .  *  .
      *  *   *  *  **        *  *   *  *  *  .        *  *  *   *  *  .
(6) onomatopeia ⟶(2) onomatopei⟨a⟩ ⟶(3) onomatopei⟨a⟩ ⟶(5a−c)

                              .  .  .  .  *  .              .  .  .  .  *  .
   *  .   *. *  .           (.  .  .  .  *) .           (* .   *. *) .
   (* *) (* *)(*) .          *  *  *  *  (*) .           (* *) (* *)(* *)
   ono mato pei⟨a⟩ ⟶(5d−g) onomato pei a ⟶(5a−c) onomato pei a


                                 .  *  .  .  .
    *  *   *  **          *  *   *  *  .          *  *   *  *  .
(7) serendipity ⟶(2) serendipit⟨y⟩ ⟶(3) serendipit⟨y⟩ ⟶(5a−c)

                        .  .  *  .  .              .  .  *  .  .
   *  *   *  .  .       (.  .   *) .  .           (* .   *  *).
   (*)(*) (* *) .        *  *  (* *) .            (* *) (*) (* *)
   se rend ipit⟨y⟩ ⟶(5d−g) serendipi t y ⟶(5a−c) serendi pit y
```

Since *onomatopeia* and *serendipity* are underived nouns, there is only a single stress plane on which are recorded the effects of both the cyclic and the noncyclic stress rules (see section 3.1). As a result of conflation by rule (5g), only a single stress—the main stress—will be generated by the stress rules in the cyclic stratum. The subsidiary stresses of the words are all generated by the Alternator, that is, by rules (5a–c) when they apply in the noncyclic stratum. Since neither Extrametricality (2) nor the Accent Rule (3) applies in the noncylic stratum, at the stage in the derivation where the Alternator applies there are no extrametrical syllables in the grid and main stress is the only stress in the word. A final consequence of this organization of the rules is that in words with main stress on the antepenult, such as *serendipity*, the Alternator will assign stress to the penultimate syllable. This extraneous asterisk is subsequently deleted by our counterpart of the *SPE* rule of Poststress Destressing. (For additional discussion, see section 7.5.)

7.1.2 Main Stress in Adjectives and Verbs

As illustrated in (8), many suffixed adjectives follow the same principles of stress placement as the nouns in (1).

(8) pérsonal   dìaléctal   ànecdótal
    vígilant   repúgnant   compláisant
    màgnánimous   mòméntous   desírous

To account for these examples, we must generalize Extrametricality as follows.

(9) *Extrametricality*

    * → . / ———]   in nouns and in certain suffixes

It was observed in *SPE* that in unsuffixed adjectives and verbs main stress is located by the same principles as in the nouns in (1) except that in the adjectives and verbs stress is displaced one syllable toward the end of the word—that is, either to the penultimate or to the final syllable. We illustrate this in (10).

(10) sólid   absúrd   supréme
       méllow   ròbúst   discréte
       cértain   diréct   ináne
       astónish   usúrp   achíeve
       detérmine tòtmént   cajóle
       fóllow   cavórt   caróuse

One difference between the examples in (10) and those in (1) is that the words in (10) are not subject to Extrametricality (9), for they are neither nouns nor words that end with a suffix. Another difference is that the two sets of words are subject to the Accent Rule (3) under somewhat different conditions than the other words discussed. In underived adjectives and verbs the line 1 asterisk is assigned to the last metrical rime if, in addition to branching, it is followed by at least one consonant. We reformulate the Accent Rule as follows.[2]

---

2. Our way of dealing with the rimes of underived adjectives and verbs differs from that of Hayes, who postulated that the last consonant in such words is extrametrical. We deviate from Hayes's procedure in this case for the technical reason that in the version of the extrametricality theory that we adopt here (Archangeli 1986) extrametricality assigned to a terminal element in the rime percolates upward and renders the entire rime extrametrical, which clearly would be incorrect in the present instance. (For details, see Archangeli 1986 and section 2.1.) We conjecture that it will be possible to eliminate the proviso in rule (11) excluding word-final consonants in the determination of syllable branchingness when we have a better grasp of the process of syllabifying phoneme sequences. A possible account might capitalize on the suggestion that syllabification proceeds not in one fell swoop but in a number of discrete steps. In particular, constituent-final consonants appear to be syllabified by a rule that is assigned to the noncyclic stratum, whereas other portions of the phoneme string are syllabified by rules ordered at the beginning of the cyclic stratum. Consequently, word-final consonants do not count in determining rime branchingness. We shall examine two further instances where constituent-final consonants must be disregarded in determining rime branchingness. For some suggestive ideas that have influenced these speculations, see Dell and Elmedlaoui (1985).

(11) *Accent Rule*

Assign a line 1 asterisk to a syllable with a branching rime with the proviso that the word-final consonant is not counted in the determination of rime branchingness in the case of the final syllable of underived verbs and adjectives.

We observed in discussing Aklan in section 1.1 that among the accented syllables of Aklan, there were (in addition to syllables with branching rimes) a number of syllables with nonbranching rimes. Whether or not a syllable is assigned a line 1 asterisk for purposes of metrical tree construction therefore cannot depend solely on its phonetic properties. The modified Accent Rule (11) of English provides yet another example of this fact. In a word such as *develop* the last rime branches, yet for purposes of rule (11) the syllable is treated on a par with syllables with nonbranching rimes; in other words, this syllable is not assigned a line 1 asterisk even though phonetically its rime is branching. We therefore need rules that allow us to mark certain syllables as heads of metrical constituents not only by virtue of the branchingness of their rime but also by virtue of properties other than phonetic, including some highly abstract as well as totally idiosyncratic ones.

In (12) we illustrate the effects of the cyclic stratum on the construction of metrical grids for unsuffixed verbs and adjectives. The representations in (12a) are produced by the application of rule (11), and those in (12b) by the subsequent application of the stress rules in (5).

(12)

```
a. .  .   .     .  *       .  *
   *  *   *     *  *       *  *
   astonish    robust     carouse
b. .  *   .     .  *       .  *
   (.  *) .    (.  *)     (.  *)
   *  (*  *)    *  (*)     *(*)
   astonish    robust     carouse
```

7.1.3 A Special Case

There are both nouns and suffixed adjectives in English that have main stress on the penult even though this syllable has no branching rime.

(13)

a. cèrebéllum   medúlla   Kentúcky   Mìssissíppi

b. cèrebéllar   medúllar   Kentúckian   Mìssissíppian

We account for the stress of these words by postulating that their stem morphemes are entered in the lexicon with a line 1 asterisk on the penultimate syllable. The stress of these words is thus lexically determined. Since these are quite marginal cases, however, their existence does not make stress a distinctive feature of English.

Selkirk (1984) has suggested accounting for the stress patterns of the words in (13) by marking these words as exceptions to Extrametricality (9); that is, stems of the class illustrated in (13) would be marked so as to block its application. However, this seems to be incorrect in view of such examples as *Kentuckian* and *Mississippian*, where main stress falls on the antepenult and not on the penult, as might have been expected if these stems caused Extrametricality to be blocked.

7.2 Subsidiary Stresses in Underived Words

In English, as in a great many other languages, nonmain stresses are assigned by a rule that is sensitive to the location of main stress and therefore must be applied after main stress has been placed by the rules in (5). As discussed in section 3.5, we shall account for the subsidiary stresses in English by assuming that rules (5a–c) are assigned both to the cyclic stratum and to the noncyclic stratum. Since the cyclic stratum includes Stress Conflation (5g), each word emerges from the cyclic stratum with a single stressed syllable, namely, the one bearing main stress. The stress effects of the noncyclic rules are recorded on the same metrical plane as those of the last pass through the cyclic rules. Since we are dealing here with underived words (words without internal constituent structure), we shall encounter only a single metrical plane on which all stress information will be recorded.

Let us consider an example. The cyclic stress rules will yield representations such as those in (14).

(14) . . . . * .   . . . . * . .
      (. . . . *) .   (. . . . *) . .
      * ** *(*) .   * * **(* *) .
      Apalachico⟨1a⟩   hamamelidanthe⟨mum⟩

We assume that extrametricality is not carried over automatically from the cyclic to the noncyclic stratum. Constituent structure assigned in the last cyclic stratum is preserved unless modified by a particular noncyclic rule, which, however, applies so as to respect previously generated heads. When

the Alternator is applied to (14), we therefore obtain the representations
in (15).

(15) .   .   .   .   *   .   .   .   .   .   *   .   .   .
      (* .   *   .   *).   (* .   *.   *)   *   .
      (* *)(* *)(* *)   (* *)(* *)(*)   (* *)
      Apa lachi cola   hamameli danthemum

The metrical grids generated in (15) are essentially correct except for the
line 1 asterisk on the penultimate syllable of *hamamelidanthemum*. This
asterisk will be deleted by our counterpart of the *SPE* rule of Poststress
Destressing (see rule (33)).

As illustrated in (16), not all underived words of English exhibit the
subsidiary stress pattern just described.

(16) Hàlicàrnássus incàrnátion òstèntátion incàntátion

These words are listed by Kenyon and Knott (1944) as having subsidiary
stresses—facultatively in some cases—on the syllable preceding the
main stress. Given the rules developed so far, this stress pattern cannot
be generated since the Alternator cannot place stress on the pretonic
syllable. The attested pattern will be produced, however, if these words
are treated as lexically marked exceptions to Stress Conflation (5g). A
word such as *Halicarnassus* will then emerge from the cyclic stratum in
the form (17). The subsequent application of the Alternator (5a–c) is
vacuous.

(17) .   .   .   *   .
      *   .   *   *   .
      (* *)(*) (*)   .
      Hali carnas⟨sus⟩

We shall show that a considerably larger class of cases are exceptions to
Stress Conflation (5g).

7.3 Word-Final Stress and Stress Retraction

As a consequence of Extrametricality (9), the rules of constituent construction in (5) will disregard the word-final syllable in nouns as well as in
suffixed words of all kinds. We should therefore expect not to find any
word-final stress in this class of words. There are, however, a number of
important exceptions to this generalization. The simplest case is that of the
nouns in (18).

(18) políce   bròcáde   baróque
     bazáar   regíme   tòupée
     àttaché   kàngaróo   Tènnessée

In general, nouns with a final rime containing a long vowel are systematic exceptions to Extrametricality (9), which must therefore be reformulated as follows.

(19) *Extrametricality*

   * → . / ———]   line 0   in nouns and in certain suffixes,
                             provided * dominates a rime with a
                             short vowel (nonbranching nucleus)

Suffixes with long vowels are thus not subject to Extrametricality (19). Words with such suffixes will therefore be stressed in the same way as the nouns in (18): they will all have main stress on their last syllable, as shown by the examples in (20a), which contrast with those in (20b).

(20)

a. i.   mìllionáire   quèstionnáire   dòctrináire
    ii. dèbàuchée   èmplòyée   nòminée
         àppòintée
    iii. ènginéer   dòminéer   elèctionéer
         vòluntéer   chàriotéer

b. i.   désignàte   exácerbàte   íllustràte
         démonstràte   álternàte
    ii. cávalcàde   ásymptòte   ánecdòte
         hỳpótenùse   fòrmáldehỳde   acétylène
         télephòne   kaléidoscòpe   áquaplàne
    iii. récognìze   sátisfỳ   jéopardìze
         díphthongìze
    iv. adúmbràte   incúlcàte   inúndàte
         elóngàte   erúctàte

The difference is that although the words in (20b) end in syllables with branching rimes, they do not have main stress on the last syllable. However, unlike the final syllables of the examples discussed in sections 7.1 and 7.2, the final syllables of these words are not stressless, but bear a subsidiary stress. Our immediate task, therefore, is to account for this fact.

English is subject to a process retracting stress from word-final syllables in such phrases as *fóurtèen yéars*, *Ténnessèe Wílliams*, and *Kálamazòo*,

Michigan. To account for such instances of stress retraction, the so-called Rhythm Rule has been generally invoked (Liberman and Prince 1977; Hayes 1980/1; Prince 1983). In these studies this rule was restricted to applying in the word-sequence stratum, to sequences of two or more words. In commenting on stress retraction in section 1.3, we proposed to extend this rule so that it would also apply within single words, which are lexically marked for this. We formulate the Rhythm Rule provisionally as follows.

(21) *Rhythm Rule*
  In a constituent C composed of a single word, retract the right boundary of C to a position immediately before the head of C, provided that the head of C is located on the last syllable of C and that it is preceded by a stressed syllable.

In view of examples such as (18) and (20a), which constitute minimal contrasts with the words illustrated in (20b), the application of the Rhythm Rule must be lexically governed; like many other stress rules, the Rhythm Rule applies not across the board but only in specially marked contexts. Thus, in addition to applying to the words in (20b), the Rhythm Rule applies to the deverbal nouns in (22); but it does not apply to the verbs from which they are derived.[3]

(22) tránsfèr   prótèst   prógrèss
     súspèct   tórmènt   íntercèpt[4]

Like all rules of stress retraction in English (and in many other languages as well), the Rhythm Rule (21) retracts the moved asterisk to the vowel with the next highest column of asterisks. If there is more than one such column, the asterisk lands on the one that is nearest. Both of these peculiarities follow automatically from the Rhythm Rule (21), for it affects the right boundary of the constituent that is coextensive with the entire word. A special proviso had to be added to the Rhythm Rule, however, to account for the fact that when no stressed syllable precedes main stress, the rule does not apply. Our impression is that this proviso reflects a general

---

3. It was observed in *SPE* (p. 95) that verbs such as *comprehend* and *introspect*, whose root morpheme is word-final, do not undergo stress retraction, whereas, as illustrated in (20), most other polysyllabic verbs retract stress. It was also noted in *SPE* (pp. 100ff.) that nouns ending in polysyllabic roots do not undergo the Rhythm Rule, as expected; compare the examples in (20bii) with *àquamaríne*.
4. See footnote 16 of chapter 1.

constraint on stress retraction rules of this type, but we have not succeeded in discovering the precise nature of this constraint.

In view of Stress Conflation (5g), words will emerge at the end of the cyclic stratum with but a single stressed syllable. The Rhythm Rule (21) must therefore be ordered in the noncyclic stratum after the Alternator (5a–c), for only after the Alternator has provided subsidiary stresses will there be stressed syllables to the left of the main stress.

Once the Rhythm Rule is included among the rules of the noncyclic word-internal stratum, it can also be used to account for the nonfinal main stress in the underived adjectives in (23). In this way the stress that is assigned to the final syllable by (5) is retracted to the antepenult.

(23) díffìcùlt   móribùnd   dérelìct   mánifèst

The examples in (24) differ from those previously discussed in that although they have a stressed final syllable, this syllable has a short rather than a long vowel and should therefore be marked extrametrical by rule (19). If this were indeed the case, stress would not appear on the word-final syllable.[5]

(24)
a. Pèkíng   Sàigón   Bèrlín
   Càntón   Hòngkóng   gazélle

b. gýmnàst   nárthèx   ínsèct
   pársnìp

c. Àdiróndàck Monádnòck   Sàskátchewàn
   Èniwétòk   Penóbscòt   Mamáronèck
   Màssapéquòd Hopátcòng   Èscúminàc
   Àgamémnòn   decáthlòn   stèreópticòn

We account for the word-final stress in (24) by assuming that these nouns are exceptions to Extrametricality (19). They will therefore emerge from the cyclic stratum with main stress on the last syllable. This distinguishes them from the nouns in (25), whose last syllable is extrametrical and hence stressless.

(25) Whéeling Lóndon   Néwton
     Óssining alúminum   témpest
     hélix   súbject   cátsup

---

5. The examples in (24c) were first discussed by Ross (1972).

Moreover, the examples in (24a) differ from those in (24b,c) in that the latter are subject to retraction by the Rhythm Rule (21), whereas the former are not.

We still must account for the fact that unlike the situation in (20b), the stress in (24c) is not uniformly retracted to the antepenult but is placed on the penultimate syllable when the latter has a branching rime. This fact can be accounted for by assuming that like the words in (16), those in (24c) are marked as exceptions to Stress Conflation (5g).

Most bisyllabic verbs in -*ate* have main stress on the initial syllable (see (26a)). They contrast with the verb in (26b), where stress is always final, and with the verbs in (26c), where stress is either final or initial.

(26)
a. stágnàte   frústràte   púlsàte
   plácàte   víbràte

b. equáte

c. díctàte   lócàte   óràte   *or*
   dictáte   lòcáte   òráte

The verbs in (26a), like those in (20bi), are subject to retraction by the Rhythm Rule, whereas *equate* is one of the few verbs in -*ate* that is never subject to the Rhythm Rule and the verbs in (26c) are subject to it only optionally.

7.3.1 Rule Summary 1
If the proposals made above are adopted, the cyclic stratum will consist of the following rules: Extrametricality (19), the Accent Rule (11), and all five parts of the Main Stress Rule (5). The noncyclic stratum will consist of only a subset of these rules, namely, parts (a–c) of the Main Stress Rule (5) (the so-called Alternator) and the Rhythm Rule (21).

The rules developed to this point are listed in (27).

(27) c   Extrametricality (19)

     c   Accent Rule (11)

         Main Stress Rule (5)

     c/n   a. Line 0 parameter settings are [+HT, +BND, left, left to right].

     c/n   b. Construct constituent boundaries on line 0.

     c/n   c. Locate the heads of line 0 constituent on line 1.

     c   d. Line 1 parameter settings are [+HT, −BND, right].

c   e. Construct constituent boundaries on line 1.

c   f. Locate the head of the line 1 constituent on line 2.

c   g. Conflate lines 1 and 2.

n   Rhythm Rule (21)

7.4 Stress Deletion

We have had repeated occasions to remark that certain syllables are subject to destressing in a position adjacent to a syllable with greater stress. In particular, the Alternator (5a–c) will assign a line 1 asterisk to the initial syllable in words such as those in (28a) and to the penultimate syllable in words such as those in (28b).

(28)

a. banana   American   devotion

b. serendipity   Aristotle   elementary

To account for the fact that these syllables surface without stress, we make use of the concept of *stress well*. We shall assume that every stressed syllable automatically induces a well under a syllable adjacent to it, provided that the stress of the latter is of lesser magnitude than the stress of the former. We illustrate the assignment of stress wells in (29).

```
(29) .   * . .     . . * . .     . . *   . .     line 2
     *   * * .     * . * * .     * . * *  .      line 1
     *   * * *     * * * * *     * * * *  * *    line 0
     American   serendipit y    elementary
     w    w w      w    w w      w    w w    stress wells
```

The required rule of destressing can now be stated in the reasonably perspicuous manner shown in (30).

(30) *Stress Deletion*
     Over stress wells, delete asterisks on line 1 and above.

As stated, however, this rule applies in too wide a number of cases.

(31)

a. màintáin   bàndána   càntánkerous

b. mìcróscopy   vìtálity   Sàigón

c. gýmnàst   plácàte   Àgamémnòn
   pársnìp

The first syllable in all forms in (31a,b) will be over a stress well since the syllable precedes the main stress. It should therefore also undergo destressing by rule (30). Since this does not in fact, happen, rule (30) must be restricted so as to apply only when the well dominates a nonbranching rime. This modification will also account for the absence of destressing in the forms in (31c), where the well is in post-stress position. Moreover, as shown in (32), Stress Deletion affects pretonic syllables with branching rimes when they terminate Latinate prefixes.

(32) sublíminal   advíce   convénient   envélop

Stress Deletion (30) will therefore have to be modified to read as follows.[6]

(33) *Stress Deletion*
Over a stress well, delete asterisks on line 1 and above, provided that the well is assigned to a syllable with a nonbranching rime or to a Latinate prefix.

7.5 Vowel Reduction

One of the most striking phonetic properties of English is the reduction of unstressed vowels to schwa. We see this most clearly when we compare words with cognate stems and different stress contours.

(34) órigin–oríginal
Páris–Parísian
mónàrch–monárchic

Following the lead of *SPE*, we account for this kind of vowel reduction by means of a rule that affects the unstressed short vowel in an open syllable —that is, an unstressed vowel linked to a skeletal slot exhaustively dominated by the syllabic nucleus. We formulate the rule of Reduction as follows.

---

6. The stress contours of words such as *certainty*, *speciality*, *dynasty*, *travesty*, *registry*, which have antepenultimate stress rather than the penultimate stress that their heavy penultimate rimes would lead us to expect, must be assumed to have a nonsyllabic /y/ in their underlying representations. Since the rule syllabifying word-final /y/ is ordered after the Alternator, there will be no subsidiary stress on the word-medial syllable. The antepenultimate stress of nouns formed with the suffix -*ity* suggests that this suffix is bisyllabic in its underlying representation.

(35) *Reduction*

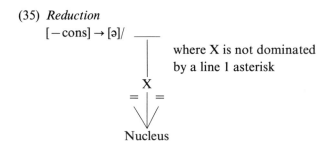

$$[-\text{cons}] \rightarrow [\text{ə}]/ \underline{\hspace{1.5cm}}$$

where X is not dominated
by a line 1 asterisk

Reduction (35) will be ordered at the very end of the phonological rules; in particular, it must follow Stress Deletion (33), because Stress Deletion feeds Reduction. Since in *SPE* stress was assumed to be a feature on a par with other features such as voicing, tenseness, and nasality, the destressing rules of *SPE*, both Pre- and Poststress Destressing, were formulated so as to assign the feature complex [−stress, −tense] to the affected vowel (see *SPE* rule (118), p. 125). Since in the present framework Stress Deletion (33) deletes asterisks in a metrical grid rather than changing the feature composition of segments, it is not an altogether straightforward matter to combine laxing with destressing. A more detailed examination of these issues is therefore in order.

In pretonic position Stress Deletion (33) seems to apply under somewhat different conditions word-medially than word-initially. Word-medially Stress Deletion affects long vowels and diphthongs (see (36a)), whereas word-initially long vowels retain stress and are therefore not reduced (see (36b)).

(36)
a. ìnvocátion   èxcitátion   rèvelátion   ìnflammátion
b. vòcátion   cìtátion   èjéction   gràdátion

We propose not to modify Stress Deletion in order to deal with these facts. This rule will destress only syllables with nonbranching rimes; it will therefore not apply to syllables with long vowels. We shall capture the difference between the words in (36a) and those in (36b) by adding to the phonology a rule that shortens pretonic vowels word-medially but not word-initially. The effect of this rule will be to render noninitial pretonic vowels in open syllables subject to Stress Deletion and hence also to Reduction (35). The necessary rule, which we shall call *Shortening over a Stress Well*, can be stated as follows.

(37) *Shortening over a Stress Well*

$$\begin{array}{ccc} X & X & X \ / \ SYL \ \underline{\hspace{1cm}} \ SYL \\ \bigvee & \rightarrow & | \\ V & & V \end{array}$$

Condition: V dominates a stress well.

This rule will apply only to syllables over stress wells, that is, to syllables adjacent to syllables with greater stress.

If we assume that Shortening (37) precedes Stress Deletion (33), the words in (36a) will undergo Stress Deletion, whereas those in (36b) will not. Words such as *denotation* and *exploitation* will be lexically marked as exceptions to Shortening; they will therefore not undergo Stress Deletion either. As already noted, Shortening applies not only in position before main stress but also in position after main stress. In particular, it shortens the poststress syllable in such words as *refectory* and *elementary*.[7]

7.6 Distinctions among Subsidiary Stresses

English differs from some other languages with subsidiary word stresses in that it distinguishes between weaker and stronger subsidiary stresses. Thus, Kenyon and Knott (1944) represent a word such as *Ticonderoga* as [ˌtaɪkandəˈrogə], where the short vertical bar on the lower half of the line indicates that the initial syllable is "more prominent than one or more others in the word, but less prominent than the strongest one in the word" (p. xxiv). They also distinguish among syllables unmarked for stress, especially between those, like the third and fifth syllables in [ˌtaɪkandəˈrogə], that contain a schwa and those, like the second syllable, that contain a full vowel. Thus, they remark that in *undone* "the first syllable is not quite without accent, but has sufficient accent (though not marked) to make it audibly more prominent than the *un-* of *unless.*"[8]

When subsidiary stresses occur on adjacent syllables, they generally differ in magnitude. This was shown in the representation of *Ticonderoga* above, where there was more stress on the first than on the second syllable.

---

7. The fact that the suffixes *-ory/-ary* are subject to rule (37) in spite of being underlyingly monosyllabic is readily captured by ordering rule (37) after the rule that syllabifies word-final /y/.

8. That the second syllable in *Ticonderoga* bears some degree of stress is shown by the aspiration of the voiceless stop [k] that constitutes the onset of this syllable. See also footnote 16 of chapter 1.

In fact, Kenyon and Knott indicate that in addition to the stress contour given above there is a second, equally acceptable pronunciation with greater stress on the second rather than on the first syllable, namely, [taɪ,kandə'rogə]. To account for this, we postulate the rule of Stress Enhancement (38), which enhances stress on the first or second syllable of a word.

(38) *Stress Enhancement*

$$* \qquad\qquad\qquad \text{line 2}$$
$$* \rightarrow * \ / \ [(\text{SYL}) \underline{\qquad} \qquad \text{line 1}$$

Stress Enhancement preserves intact the previously established distinction between main and subsidiary stresses. To implement this formally, we assume that Stress Enhancement is preceded in the noncyclic stratum by a set of rules essentially identical with the rules assigning main stress (5d–f).

(39)

a. Line 2 parameter settings are [+HT, −BND, right].

b. On line 2 construct constituent boundaries.

c. Locate the line 2 constituent head on line 3.

If the rules in (39) are ordered before Stress Enhancement (38), the application of Stress Enhancement will not obliterate the distinction between main and subsidiary stresses.[9]

There are a number of arguments in favor of the solution just proposed. We noted in section 1.2 that in order for the rules of stress subordination to apply properly, the main stresses of all words must be of the same magnitude. In particular, the main stress of words such as *póison, fórt* that lack subsidiary stresses must be of the same magnitude as the main stresses of words with several subsidiary stresses such as *fòrmáldehỳde, Tìcònderóga*. The rules in (39) ensure that all words will surface with their main stress marked by a line 3 asterisk, thus formally implementing the equality of all main stresses of words pronounced in isolation.

We shall argue in section. 7.8 that rule (39) is required to account for the stress patterns of nouns of the type *electrode, hominoid, contemplative, articulatory*, which have main stress on a presuffixal syllable and secondary stress on the suffix.

---

9. The obvious similarity between rules (5d–f) and (39) suggests that they are special cases of a single rule. We shall not incorporate this further generalization into the present description.

The line 2 asterisks assigned by Stress Enhancement (38) are heads of metrical constituents defined by the rules (5d–f), which are the basis of line 1 constituents. We illustrate this in (40).

(40) a.   b.   c.

```
.  .  .  *  .          .  .  .  *  .          .  .  .  *  .     line 3
(*  .  .  *) .          (.  *  .  *).          (       .  *).    line 2
(*)(*  .  *) .          (*  *)(.  *).          *  *  (.  *).     line 1
(*)(*  *)(*   *)        (*)(*   *)(*  *)        (*)(*   *)(*  *)  line 0
Winnipe saukee          a pothe osis           Ti conde roga

.  .  .  *  .          .  .  .  *  .          .  .  .  *  .     line 3
(*  .  .  *) .          (.  *  .  *).          (       .  *)     line 2
(*)(*  .  *) .          (*  *)(.  *).          *  *(.  *).       line 1
(*)(*  *)(*   *)        (*)(*   *)(*  *)        (*)(*  *)(*  *)   line 0
abraca dabra            Mo nonga hel a         a cademician
```

The cyclic Main Stress Rule (5) and its noncyclic counterpart ((5a–c) and (39)) generate grids in which the first two syllables of these words have line 1 asterisks and the main stress is represented by a line 3 asterisk. At a subsequent point in the derivation Stress Enhancement (38) applies, yielding the representations in (40). In the words in (40a) a line 2 asterisk is placed on the first syllable; in those in (40b) it is placed on the second syllable; and in those in (40c) it is placed on either the first or the second syllable. (To indicate the latter indeterminacy, we have left the space blank.) Stress Deletion (33) applies next and destresses the syllable with lesser stress, provided it has a nonbranching rime. The rule applies without exception when the two syllables beginning the word have nonbranching rimes (see (41a,b)) or when the first syllable does not branch and the second does (see (41c)). Reduction appears to be rather less systematic when the first syllable has greater stress and branches and the second syllable does not branch (see (41d)).

(41)

a. pàraphernália   mèmorabília   fòraminífera   Tàtamagóuchi

b. amànuénsis   apòtheósis   Epàminóndas

c. epìstemólogy   Colùmbiána   Epìscopálian   Atàscadéro

d. icònoclástic   icòsahédron   dègènerátion   Dòdècanésus

Kenyon and Knott (1944) observe that "in actual speech, such alternative accentuations as *a,cade'mician* or *,acade'mician*, *im,penetra'bility* or

ˌimpenetraˈbility, inˌferiˈority or ˌinferiˈority are very common, and do not represent more or less desirable pronunciations . . ." (p. xxv).[10]

Since the final syllable of the words in (41) is stressless, these words are not subject to the Rhythm Rule (21). Among words with final stress we would expect to find the same contrasting application of Stress Enhancement (38). Since the Rhythm Rule could apply to such words, we would expect to find the contrasting application of Stress Enhancement to be reflected in the position of main stress. In particular, we would expect to find, corresponding to the contrast between (41a) and (41b), a contrast between words with main stress on the first and on the second syllable. As illustrated in (42a) and (42b), this expectation is borne out to some extent.

(42)

a. cátamaràn   húllabalòo   rígamaròle
   óxygenàte   álienàte

b. hỳpótenùse   acétylène   fòrmáldehỳde
   amélioràte   detérioràte

c. dòmicíliàte   rècapítulàte   dìfferéntiàte
   còunteríndicàte ìntercommúnicàte trànssubstántiàte
   cìrcumámbulàte   dèphlogísticàte

The only verbs in -ate that exhibit the expected contrasts are quadrisyllabic. In these verbs the Alternator places stress on both the first and the second syllables, one of which subsequently undergoes Stress Enhancement (38). Verbs in -ate that are five or six syllables long never retract stress to the initial syllable. These restrictions can be readily expressed by appropriate amendments to the rule of Stress Enhancement.[11]

Consider finally the stress contours of words such as those in (43), where

---

10. Kenyon and Knott fail to draw explicit attention to the fact noted in the text and reflected in their transcriptions that stress shift is frequently, although not invariably, accompanied by vowel reduction.

11. A possible way of capturing this difference formally is by positing that in the derivation of the words in (41a) the Rhythm Rule (21) follows Stress Enhancement (38), whereas in the derivation of the words in (41c) the order is reversed. As we have encountered such local variability in rule ordering elsewhere (see section 6.3), we might have recourse to it here as well. We would then assume that in the basic rule order the Rhythm Rule (21) precedes Stress Enhancement (38) but that the order is reversed in deriving the marked class of words in (41a). Such variability in rule order is extremely limited in actual cases, and the reason for this restrictiveness is at present unknown.

Kenyon and Knott indicate secondary stress both on the first syllable and on the third.

(43) Àpalàchicóla   hàmamèlidánthemum   ònomàtopéia

As stated in (38), Stress Enhancement would supply additional stress only to the word-initial syllable and thus predicts that the first syllable has more stress than the third, apparently contradicting Kenyon and Knott. There is some evidence that this prediction is, in fact, correct. Prince (1983, 43ff.) observes that in compounds such as *Apalachicola Falls* the main stress of the first word is retracted to the initial rather than to the third syllable. Since the Rhythm Rule retracts stress to the preceding syllable with greatest stress, the retraction facts indicate that the initial syllable has more stress than the third syllable, as predicted by Stress Enhancement (38).

The above treatment of the placement of secondary stress differs fundamentally from that proposed by Kiparsky (1979), where the placement of secondary stress reflects the assignment of main stress on a previous cycle. Kiparsky states that in "all the following words" his rule "predicts that the most prominent secondary stress is on the second syllable, not on the first" (p. 423).

(44) iconoclastic   anticipation   totalitarian
     egalitarian   inferiority   posteriority
     theatricality superiority

Of the eight words cited by Kiparsky, Kenyon and Knott list seven. For four of these they indicate that either of the two first syllables may have the stronger stress; for three others (*egalitarian, posteriority, superiority*) they indicate stronger stress on the second syllable only. In view of the fact that for Kenyon and Knott *totalitarian* and *inferiority* can have either stress (recall their remark concerning the orthoepical equality of the different alternatives of *inferiority*), it would appear that the absence of a second alternative for *egalitarian, posteriority, superiority* is more likely to be an oversight than a systematic gap to be accounted for in a phonological description of the language.[12] It would thus seem that at least for the

---

12. A check of the first half of Kenyon and Knott's dictionary (letter *a* through *m*) reveals the following 97 entries with alternative stress patterns on the first two syllables: *academician, acceptability, acceleration, accessibility, antipathetic, apotheosis, aristocratic, arithmetician, articulation, asphyxiation, authentication, canalization, certification, coagulation, cooperation, decapitation, deceleration, delectation, degeneration, delimitation, demagnetization, demobilization, depolarization, di-*

dialect(s) represented by Kenyon and Knott, the cyclic account proposed by Kiparsky does not hold.

7.6.1 Rule Summary 2

We list in (45) the rules that have been discussed to this point in our exposition of the English stress pattern. The rules are listed in the order of their application, with the proviso that there is variability in the relative ordering of the Rhythm Rule and Stress Enhancement.

(45) c   Extrametricality (19)

    c   Accent Rule (11)

    c/n   Binary Constituent Construction/Alternator (5a–c)

    c   Unbounded Constituent Construction on line 1 and Stress Conflation (5d–g)

    n   Unbounded Constituent Construction on line 2 (39)

    n   Rhythm Rule (21)

    n   Stress Enhancement (38)

    n y-Syllabification

    n   Shortening over a Stress Well (37)

    n   Stress Deletion (33)

    n   Reduction (35)

7.7 The Stressing of Derived Words

The study of words that have internal constituent structure has led to the important discovery that stresses assigned to some of the embedded con-

---

cotyledon, disapprobation, disconsolation, disembarkation, disfiguration, disingenuous, disintegration, disorganization, disqualification, domesticity, elasticity, electricity, ellipticity, experimental, humanitarian, humiliation, immobilization, immovability, immutability, impalpability, impassability, impeachability, impeccability, impedimenta, impenetrability, imperatorial, imperishability, impermeability, impersonality, impersonation, implacability, imponderability, impossibility, impracticability, impracticality, impressibility, inalienability, inamorata, inapplicability, inaudibility, incalculability, incapability, incomparability, inconsequentiality, incredibility, incrimination, indisputability, indissolubility, indoctrination, inedibility, ineffability, ineligibility, inferiority, infinitival, inquisitorial, insatiability, inscrutability, insemination, insensibility, inseparability, insociability, invariability, invincibility, inviolability, invisibility, invulnerability, irrefutability, irregularity, irreparability, irresolution, Louisiana, metempsychosis, misericord, misestimation.

stituents appear with reduced magnitude in the stress contour of the derived word. Thus, it was noted in *SPE* that the contrast in stress contour between words like *còndènsátion* and *còmpensátion* is due to the fact that *condénse* but not *cómpensàte* has stress on the second syllable. It was therefore suggested in *SPE* that stress assignment must be cyclic—in other words, that in deriving the stress contour of a complex word, the stress contour of each of its embedded constituents must be taken into account. The precise details of how this is to be done depend, of course, on the theoretical apparatus employed for computing the stress contours of words. The machinery employed in chapter 3 of *SPE*, where stress facts were represented without recourse to metrical trees, has therefore differed greatly from that employed by Hayes (1980/1) or Kiparsky (1979), for whom labeled metrical trees—but not metrical grids—are the primary device for the notation of stress. Since the devices we employ here differ from those of our predecessors, our way of dealing with these phenomena will of necessity differ in important details from theirs.

The heart of our proposal concerning the preservation of stresses of embedded constituents follows directly from our assumption that the application of the stress rules to each cyclic constituent is recorded on a separate metrical plane and that information from earlier planes is not automatically carried over to later planes. As pointed out in chapter 3, unlike Vedic Sanskrit and Spanish, but like Chamorro and Lenakel, English preserves a "memory" of the fact that a particular syllable received main stress on a previous pass through the cyclic stress rules. As is well known, such syllables frequently surface with some degree of stress that renders them immune to Vowel Reduction. We shall capture this fact by postulating the rule of Stress Copy (46).

(46) *Stress Copy*
Place a line 1 asterisk over an element that has stress on any metrical plane.

Like the Accent Rule (11), Stress Copy determines the effects of the stress rules in (5) and will therefore be ordered before them. The rules differ in that the Accent Rule is assigned to the cyclic stratum and Stress Copy to the noncyclic stratum. In view of this, the question arises whether there is any need for a separate rule of Stress Copy. Would it not be possible to account for all instances of "cyclic" stress by assigning the Accent Rule to the noncyclic stratum as well and by making it obligatory for all derived words? The contrast between words such as *compensation* with a reduced (unstressed) pretonic vowel and *condensation* with a nonreduced (stressed) pretonic vowel shows that this proposal is inadequate. Since both are derived words, both would be subject to the Accent Rule in the noncyclic stratum. Since in both words the pretonic syllable has a branching rime, the Accent Rule would treat the two words alike, but this is contrary to fact. The proposal to include the Accent Rule in the noncyclic stratum is therefore not viable.

What distinguishes the two words is their derivational history. *Còndènsátion* has stress on the syllable before main stress because it derives from the verb *condénse*. *Còmpensátion* lacks stress on the syllable before main stress because it derives from the verb *còmpensáte*. This difference is reflected straightforwardly if both words are subject to Stress Copy but not to the Accent Rule in the noncyclic stratum. These facts further support our treatment of the Accent Rule as applying in the cyclic stratum only.

We illustrate the functioning of Stress Copy (46) with the derivation of the stress contour of the derived noun *instrumentality*. On the first cycle we obtain the metrical grid and constituents in (47).

```
(47)  *     .     .
      (*    .)    .
      (*    *)    .
      instru⟨ment⟩
```

In the course of this derivation the word-final syllable is marked extrametrical by Extrametricality (19). The Accent Rule (11) does not apply and the Main Stress rules (5) then generate the representation in (47). Since the suffix -*al* is not a domain for stress, the stress assigned on the first cycle is not copied onto the plane of the suffix and the derivation begins with a matrix that has no line 1 asterisks. The same rules as those operating on the first cycle then generate the metrical constituent grid in (48).

```
(48)  .     .     *     .
      (.    .     *)    .
      *     *(    *)    .
      instrument⟨al⟩
```

In the next and last pass through the cycle (49) is generated.

```
(49)  .     .     .     *    .    .
      (.    .     .     *).    .
      *     *     *    (*    *).
      instrumentali⟨ty⟩
```

Since no further cyclic suffixes are present, (49) is submitted to the noncyclic stratum. The first rule to apply there is Stress Copy (46), which generates (50).

(50) .   .   . * . .   line 2
     (*   .   * *) . .   line 1
      *   *   * (* *)*   line 0
     instrumentalit y

The Alternator (5a–c) applies next, but its effect is vacuous except for placing a line 1 asterisk on the penultimate syllable and locating constituent boundaries on line 0.[13] Then the noncyclic Main Stress Rule (39) applies, followed by Stress Enhancement (38). The last rule to apply is Stress Deletion (33), which deletes the asterisk assigned by the Alternator to the penultimate syllable. We thus obtain the representation (51), which correctly reflects the surface stress contour of this word.

(51) .   .   . * . .
      *   .   . * . .
      *   .   * * . .
      *   *   * * * *
     instrumentality

Consider next the noun *classification*. The innermost constituent is subject to the stress rules of the cyclic stratum, whose application results in the representation (52).

(52)   .   . *
       .   . *
       *   * *
     classi fy

If we were deriving the stress contour of the verb, we would next enter the noncyclic stratum and go through the derivation in (53), which begins with the vacuous application of Stress Copy (46) and then proceeds as shown.

(53)   . . *   * . .
       . . *   . . *   * . *   * . *
       . . *   * . *   * . *   * . *
       * **   * **   * **   * **
     classify $\xrightarrow{(5a-c)}$ classify $\xrightarrow{(38)}$ classify $\xrightarrow{(21)}$ classify

---

13. Except where especially relevant to the point under discussion, metrical constituent structure generated by stress rules of the noncyclic stratum is omitted in the representations to follow.

As our objective is to derive the stress contour of the noun *classification*, however, we must go through another application of the cyclic rules before entering the noncyclic stratum. The cyclic rules will generate the first representation in (54), and the rules in the noncyclic stratum will then apply as indicated.

(54)

```
 .  . . * .              .  . . * .              .  . . * .
 .  . . * .              .  . . * * .            *  . . * * .
 *  * * * *              *  * * * *              *  * * * *
classification  ──(46)→  classification  ──(5a–b)→  classification


            .  . . * .              .  . . * .
            *  . . * .              *  . . * .
            *  . * * .              *  . . * .
            *  * * * *              *  * * * *
  ──(38)→  classification  ──(37),(33)→  classification
```

The derivation of the noun *solicitation* proceeds in exactly the same way, except that since in *solicitation* the second syllable is stressed on the first cycle, Stress Enhancement (38) has, in principle, a choice of enhancing the stress on either the first or the second syllable. As noted previously, Kenyon and Knott believe that there is no preferred stressing for many words in this category. On the other hand, for words like *solicitation* the alternative with secondary stress on the first syllable seems to be excluded for everyone we have consulted. The obvious factor at work here is etymology: since *solicit* has stress on the second syllable, this stress is preserved in the derived noun. This cannot be the whole story, however, (as shown by many of the words cited in footnote 12) the etymology is often not decisive. We have not found an especially insightful solution to this problem and leave it with the observation that the topic requires further study.

Consider next the nouns *inflammation* and *condemnation*. On the innermost cycle main stress will be assigned to the last syllable of the verb. In the outer cycle the nouns will be stressed on the suffix *-ation*. In the noncyclic stratum Stress Copy (46) and the Alternator (5a–c) will supply line 1 asterisks to both syllables preceding main stress, and Stress Enhancement (38) will enhance the stress on the first syllable, yielding the representations in (55).

(55)

```
 .  .    * .              .  .    * .
 *  .    * .              *  .    * .
 *  *    * .              *  *    * .
 *  *    * *              *  *    * *
 inflammation             condemnation
```

Shortening (37) and Stress Deletion (33) then apply to the second syllable of *inflammation*, but not to that of *condemnation*. As a result, the second syllable is reduced in the former word, but not in the latter.

According to Kenyon and Knott, *condemnation* has an alternative pronunciation with a reduced vowel in position before main stress. Their dictionary contains a number of derived nouns with such alternative pronunciations, for example, *adaptation, affection, condemnation, deformation, emendation, exhortation*. A somewhat larger number of derived nouns are systematically given a reduced pronunciation: *affirmation, confirmation, conservation, consultation, conversation, information, lamentation, preservation, transportation, usurpation*. The stems of all of these nouns end with a sonorant cluster, but not all nouns with such stems have a reduced vowel in the syllable preceding main stress. The largest group, close to a majority, are given only with an unreduced vowel in the pretonic syllable: *annexation, attestation, condensation, deportation, exaltation, expectation, exportation, exultation, importation, indentation, infestation, prolongation, retardation, relaxation, sequestration, subornation*. We shall follow *SPE* (p. 112) and postulate that the nouns with reduced vowels in pretonic position are derived from representations without internal constituent structure (*trans + port + at + ion*), whereas those with unreduced vowels have such internal structure ([[*ex + port*] + at + ion]). Either of these underlying representations is well formed by the rules of English word formation, and speakers have the choice between the two alternatives. It is therefore to be expected that different speakers will make somewhat different choices for different words.

Finally, there are underived words of the type *in + cant + at + ion*, which have an unreduced (stressed) vowel in the syllable immediately preceding main stress. As noted in section 7.2 these words will be marked as exceptionally not undergoing Stress Conflation (5g) in the cyclic stratum, and it is this marking that distinguishes them from nouns of the *affirmation* class.

7.8 Shortening and the Treatment of Suffixes That Are Stress Domains

7.8.1 The Shortening of Stressed Vowels
It is well known that English vowels shorten under stress in certain contexts. Alternations such as *five ~ fifth* and *abstain ~ abstention* show that stressed vowels are shortened in closed syllables. This shortening process is evidently cyclic, for it does not apply in underived stems such as *lounge*,

field, paste. It thus differs fundamentally from Shortening (37), which is part of the noncyclic rule stratum.[14]

Shortening of stressed vowels has been investigated by Myers (1985), who proposes that all types of shortening under stress are special instances of shortening in a closed syllable. Embracing a suggestion by Borowsky (1984), Myers asserts that both so-called Trisyllabic Shortening and shortening before suffixes such as *-ic, -id, -ion* are special instances of closed syllable shortening. According to Myers, shortening in the latter cases is brought about by a special rule of resyllabification that links a syllable-initial consonant of an unstressed syllable to the rime of the immediately preceding stressed syllable (Myers's rule (8)). Resyllabification creates the closed syllable that feeds the rule shortening vowels in closed syllables. In Myers's account, the resyllabification rule applies therefore in forms such as those in (56a) but not in forms such as those in (56b).[15]

(56)
a. exilic   phallic   apostolic   metallic
b. solar   callous   phallus   medullar

Since there is no evidence of any difference in the pronunciation of the /1/ or in other possible consequences of different syllabifications in the two sets of words and since Myers offers none, it is difficult to accept his account as it stands. At the very least, the account must be supplemented by a special rule that would eliminate the postulated difference in the syllabification of the two sets of words. The need to add such a rule to the account, however, renders Myers's proposal less desirable than the alternative of replacing his rule of resyllabification by a rule that shortens vowels in the identical environment. Put differently, the necessity of adding the

---

14. There may seem to be a technical problem with the application of Shortening to words such as *abstention, fifth*. Since Strict Cyclicity prevents cyclic rules from applying in contexts that were present on an earlier pass through the cyclic rules, it would appear that Shortening cannot apply in these words because the syllables are already closed in the constituent to which the word-final suffixes are added. We believe that the solution concerns the way in which phoneme sequences are syllabified in English. It was suggested in footnote 2 that constituent-final consonants are syllabified only by a rule assigned to the noncyclic stratum. As a result, the presuffixal consonants in *fif-th, absten-tion* are first syllabified on the final pass through the cyclic rules. If this explanation is correct, then Strict Cyclicity would not prevent application of Shortening.

15. We discuss the manner in which the two classes of words are distinguished directly below in the text.

above rule implies that Myers's proposed generalization that shortening of stressed vowels takes place only in closed syllables is spurious: it can be maintained only at the cost of adding an otewise unnecessary fix-up rule.[16]

The elimination of this claim, however, does not affect the validity of any other points made in Myers's valuable paper. In fact, the only modifications needed are to eliminate the resyllabification rule and to postulate two environments for shortening under stress: in closed syllables and before stressless syllables, or, more precisely, in syllables that are heads of binary metrical constituents. We state the latter rule formally in (57).

(57) *Shortening*

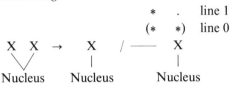

This formulation also accounts for the examples in (56b), where the conditions for shortening are met but where shortening does not take place. Myers points out that the forms in (56b), unlike those in (56a), end with an extrametrical suffix. Since extrametrical syllables are not visible to the rules of metrical constituent construction, the forms in (56b) cannot undergo rule (57).[17]

Modified as we have just suggested, Shortening (57) replaces the rule of Trisyllabic Shortening (or Laxing) that has played a pivotal role in many previous discussions of English stress. The fact that Shortening (57) is more general than the old Trisyllabic Shortening rule is not the only argument in its favor. Another is that it provides a single account for two distinct

---

16. Myers's rule of resyllabification applies in many other contexts in addition to those illustrated in (56), and in some of these it yields grossly incorrect syllabifications: for example, *punct.u.al, tem.pest.u.ous, text.u.al.*

17. The formalization adopted in this study allows us to bring out a further parallel between the two contexts for shortening under stress: in (57) and in closed syllables. In both cases the head of the shortened rime governs another syllabic position. In the closed syllable the governed position is the syllable-final consonant, and government is effected within the rime constituent. In (57) the governed position is the following stress-bearing unit in the foot (binary constituent) headed by the shortened vowel, and government is effected within the metrical constituent structure. This more abstract parallel explains why shortening in (57) obtains only before unstressed syllables that belong to the same metrical constituent as the head.

properties of suffixes such as -ic, -id. By marking these suffixes as not subject to Extrametricality, we account not only for the fact that they regularly shorten the presuffixal vowel but also for the fact that they invariably assign stress to it as well.[18] In the account with Trisyllabic Shortening the shortening triggered by these suffixes had to be treated by adding a third shortening rule to the grammar and by including a separate context in the rule of primary stress placement.

As Myers points out, the other large class of exceptions to shortening is made up of the words that are subject to lengthening of nonhigh vowels before a single consonant followed by /i/ or /y/ and a stressless vowel, such as *Caucasian, remedial, Arabian, Iranian, Newtonian*. Myers suggests that these facts should be dealt with by assuming that the Lengthening rule is ordered before Shortening (57) and is disjunctive with respect to it, so that Shortening may not apply to any form to which Lengthening has applied. This suggestion seems to us exactly right. Since the theoretical issues it raises are both extremely complex and somewhat tangential to the issues at hand, we shall not address them here.

7.8.2 Suffixes That Are Stress Domains

As shown in section 7.3, in a great many instances the Rhythm Rule (21) retracts stress from a word-final syllable. We accounted there for the fact that stress retraction may or may not be sensitive to the rime structure of the pretonic syllable by marking certain words as exceptions to Stress Conflation (5g). This device is inapplicable in the case of words such as those in (58).

(58)

a. álkalòid   hóminòid   céllulòid
   aráchnòid   ellípsòid   mollúscòid

b. dýnamìte   mágnetìte   molýbdenìte
   stalágmìte   staláctìte   smarágdìte

c. inhíbitòry   admónitòry   sécretàry
   perfúnctory   reféctory   èleméntary

These examples pose two related questions: how is the sensitivity to rime structure that they manifest to be formally reflected in the description? and

---

18. Examples such as *geodesic, basic, scenic* are lexically marked exceptions to Shortening (57).

how is the difference between them and the examples in (20a) to be accounted for?

A possible way of dealing with these problems is to posit that retraction by the Rhythm Rule (21) takes place only in the examples in (20b), whereas the suffixes in (58), like many other suffixes, are subject to Extrametricality (19) but differ from such ordinary suffixes as *-al*, *-ous*, *-ent* in being accented, underlyingly stressed.

This proposal encounters a number of difficulties, which become especially apparent when we try to extend it to cover the examples in (59) and (60), which exhibit the same stress contours as those in (58).

(59)

a. àntícipatòry   àrtículatòry   gèstículatòry

b. confíscatòry   compénsatòry   obsérvatòry

c. defámatòry   explánatòry   decláratòry

d. réspiratòry   pacíficatòry   óbligatòry

e. appróbatòry   víbratòry   rótatòry

(60)

a. agglútinative   imáginative   assóciative   commémorative

b. ínnovàtive   quálitàtive   législàtive   àuthóritàtive

c. derívative   provócative   exclámative   declárative
   altérnative   infórmative   consérvative   sédative

If the suffixes in (59) and (60) are to undergo Extrametricality (19), a number of possible restrictions that might be imposed on this rule will no longer hold. To this point all suffixes undergoing (19) have been monosyllabic and unaccented. If we adopt the proposed solution, we will have to admit that extrametricality may also be assigned to suffixes that are polysyllabic (or polymorphemic) and/or accented.

The most serious difficulty facing the proposed solution, however, is connected with the fact that in addition to being bisyllabic, the suffixes in (59) and (60) differ from those in (58) in that they shorten the presuffixal vowel as shown in (59c) and (60c).[19] Since an essential feature of Shortening (57) is that it applies only before metrical syllables, it is impossible to sustain the proposal that the suffixes *-ative*, *-atory* (see (59) and (60)) are extrametrical, because these suffixes trigger Shortening. We must therefore

---

19. Shortening does not apply in (59e). We assume that these examples are lexically marked exceptions to Shortening.

explore the alternative that, like the suffixes of Diyari (section 3.2.2) and unlike suffixes such as *-ent, -al, -ity*, the stressed suffixes under discussion here constitute domains of the stress rules.

By positing that these suffixes are domains of the stress rules, we also imply that the words in which they figure consist of two independent elements, each of which is a domain of the stress rules. We are therefore dealing with forms such as those in (61).[20]

(61) ((mollusc)(oid))   ((dynam)(ite))   ((refect)(ory))

In the last pass through the cyclic rules none of the stress rules can apply since the metrical structure supplied to the morphemes on previous passes through the cyclic rules remains intact (see condition (7) of chapter 3). A word such as *molluscoid* emerges from the cyclic stratum as shown in the left-hand form in (62). In the noncyclic stratum the word is subject to the Alternator (5a–c) and then to the Main Stress Rule (39), which enhances the main stress on the word-final syllable.[21] The Rhythm Rule (21) and Stress Deletion (33) complete the derivation.

(62)

	. . *	. * .	line 3
. * *	(. * *)	(. *) *	line 2
(. *) (*)	(* *) (*)	(. *) (*)	line 1
* (*) (*)	(*)(*) (*)	* (*) (*)	line 0
mollusc-oid $\xrightarrow[(39)]{(5a-c)}$	mollusc-oid $\xrightarrow[(33)]{(21)}$	mollusc-oid	

Among the suffixes that are domains for the stress rules are *-ory* and *-ary*, as well as the previously mentioned *-ative, -atory, -ite, -ode*. We next discuss some of these.

7.8.2.1 The Suffixes *-ory/-ary* and Sonorant Destressing
As illustrated in (58c), reproduced here as (63), the suffixes *-ory/-ary* exhibit essentially the same stress contours as the noun *molluscoid*.

(63) inhíbitòry   admónitòry   sécretàry
      perfúnctory   reféctory   èleméntary

---

20. The status of such stems as *dynam* or *refect* does not constitute a serious problem for the proposed representation, for nonword stems are standardly domains for the stress rules: *nat-ive, nat-ion; hap-less; hospit-able, incorrig-ible*.

21. Recall that rules constructing constituent boundaries such as (5b) and (39b) respect previously assigned asterisks. Note also that Stress Copy (46) applies vacuously here.

We add the suffixes *-ory/-ary* to the list of suffixes that constitute domains for the stress rules and derive the stress contours of the words in (63) as illustrated in (62). As already noted, like *SPE* and like most other writers on the subject, we assume that in the underlying representation these suffixes are monosyllabic and that their final [iy] is underlyingly the glide /y/, which is syllabified by a rule that is ordered after the stress rules in the noncyclic stratum. The main stress will then be placed, as required, on the presuffixal syllable if its rime branches, and on the syllable before that otherwise. On the account just given, subsidiary stress should fall on the suffix in all of the words in (63). We shall follow *SPE* here in accounting for the absence of stress on the suffix in posttonic position by attributing it to the operation of Stress Deletion (33).

Kiparsky (1979) has drawn attention to the fact that the preceding account of main stress assignment fails in words such as those in (64).

(64) légendàry   mómentàry   frágmentàry   sédentàry
     dýsentèry   ínventòry   vóluntàry   répertòry

Kiparsky observes that in these examples the poststress syllable has a rime ending with a sonorant, and he proposes (p. 428) that these syllables are subject to a special rule of Sonorant Destressing that, as shown by the examples in (65a), is not restricted to words ending in *-ory/-ary*.

(65)
a. ínfantìle   sérpentìne   Gílbertìte
b. projéctìle   smarágdìne   staláctìte

As shown in (65b), destressing does not take place in case the syllable ends with an obstruent. Nor does it apply to words such as those in (66) where the syllable in question is preceded by more than one syllable.

(66) èleméntary   rùdiméntary   ànnivérsary   èlephántìne

We propose to formalize Kiparsky's suggestion that the words in (64) and (65a) are subject to destressing by means of the rule (67).

(67) *Sonorant Destressing*

$$* \rightarrow . \; / \quad * \underline{\quad} * \quad \text{line 1}$$
$$\# * \quad * \quad * \# \quad \text{line 0}$$

where # represents a word boundary
Condition: ____ dominates a rime ending with a sonorant.

Rule (67) applies in trisyllabic words whose middle syllable ends with a sonorant. Its direct effect is to render the affected syllable stressless. When

it applies to representations such as those generated in (64) or (65a) its
effect will be to shift main stress one syllable to the left, as we show in (68).

(68)

```
                      . . *        . * .        * . .
      . * *          (. * *)      (. *) *      (*). *
     (. *)(*)        (* *)(*)     (* *)(*)     (*). (*)
     *(*)(*)         (*)(*)(*)    (*)(*)(*)    (*)* (*)
```

sedentary $\xrightarrow[(39)]{(5a-c)}$ se dentary $\xrightarrow{(21)}$ se dentary $\xrightarrow{(67)}$ sedentary

The derivation in (68) begins with the output of the rules of the cyclic
stratum. The first rule of the noncyclic stratum is the Alternator (5a–c),
and it is followed by the noncyclic Main Stress Rule (39). Next the Rhythm
Rule (21) retracts the main stress to the penultimate syllable. At this point
Sonorant Destressing (67) applies and eliminates the line 1 asterisk over
the penultimate syllable. This also automatically eliminates the line 0
constituent composed of this syllable. The line 1 constituent is not eliminated, since it still includes a stressable element, but it is restructured
so that its right boundary directly adjoins its head. The head of this
constituent is then represented on line 2. The elimination of the line 1
asterisk automatically triggers the elimination of the line 2 asterisk above
it, and the procedure just sketched is repeated, resulting in the output in
(68).

In his discussion of this phenomenon Hayes (1980/1, 175) observes that
the exceptional stressing of words noted by Kiparsky is not limited to
suffixed words but "that it applies pervasively among monomorphemic
words as well." In (69) we reproduce three of the examples cited by Hayes.

(69) Háckensàck   Álgernòn   Hóttentòt

The derivation of the stress patterns of these words is identical with that
of *sedentary* in (68). It should be noted that the words in (69), like the
nouns in (24c) and unlike the nouns in (1), will be marked as exceptions
to Extrametricality (19). The nouns in (24c) do not undergo Sonorant
Destressing (67) because they do not meet its structural description.

We list in (70) a number of nouns with stressless final syllables that seem
to undergo Sonorant Destressing (67) although they do not fully meet its
structural description.

(70) Wáshington   Pálmerston   Bírmingham
     Rútherford   Lívingston   Wéstminster

If these words are to be dealt with as instances of Sonorant Destressing, it would be necessary to drop the condition in (67) requiring that the word-final syllable bear stress. It is obvious that this condition can be dropped only in the case of specifically marked words, because trisyllabic words whose last syllable is unstressed do not normally retract stress (for examples, see (1), (8)).[22]

Kiparsky notes that forms such as those in (71) surface with main stress on the second syllable, rather than on the expected initial syllable.

(71) infírmary   dispénsary   compúlsory
     respónsary   placéntary

Both Kiparsky and Hayes treat these forms by attributing internal constituent structure to them. The assumption implicit in their analysis that *infirmary* is derived from *infirm* and *dispensary* from *dispense* seems to us dubious. The connection between these pairs of words appears to be no less tenuous than that between *pròtést* and *Prótestant*, which Kiparsky (p. 431) specifically rejects. Moreover, the cyclic derivation would require us to account in the phonology for alternations such as *pel ~ puls, spond ~ spons* and to include truncation rules in the phonology as well to handle words such as *placentary*. Since none of these moves is readily motivated, we see no advantage in accounting for the forms in (71) by means of the cycle rather than by straightforwardly marking them as exceptions to Sonorant Destressing (67).

7.8.2.2 The Suffix -atory The derivation of the stress contour of the adjectives in *-atory* exemplified in (59), reproduced here in (72), proceeds in the same fashion as that of the noun *molluscoid* in (62).

---

22. Myers (1985) has suggested that the antepenultimate stress in words such as *reverent, resident, president, impotent, confident, prevalent, pertinent, abstinent* should be accounted for by extending Sonorant Destressing (67) to these cases as well. However, this attractive proposal has a number of inherent difficulties that must be resolved if it is to be adopted. First, like the examples in (70), none of these words has stress on the final syllable, and each will therefore have to be marked to undergo Sonorant Destressing (67). Second, unlike all other cases of Sonorant Destressing, the syllable undergoing destressing does not end with a sonorant consonant. In fact, syllables ending with a sonorant consonant do *not* ever undergo destressing in words of this class, as shown by such examples as *redundant, informant, dependent, respondent, descendant, conversant, triumphant*. Finally, as B. Sietsema (personal communication) has pointed out, there are numerous trisyllabic words with medial long vowel that do not undergo Sonorant Destressing, such as, *assailant, adherent, coherent, opponent, complacent*.

(72)

a. àntícipatòry   àrtículatòry   gèstículatòry

b. confíscatòry   compénsatòry   obsérvatòry

c. defámatòry   explánatòry   decláratòry

d. réspiratòry   pacíficatòry   óbligatòry

e. appróbatòry   víbratòry   rótatòry

As illustrated in (73), the two constituents of the adjective emerge from the cyclic stress rules in (5) with two main stresses, one on the stem and the other on the suffix.[23] In the last pass through the rules of the cyclic stratum, after stresses have already been assigned, the word is subject to the rule of Shortening (57). No shortening takes place in *anticipatory*, but it is amply attested before this suffix; for examples, see (72c). As in the case of *molluscoid* (see (62)), none of the stress rules will apply on the last pass through the cyclic stratum since the metrical structure derived on earlier passes through the rules is preserved by virtue of condition (7) of chapter 3. Stress Conflation (5g) may apply, but its effect are vacuous. In the noncyclic stratum the Alternator (5a–c) and the Main Stress Rule (39) apply with the results shown in the middle form of (73). It is worth noting that although the Alternator applies so as to respect previously assigned asterisks, it changes the constituent boundary locations so that the output consists uniquely of binary constituents.[24]

---

23. As noted, we assume that in its underlying representation the suffix *-ory* is monosyllabic.

24. In order to account for the fact that the constituent *anticip* emerges from the cyclic stress rules with stress on the penultimate syllable, it is necessary to assume that the constituent-final consonant does not count in determining the branchingness of the constituent-final rime. This is yet another instance of the suggestion made in footnote 2 and elsewhere that constituent-final consonants are syllabified only in the noncyclic stratum and remain unsyllabified as far as the rules of the cyclic stratum are concerned.

On the account presented, adjectives derived from verbs in *-(if)y* such as *classificatory, pacificatory, multiplicatory* should emerge with main stress on the third syllable. An informal inquiry among colleagues indicates that for most, main stress in *classificatory* falls on the first syllable, rather than on the third. Opinions were split concerning *pacificatory* and *multiplicatory*, the only other two adjectives of this type that had any currency among our informants. In order to obtain initial stress, we should have to assume underlying representations in which the suffix is *-icatory* rather than *-atory*.

(73)
```
  .  . . . .                  .  . . . *              .  * . . .
  .  * . . *               (.  * . . *)            (.  *). . *
 (.  *). (. *)             (*  *) * (. *)          (*  *). (. *)
 *  (* *) *(*)             (*) (*)(* *)(*)         (*) (*)* *(*)
anticip-atory  ──(5a−c)──▶  anti cip-a tory ──(21)──▶  anticip-atory
                 (39)                         (33)
```

7.8.2.3 The Suffixes -*ive* and -*ative* Like suffixes such as -*al*, -*our*, -*ent*, the suffix -*ive* assigns stress to the presuffixal syllable if it has a branching rime and to the syllable before that otherwise.

(74)
a. efféctive,   decísive   elúsive
   emótive   apprehénsive

b. pósitive   prohíbitive   cógnitive
   sénsitive   púnitive

c. cóvetous   ríotous   dígital
   génital   cómpetent   pénitent

An informal survey conducted among a small number of native speakers of American English suggests that there is an interesting difference between -*ive* and the suffixes in (74c) with respect to the extent to which the presuffixal /t/ can be implemented with a dental flap. It would seem that /t/-flapping is much more restricted before -*ive* than before the suffixes in (74c). Since flapping takes place only before stressless syllables, we offer as an explanation for this difference the suggestion that -*ive* is stressed, whereas the suffixes in (74c) are stressless. The assumption that -*ive* is stressed accounts for a number of additional special facts connected with this suffix.

We shall account for the stress on -*ive* the same way we have accounted for stress on all other suffixes: by positing that -*ive* constitutes a domain for the stress rules. This assumption will also explain why this suffix does not trigger Shortening (57), for Shortening takes place only before a stressless syllable. We account for the stress patterns of the adjectives in -*ative* illustrated in (60), reproduced here as (75), by postulating that the suffix -*ative* is a stress domain.

(75)
a. agglútinative   imáginative   assóciative   commémorative

b. ínnovàtive   quálitàtive   législàtive   authóritàtive

c. derívative   provócative   exclámative   declárative

d. altérnative   infórmative   consérvative   sédative

As shown in (76), we derive the stress contours of the adjective in (75b) without further difficulty provided that -*at*- is assumed to have a long vowel in its underlying representation.

(76)
```
                      .   . . * .            .   * . . .
  .    * . * .       (.   * . * .)         (.   *). . * .
 (.   * .) (* .)     (*   * . * .)         (*   * .) (* .)
 *   (* *)(* *)      (*)  (* *)(* *)       (*)  (* *)(* *)
 authorit -ative  ──(5a–c)──▶  authorit -ative  ──(21)──▶  authorit -ative
                     (39)                        (33)
```

To obtain the stress contours in (75a,c,d), we postulate a special rule that renders -*at*- non-stress-bearing. Once the line 0 asterisk over -*at*- is deleted, the stress shifts automatically to -*ive*. We illustrate this in (77).

(77)
```
 .    * . . .             .   * . . .
(.    *). * .            (.   *). . *
(*   * .) (* .)          (*   * .) (. *)
(*)  (* *)(* *)          (*)  (* *)(. *)
 agglutin-ative  ──−ative Rule──▶  agglutin-ative
```

Nanni (1977) has suggested that in the adjectives to which (in the present account) the -*ative* Rule applies, the onset of the syllable containing the suffix -*at*- begins with a sonorant—hence, *authóritàtive* but *imáginatìve*. Interestingly, this contrast is not reflected by Kenyon and Knott, who give both words with subsidiary stress on -*at*-. Webster's Third lists both alternatives for these as well as for all other words in -*ative*, and a limited inquiry among a few native speakers of American English reveals considerable uncertainty about how individual words are stressed. We conclude that Nanni's generalization holds for only a limited group of speakers and that for the rest the -*ative* Rule applies only to specifically marked words.

7.8.3 Rule Summary 3
In (78) we list all the rules developed to this point in this chapter.

(78) c   Extrametricality (19)

   c   Accent Rule (11)

   n   Stress Copy (46)

   c/n Binary Constituent Construction/Alternator (5a–c)

   c   Unbounded Constituent Construction on line 1 (5d–f)

   c   Stress Conflation (5g)

c   Shortening (57)

n   Unbounded Constituent Construction on line 2 (39)

n   Rhythm Rule (21)

n   Stress Enhancement (38)

n   Sonorant Destressing (67)

n   *-ative* Rule

n   *y*-Syllabification

n   Shortening over a Stress Well (37)

n   Stress Deletion (33)

n   Reduction (35)

7.9 The Stress of Phrases and Compound Words

To this point we have restricted attention to the stress contours of single words. The rules listed in (78) are part of the two strata that compose the word phonology of English. Phonological regularities whose domain extends beyond a single word are dealt with by rules assigned to the two strata of the word-external phonology (see section 3.1). In this section we investigate the stress contours of English phrases and compounds, all of which are composed of two or more words. Accounting for these stress contours calls for two rules that apply cyclically. These rules constitute only a fraction of the word-external phonology of English, which also includes a noncyclic stratum. Since the latter rules appear to have no effects on the stress contours of words and phrases, we do not discuss them here.[25]

7.9.1 The Nuclear Stress Rule
When English words are joined to form phrases or compound words, the stress contours of the individual words are largely unaffected. The fact that a sequence of words constitutes a phrase or a compound is signaled phonetically by giving greater prominence to the main stress of one word than to the main stresses of the rest. Formally, we propose to capture

---

25. As noted in section 3.1, the cyclic stratum of the word phonology corresponds in the main to the *lexical* strata of Halle and Mohanan (1985), whereas the noncyclic stratum corresponds to their *postlexical* stratum. In other studies written in the framework of Lexicalist Phonology the postlexical stratum also includes rules applying across word boundaries.

these two facts in the following way. Whenever two words form a syntactic constituent (phrase or compound), we shall interpret the constituent boundaries as boundaries of metrical constituents, and we shall assume that these constituents are unbounded and right-headed. The effect of this procedure will be to add a new line to the metrical grid. Since nothing else is changed, the stress contours of the individual words remain intact. We illustrate this in (79), where the asterisks on line 3 represent the main stresses of the individual words and the head of the newly created constituent is located on line 4.[26]

```
(79) . .    *           . . .   * . .    line 4
     ------------      ------------------
     (* .    *)        (* . .   *) . .    line 3
     Jesus wept        Madison Avenue
```

The Nuclear Stress Rule can be formally expressed by the rules in (80), which are assigned to the cyclic stratum of the word-sequence phonology of English.

(80) *Nuclear Stress Rule*
    a. Parameter settings on line N (N $\geq$ 3) are [$-$BND, $+$HT, right].
    b. Interpret boundaries of syntactic constituents composed of two or more stressed words as metrical boundaries.
    c. Locate the heads of line N constituents on line N$+$1.

The Nuclear Stress Rule (80) systematically skips over constituents where one of the elements is a stressless word (clitic), since such clitics have no effect on the stress contour of the phrase. Thus, of the four nested constituents in the prepositional phrase in (81),

(81) [to [the [people [of Judea]]]]

the boundaries of only one, shown in (82), are interpreted as metrical boundaries.

(82) to the (people of Judea)

    The Nuclear Stress Rule is thus identical with the rules assigning main stress (5d–f) and (39) except for the line to which the rule applies. The latter two rules apply to grid lines 1 and 2; the Nuclear Stress Rule applies

---

26. Word-internal metrical structure other than main stress location is omitted here and below except where especially relevant to matters under discussion. We discuss the stress contours of compounds such as *Madison Street*, which differs from that of phrases, in section 7.9.3.

to grid lines 3 and above. It is obvious that this almost total identity of the rules must be reflected formally in the description. Unfortunately, the evidence reviewed here provides few hints as to how this is to be done. We therefore leave this question open, hoping to return to it in a future study.

The procedure sketched above will fail in cases where the phrases or compounds form part of a larger constituent, as, for example, in [*Jesus* [*preached* [*to the people* [*of Judea*]]]], for as shown in (83) it will not reflect the fact that *Jesus* has more stress than *preached*, and *preached* has more stress than *people*.

(83)　　.　　　　　.　　　　　　　.　　　　　　*

　　　　(.　　　　　.　　　　　　　.　　　　　*　　)

　　　　　.　　(.　　　　　　　.　　　　　*　　)

　　　　　　　　　　　---
　　　　*　　*　　　　　　(*　　　　*)
　　　　[Jesus [preached [to [the [people [of [Judea]]]]]]]

In order to reflect the stress contours of such phrases correctly, we postulate that stress rules are subject to the Stress Equalization Convention (84).

(84) *Stress Equalization Convention*
　　　When two or more constituents are conjoined into a single higher-level constituent, the asterisk columns of the heads of the constituents are equalized by adding asterisks to the lesser column(s).

We illustrate the effects of (84) in (85), where the asterisks added by (84) are enclosed in braces { }.

(85)
line 6　　.　　　　　.　　　　　　　.　　　　　*

line 5　{*}　　　.　　　　　　　.　　　　　*

　　　　　---
line 4　{*}　　{*}　　　　　.　　　　　*

　　　　　　　　　-----------------------------------
line 3　*　　*　　　　　*　　　　*
　　　　(Jesus (preached to the (people of Judea)))

Given the procedure just outlined, the number of lines in the metrical grid is equal to $3+n$, where n is the number of metrically interpreted constituents of the most deeply embedded word. Since there is no upper bound on the depth of embedding, there is also no upper bound on the number of stress distinctions. Phonetically, however, speakers make fewer distinctions than are provided by this procedure. To reflect this fact, we propose the Grid Simplification Convention (86).

(86) *Grid Simplification Convention*
Lines in the metrical grid may be eliminated beginning with the line immediately above the word layer and proceeding upward without skipping. This process may stop at any line but must leave at least the top line in the grid intact.

7.9.2 The Rhythm Rule in the Word-Sequence Phonology

We have had occasion to examine a number of instances where main stress in a word is displaced from the position where it was originally located by the Main Stress Rules in (5) and (39) (see section 7.3), and we have accounted for these displacements by means of the Rhythm Rule (21). There are a number of additional contexts where stress is displaced and where the Rhythm Rule might play a role.[27]

It seems to us that not all phenomena that have been discussed under the rubric of the Rhythm Rule do in fact belong under a single heading. For instance, given the theory described here, example (87b), but not (87a), is a bona fide instance of a stress retraction process.[28]

(87)

$$\overset{2}{\text{a. Far}}\text{rah }\overset{1}{\text{Faw}}\text{cett-}\overset{3}{\text{Ma}}\text{jors}$$

$$\overset{2}{\text{b. Ma}}\text{ry-}\overset{1}{\text{El}}\text{len }\overset{3}{\text{Ma}}\text{thers}$$

As shown in (88), the stress contour of (87a) falls out directly from the normal cyclic application of the Nuclear Stress Rule.

(88)

$$[\text{F }[\text{F-M}]] \xrightarrow{(80)} [\text{F }[\text{F-M}]] \xrightarrow{(84)} [\text{F F-M}] \xrightarrow{(80)} \text{F F-M}$$

---

27. Many of the facts discussed here have been previously dealt with by other investigators. Excellent ideas on this subject are to be found in Liberman and Prince (1977), Prince (1983), and Hayes (1984), from all of which we have learned a great deal.

28. Here and below the numerals above the syllables represent the number of asterisks associated with the vowels in question. To simplify the arithmetic, we have arbitrarily disregarded all but the main stress in each word.

As shown in (89), example (87b) does not result in the correct stress contour when only the Nuclear Stress Rule applies.

(89)
```
                                                                          *
                        *                    * *                 * *
          *   *   *           *   *          * * *               * * *
     [[M-E] M] ──(80)→ [[M-E] M] ──(84)→ [M-E  M] ──(80)→  M-E  M
```

To obtain the correct stress contour in this example, we need to move the top asterisk of the word *Ellen* to the left so that it lands over the top asterisk of the word *Mary*. This is accomplished by the Rhythm Rule (90) for word sequences, which is partially identical with the word-internal Rhythm Rule (21).

(90) *Rhythm Rule*

In a constituent C composed of two or more words, retract the right boundary of the prefinal subconstituent S of C to a position immediately before the head of S, provided that the head of S is located in the last word of S (with further restrictions if the subconstituent S consists of a single word).

Given the formulation in (90), the Rhythm Rule will shift the main stress not of the entire string but only of its prefinal constituent. It will therefore ensure that in *Mary-Ellen Mathers* greater stress falls on *Mary* than on *Ellen*. By the same token, rule (90) will see to it that in *Caroline-Mary Mathers* greater stress falls on *Caroline* than on *Mary*, even though the last syllable of *Caroline* bears a stress of its own. The same would be true in *Mary-Louise Mathers*, where the first syllable of *Louise* bears its own stress. On the other hand, in *Louise-Mary Mathers* the stress is retracted only to the second syllable of *Louise*, since this syllable becomes the head of the prefinal constituent.

One of the many penetrating insights of Prince (1983) is that the "Rhythm rule is universally constrained from moving the absolute stress peak of the phrase to which it applies" (p. 33). We have reflected this constraint in our formulation of the rule by restricting it to *the prefinal constituent S of C*. As stated in (90), the rule handles many additional examples, a few of which we give in (91).

(91)

$$
\text{a. the } \overset{2}{\text{Saginaw}} \ \overset{1}{\text{Michigan}} \left\{ \begin{array}{c} \overset{3}{\text{Journal}} \\ \overset{3}{\text{Gazette}} \end{array} \right\}
$$

b. $\overset{3}{\text{one}} \ \overset{2}{\text{twenty}} \ \overset{4}{\text{Jay}} \ \overset{1}{\text{Street}}$

c. a hundred twenty fortifications
   3   2   (1)   4

   3   1   2   4
d. New York Maine Route

   3   1   2   4
e. Maine New York Route

Like the Nuclear Stress Rule (80), the Rhythm Rule for word sequences (90) applies cyclically. As a result, it affects *New York* differently in (91d) than in (91e). We illustrate this in (92).

(92)

[[Maine [New York]] Route]				[[[New York] Maine] Route]				
	1	1			1	1		
								NSR (80)
	1	2			1	2		
								SEC (84)
2	1	2			1	2	2	
								NSR (80)
2	1	3			1	2	3	
								RR (90)
not applicable				2	1	3		
								SEC (84)
2	1	3	3	2	1	3	3	
								NSR (80)
2	1	3	4	2	1	3	4	
								RR (90)
3	1	2	4	3	1	2	4	

Rule (90) retracts stress both in word sequences and word-internally. Examples of word-internal stress retraction by rule (90) are given in (93).

(93)

   3   2   1   4
a. nineteen explanations

   3   2   4
b. Kalamazoo, Michigan

   3 2   1   4
c. Chinese bamboo

   3   2   4
d. achromatic lens

In (93) stress displacement is word-internal, as in the cases for which (21) was postulated. However, unlike what happens in the cases handled by (21), displacement takes place in (93) only when the word is followed by another word—that is, in the prefinal constituent. Moreover, as shown by

(93d), the rule applies even when the affected word does not have stress on its last syllable. Prince (1983) observes that when the topmost asterisk is not on the last word of the subconstituent, the Rhythm Rule does not apply. It is for this reason that we have limited rule (90) to applying only if the asterisk to be moved is "located in the last word of S." We give some examples of this in (94).

(94)

a. Tom Paine Street blues
   (1 3 2 4)

b. American Can Company Times
   (1 3 2 4)

c. Boston Symphony Orchestra anniversary
   (1 3 1 4)

In the prefinal constituent of these examples—for example, in *Tom Paine Street*—the head is not located in the last word. Rule (90) therefore cannot apply here, and the subconstituent surfaces with a rising-falling stress contour. We illustrate this in the derivation in (95), where we detail the last pass through the cyclic rules of the string *Tom Paine Street blues*.

(95) Tom Paine Street blues
       1   3   2   1
                                    SEC (84)
       1   3   2   3
                                    NSR (80)
       1   3   2   4
                                    RR (90)
           does not apply

By contrast, when the head of the prefinal subconstituent is located on the last word—as is the case in *New York Maine Railroad*—rule (90) does apply, and the subconstituent surfaces with a falling-rising stress contour.

There are, however, numerous exceptions to the rule (90), a fact we have reflected by means of the parenthesized phrase in (90). Among these exceptions Hayes (1984, 56ff.) gives the examples in (96).

(96)

a. Montana governor
   (1 3 4)

b. titanic struggle
   (1 3 4)

c. Alberta, Canada
   (1 3 4)

d. grotesque clown
   (1 3 4)

To these idiosyncratic exceptions to the Rhythm Rule we must add a number of systematic ones. On the one hand, because stress retraction in English requires that the landing site have some degree of stress, the Rhythm Rule cannot apply in words where the potential landing site lacks stress. As a result, it applies to the left-hand but not to the right-hand examples in (97).

(98)

a. 3 2 4
    antique chair   vs.   3   4
                               divine wrath

b. 3 2 4
    fifteen summers   vs.   3   4
                               serene summers

c. 3   2   4
    Tennessee Williams   vs.   3   4
                               Elaine Williams

Moreover, as illustrated in (98), words in which main stress falls on the antepenultimate syllable systematically fail to undergo the Rhythm Rule (90).

(98)

a. 1 3   4
    cantankerous comment

b. 1 3   4
    asynchronous motor

c. 1   3   4
    editorial view

d. 1   3   4
    Episcopalian ceremony

Hayes (1984) has suggested that word-internally retraction tends not to occur when more than two syllables intervene between main stress and the asterisk to be moved. He cites such contrasts as those in (99).

(99)

a. 2   1   3
    Mississippi Mabel   vs.   1   2   3
                                   Minneapolis Mike

b. 2   1   3
    Mississippi legislature vs.   1   2   3
                                   Mississsippi legislation

With numerals, however, this restriction does not seem to hold.

(100)   2   1   3   2   1   ⎧   3   ⎫
        nineteen chairs   vs.   nineteen ⎨ fortifications   ⎬
                                          ⎪ Episcopalians   ⎪
                                          ⎪ delegations   ⎪
                                          ⎩ appointments   ⎭

Finally, Liberman and Prince (1977) have noted that although speakers readily accept retraction in *Marcel Proust*, they are less certain about retraction in *Marcel's book* and tend to reject it in the sentence *Marcel left*.[29]

As noted above, when the Rhythm Rule (90) applies to single words, there are special subregularities as well as a number of idiosyncratic exceptions, all of which must be taken into account in a full description of the English stress pattern. We have subsumed these restrictions in our statement of the Rhythm Rule (90) under "further restrictions if the subconstituent S consists of a single word." However, the nature of these further restrictions is at present unexplored territory.

7.9.3 The Compound Stress Rule

A most characteristic feature of English is the special stress contour that it assigns to compound words. In this type of constituent, consisting of two or more words dominated by a lexical category, the greatest stress is generally found on the prefinal subconstituent. Thus, in binary compounds the main stress is located on the first subconstituent.

(101)

a. $\overset{2}{\text{Madison}} \; \overset{1}{\text{Street}}$

$\overset{2}{\text{evening}} \; \overset{1}{\text{class}}$

$\overset{2}{\text{teachers}} \; \overset{1}{\text{union}}$

b. $\overset{3}{\text{teachers}} \; \overset{1}{\text{union}} \; \overset{2}{\text{president}}$

$\overset{3}{\text{Madison}} \; \overset{1}{\text{Street}} \; \overset{2}{\text{bus}}$

c. $\overset{4}{\text{teachers}} \; \overset{1}{\text{union}} \; \overset{2}{\text{president}} \; \overset{3}{\text{election}}$

$\overset{4}{\text{Madison}} \; \overset{1}{\text{Street}} \; \overset{2}{\text{bus}} \; \overset{3}{\text{schedule}}$

---

29. It appears that the word-internal application of the Rhythm Rule (90) is restricted to lexical compounds. This explains why retraction is (almost) obligatory in *Marcel Proust*, but (almost) impossible in *Marcel left*: the former is a lexical compound, whereas the latter is formed in the syntax. The optionality of stress retraction in *Marcel's book* would then be attributed to the ambiguous nature of the construction: it can be analyzed either as a lexical compound or as a syntactic collocation. In the former case retraction is obligatory; in the latter it is impossible. This difference is brought out more clearly by such examples as *We know about Marcel's book, but not yet about Mary's*. In this sentence *Marcel's book* must be pronounced without retraction because the pronominal relation that holds between *book* and the empty noun following *Mary's* forces the syntactic analysis of the collocation.

At first sight, it might appear that a separate rule is needed to account for the stressing of compounds. In fact, no new rule is required, for the stress contours of compound words result from the interaction of two rules already postulated and justified. In particular, we propose to account for compound stress by assuming that the Nuclear Stress Rule (80) freely applies to all constituents composed of two or more full words (that is, not clitics). In fact, as stated in (80), the rule will apply to compounds as well as to noncompounds and will place an extra asterisk on the rightmost subconstituent. This is necessary in any event, since the language abounds in compound nouns whose stress contour is identical with that of (non-compound) phrases. In addition to those in (87), we cite the examples in (102).

(102)

a. $\overset{1}{\text{Ma}}$dison $\overset{2}{\text{A}}$venue

   $\overset{1}{\text{Ma}}$ry-$\overset{2}{\text{E}}$lizabeth

   $\overset{1}{\text{Ma}}$rcel $\overset{2}{\text{P}}$roust

   $\overset{1}{\text{Ha}}$rvard $\overset{2}{\text{U}}$niversity

   $\overset{1}{\text{Pe}}$nn $\overset{2}{\text{S}}$tation

   $\overset{1}{\text{Gra}}$nd $\overset{2}{\text{C}}$entral

b. $\overset{2}{\text{Ma}}$ry-$\overset{1}{\text{E}}$lizabeth $\overset{3}{\text{Ma}}$thers

   $\overset{2}{\text{Gra}}$nd $\overset{1}{\text{C}}$entral $\overset{3}{\text{S}}$tation

Since we have already discussed examples such as those in (102) (see (88), (89)), we shall not examine them again here.

A plausible approach to accounting for the stress contours of the compounds in (101) is to assume that they are subject to a special rule, which retracts the main stress from the last to the prefinal subconstituent of the compound word. Liberman and Prince (1977) have shown that it is necessary to restrict the rule further so that it applies only if the maximum peak is located in the last word of the expression. We therefore state the Compound Stress Rule as follows.

(103) *Compound Stress Rule*

   In a constitutent C composed of two or more words, retract the right boundary of C to a position immediately before the head of C, provided that C is dominated by a lexical category and that the head of C is located in the last word of C.

In left-branching compounds such as those illustrated in (101), rule (103) will place main stress on the leftmost of the two constituents, since the rightmost constituent is also the last word. As shown by Liberman and Prince (1977), the restriction imposed on the rule so that it retracts the main stress only if the latter is located in the last word is needed in order to prevent it from applying to compounds such as those in (104) that do not have exclusively right-branching structure.

(104)

a. $\overset{2}{\text{ki}}$tchen $\overset{3}{\text{towel}}$ $\overset{1}{\text{rack}}$

b. $\overset{2}{\text{teachers}}$ $\overset{3}{\text{pension}}$ $\overset{1}{\text{fund}}$

c. $\overset{2}{\text{evening}}$ $\overset{3}{\text{chemistry}}$ $\overset{1}{\text{class}}$

d. $\overset{2}{\text{law}}$ $\overset{1}{\text{school}}$ $\overset{3}{\text{language}}$ $\overset{1}{\text{exam}}$

e. $\overset{2}{\text{labor}}$ $\overset{1}{\text{union}}$ $\overset{3}{\text{vacation}}$ $\overset{1}{\text{colony}}$

In such compounds the Compound Stress rule (103) will fail to apply on the last pass through the cyclic rules since the topmost asterisk will not be located in the last word. The compounds in (102) will be treated as specially marked exceptions to rule (103).

Obviously, the Compound Stress Rule (103) is in many respects identical with the Rhythm Rule (90). Both rules move the right boundary of a right-headed constituent to a position before the constituent head and both rules are restricted so that they apply only when the topmost asterisk is located in the last word. Since this restriction is rather special, it is a priori unlikely that we should be dealing here with two distinct processes subject to the same highly idiosyncratic constraint. It is far more plausible that we are dealing with a single phonological process that should be captured by a single rule.

This suspicion is heightened when we investigate the ordering of the two rules. As shown in (105), if the Rhythm Rule (90) is ordered before the Compound Stress Rule (103), the result is incorrect.

(105) Madison Avenue bus
           1   1
                              NSR (80)
           1   2
                              RR (90)
           not applicable
                              CSR (103)

exception

1	2	1

SEC (84)

1	2	2

NSR (80)

1	2	3

RR (90)

2	1	3

CSR (103)

3	1	2*

As shown in (106), if the order is reversed, the output is again incorrect.

(106) Madison Avenue bus

1	1

NSR (80)

1	2

CSR (103)

exception

RR (90)

not applicable

1	2	1

SEC (84)

1	2	2

NSR (80)

1	2	3

CSR (103)

1	3	2

RR (90)

3	2	2*

It is significant that although the last derivation yields an incorrect result, it would produce the required output if the Rhythm Rule (90) were prevented from applying. In other words, we have here a situation where ordering the Compound Stress Rule (103) before the Rhythm Rule (90) produces the correct result if application of the Compound Stress Rule blocks application of the Rhythm Rule.

This type of disjunctive ordering of rules has long been familiar to phonologists. It was suggested in *SPE* that partially identical rules that could be formulated so the less specific, more general rules could be derived from the more specific by means of deletion constitute a disjunctive block:

they are to be applied in order of specificity, beginning with the most specific, and once a given rule is found to apply, no further rules in the block can be applied. Kiparsky (1973) has suggested that this conception of specificity, which identifies it with length (number of symbols), is too rudimentary and that a more sophisticated notion of specificity of rule is in order. A comparison of the Compound Stress and Rhythm Rule suggests where to look for this notion. The more specific Compound Stress Rule refers to the fact that its domain is a lexical category. The less specific Rhythm Rule refers to the fact that a subconstituent of any sort must follow the word where the topmost asterisk is located. Formally, the difference may be expressed as that between (107a) and (107b).

(107)
a. _____] A   where A is a constituent dominated by a lexical category
           (X^0)

b. _____ B]   where B is a constituent (of any kind (X))

The difference in specificity of the rules derives from the definition of the two entities A and B. Since the Compound Stress Rule (107a) is the more specific rule and the Rhythm Rule (107b) the less specific, we must conclude that the characterization of an entity as being dominated by a lexical category is more specific than the characterization of an entity as being a constituent of any kind.

These two rules obviously share a number of salient properties with the word-internal Rhythm Rule (21), reproduced here as (108).

(108) In a constituent C composed of a single word, retract the right boundary of C to a position immediately before the head of C, provided that the head of C is located on the last syllable of C and that it is preceded by a stressed syllable.

But there are also differences between the word-internal Rhythm Rule (108) (= (21)) and the two word-sequence rules in (107). First, whereas the latter apply in a constituent composed of two or more words, rule (108) applies in a constituent composed of a single word. It is likely, however, that this difference will not have to be directly stated in the rules but can be derived from the fact that rule (108) is assigned to the noncyclic word stratum whereas the Compound Stress and Rhythm Rules (90) and (103) are assigned to the cyclic word-sequence stratum. The second difference between rule (108), on the one hand, and the rules (90) and (103), on the other, is that the head of the constituent undergoing the rule must be on the last *syllable* in the former and on the last *word* in the latter. It would seem that this distinction, too, might not have to be directly stated in the rules but could be derived from the fact that (108) is assigned to the noncyclic stratum of the word phonology, where only single words are considered, whereas rules (90) and (103) are part of the stratum, where word sequences are dealt with. Since it is not self-evident how these simplifications in the rules are to be implemented, we have not instituted them in the formal statement of the rules.

In (109) we have collapsed the three rules into a single statement so as to bring out both their similarities and their differences.

(109) In a constituent C composed of $\left\{ \begin{array}{l} \langle \text{a single word} \rangle_{(108)} \\ \langle \text{two or more words} \rangle_{(103),(90)} \end{array} \right\}$

retract the right boundary of $\langle$the prefinal constituent S of$\rangle_{(90)}$ C

to a position immediately before the head of $\left\{ \begin{array}{l} \langle S \rangle_{(90)} \\ \langle C \rangle_{(103),(108)} \end{array} \right\}$,

provided $\langle$that C is dominated by a lexical category and$\rangle_{(108),(103)}$

that the head of $\left\{ \begin{array}{l} \langle S \rangle_{(90)} \\ \langle C \rangle_{(108),(103)} \end{array} \right\}$ is located on the last

$\left\{ \begin{array}{l} \langle \text{syllable} \rangle_{(108)} \\ \langle \text{word} \rangle_{(90),(103)} \end{array} \right\}$ of $\langle$the subconstituent S of$\rangle_{(90)}$ C

$\langle$and that it is preceded by a stressed syllable$\rangle_{(108)}$.

Postface
Retrospect and Prospects

The theory of stress developed in the preceding chapters has the following main features.

Stress is represented on a separate autosegmental plane by means of metrical constituent structure. Each constituent includes an element that is its head, and this head element is projected upward onto a higher line where it represents the entire constituent. There is in general more than one line of constituent structure, and this stacking of constituent structures gives rise to columns of projections of various heights. All other things being equal, the height of a column reflects the degree of prominence of the corresponding position on the bottom line (line 0).

Languages have special rules for constructing constituents. These rules involve parameters whose values must be stipulated for each particular case. Specifically, the parameters to be set determine whether the constituents are bounded or not, whether government is directional or not (whether or not the heads of the constituents are terminal), and, if heads are terminal, whether they are located at the right or the left extremity of the constituent. If constituents are bounded, the direction of constituent construction must also be stipulated.

Constituents are constructed in two steps. First, boundaries are constructed or, in the absence of a construction rule, are identified. Then heads are located. The process of head location is subject to the Recoverability Condition, which requires that constituent structure always be recoverable from the location of the heads and the specification of the direction of government. This condition accounts for the fact that in unbounded constituents the heads are always terminal, whereas direction of government may be left unspecified in bounded constituents. In addition, it forbids maximally degenerate ternary constituents.

In addition to locating the heads of constructed constituents, languages have other means for assigning headship to particular elements. Certain elements can be idiosyncratically marked as heads (accented) in the lexicon. Moreover, there may be a rule marking elements as heads in specified phonetic contexts, such as in closed syllables.

Constituent boundaries may be moved laterally, triggering the concomitant movement of the associated heads. This movement is the only type of transformation that metrical constituent structure may undergo.

A separate major concern of the book is the theory of Lexical Phonology. The evidence presented in chapter 3 suggests that the strong version of Lexical Phonology advanced, for example, by Pesetsky (1979) cannot be maintained. Instead, we assume a weakened version of the theory proposed by Halle and Mohanan (1985). In this version the rules of the morphology are distinct from the rules of the phonology in the sense that the former generate objects to which the latter apply. Morphology distinguishes cyclic from noncyclic morphemes. Each cyclic morpheme is represented on a separate autosegmental plane, whereas a noncyclic morpheme is represented on the same plane as the stem to which it is affixed. The morphology therefore represents a complex word with several cyclic morphemes as a series of half-planes intersecting in a single line, the central line of phonemes (to be more accurate, the line of intersection consists of timing slots themselves devoid of phonological content but linked to segments composed of feature complexes).

As in Halle and Mohanan (1985), the rules of the phonology are organized into several ordered strata. The strata are stipulated to be either cyclic or noncyclic, and a given rule may be assigned to more than one stratum. The cyclic rules apply to each cyclic constituent in turn. On each pass through the cycle the cyclic planes are conflated; that is, the content of the previous cyclic constituent is copied onto the plane of the current cyclic morpheme. Not all phonological properties are copied in this process. In particular, stress information developed on earlier cycles is systematically omitted. After all cyclic rules have applied, the rules of the noncyclic stratum are applied in one fell swoop.

An important respect in which this framework differs from that of *SPE* is that here the organization of the rule system is governed by two independent principles. Rules are ordered in the linear manner familiar from *SPE* but are also assigned to particular rule strata. These two principles function independently, and, as a result, a rule R1 ordered before a rule R2 may consistently apply after R2 if it is assigned to the noncyclic stratum and R2 is assigned exclusively to the cyclic stratum.

Another major difference between the theory advanced here and that of *SPE* is that all processes considered here have been characterized as local.

In the *SPE* framework rules could include variables ranging over strings of segments or syllables of arbitrary length. In fact, given the restrictive linear formalism adopted in *SPE*, a great number of phonological rules had to refer to variable strings. For example, the stress rule for Sanskrit would have to be formulated as follows within an *SPE*-type grammar.

$$(1) \quad V \rightarrow [+\text{stress}] \,/ \left(\left(C_0 \begin{bmatrix} V \\ -\text{accent} \end{bmatrix} \right)^* \right)_a C_0 \underline{}$$
$$([+\text{accent}])_b$$

   Condition: a iff b

In the present framework the stress pattern of Sanskrit is described without recourse to variables. The constituent structure that underlies this pattern is constructed by means of purely local rules, which identify the natural brackets induced by the accented elements, the beginning, and the end of the string.

   A still more crucial case of elimination of variables is found in the characterization of alternating patterns. Within the formalization of *SPE* such patterns require rules that depart significantly from other rules, including rules like (1), in that the rules for alternating patterns correspond to what is called in automata theory "counting events" (as defined in McNaughton and Papert 1971). All other rules of phonology are non-counting events. Within the framework developed here the special case of alternating patterns arises from the iterative application of a local rule, which expresses the bounded character of the metrical constituents involved. The iterativity of the rule is itself a consequence of the formalization of constituents and of the notion of boundedness and need not be stipulated as an independent property.

   The elimination of variables from the grammatical formalism is of course not incompatible with the existence of phonological phenomena that involve unbounded strings or repetition of some basic motif. This elimination means that the category of unbounded strings or repetitive motifs that are found in natural languages falls into a restricted class of patterns that can be described as by-products of simple local higher-order notions and principles. These higher-order notions and principles permit us to retain the central and natural condition that all processes will be characterized as involving adjacent elements. For example, the lines in the metrical grid allow us to refer to consecutive head elements as adjacent, although such elements may be separated by an unbounded sequence of governed elements. The proposed extension of adjacency does not render the notion vacuous, for it still excludes innumerable configurations involving unbounded strings or repetitive motifs.

The theory of metrical phonology—the theory underlying the metrical constituents—is one of the modules of a grammar and interacts in complex and illuminating ways with other modules of the grammar. We have devoted much attention to the effect that nonstress rules have on the stress pattern of words. Examining rules of deletion and epenthesis in this light, we have shown that their effects on the stress patterns of words can be understood only if metrical constituent structure is hypothesized. The examples discussed in this connection bring out the fact that phonology "is divided into distinct and coherent subtheories, each with its own laws ... (and that in it) the dimensions of linguistic variation—i.e., the ways in which languages can differ from one another—are parcelled out among the modules" (Williams 1984). In addition, the theory of metrical phonology is itself analyzed into more specific subtheories or modules. Insight into this "submodularity" can be obtained by looking at particular patterns and seeing how the fixing of parameters determines the form of the pattern, as in our treatment of such complex cases as English, Lithuanian, Chamorro, Tiberian Hebrew, and Winnebago.

The role of parameters in the theory needs to be especially emphasized. Our theory differs from that of *SPE* in that it rejects the fundamental proposition of *SPE* that every grammatical description at every level is given in terms of a general rule-writing system. In our theory the different modules are not conceived as rule-writing systems.

Nonetheless, we have made use here of various aspects of the rule-writing formalism of *SPE*. In particular, we have argued that the parenthesis notation and the disjunctive ordering that it triggers are crucially involved in the description of alternating patterns. There is of course no contradiction between the theoretical position adopted here, which is to dispense with general rule-writing systems, and the fact that we have made use of particular aspects of the formalization in *SPE*. On the other hand, the use of the latter formalization within a framework such as ours requires some explanation. We propose the following account.

Language can be usefully viewed as a computational object that relates phenomena of a distinct nature, for example, sound and meaning, lexical representations and syntactic representations, morphological representations and their phonological implementations, and—the subject matter of this book—patterns of stress prominence and metrical organization of strings. In studying computational objects of any complexity, it is always necessary to distinguish several levels of description that differ in degree of abstractness, and in the case of such artificial computational objects the lowest level is that of the machine language, which must be shared by all such objects because it establishes the ultimate relation of the object to the hardware in which it is implemented. At higher levels of abstraction we find for example such programming languages as Pascal, Lisp, and Prolog.

We suggest that in the study of phonological phenomena, including stress, the analogue of the machine language is the formal theory of rules and representations developed in *SPE*. The work carried out since the publication of *SPE* has shown the need, not for eliminating the *SPE* theory, but for supplementing it with more abstract modules. These more abstract modules have been embodied in what have come to be known as autosegmental phonology and metrical phonology.

The theoretical framework summarized above incorporates ideas from *SPE* as well as from more recent developments, because our analyses are carried out at both the lower and the higher levels of description. On the higher level we characterize metrical constituents by means of a set of constraints and parameters. Thus, all metrical constituents are described in terms of boundedness and direction of headedness, and a given grammar for stress will consist of statements assigning values to the corresponding parameters and selecting appropriate constraints. On the lower level we carry out the construction of metrical constituent boundaries and heads, and it is there that we encounter such requirements as the one that constituent boundaries must be recoverable from the location of the heads and the direction of government. It is also at this lower level that the *SPE* constraint of disjunctive ordering applies. As shown in chapter 4, the parenthesis notation of *SPE* plays a crucial role in accounting for the form of alternating patterns, as well as for the location of main stress in such languages as English, Polish, and Latin. This was in fact the original hypothesis in *SPE*.

The structure of an alternating pattern of stresses (and of the patterns that underlie the placement of main stress in the languages just mentioned) is described at the higher level by positing the general rule "Construct boundaries." At the lower level the effective construction process is described by means of a rule written in the *SPE* format. This rule inserts a metrical boundary at the appropriate distance from an already present constituent boundary and applies iteratively in the direction stipulated by the grammar. It is this rule that makes use of the *SPE* parenthesis notation and is subject to the convention of disjunctive ordering.

The fact that we are rejecting the characterization of grammatical theory at all levels as a general rule-writing system of course does not mean that the question of the form of grammatical statements within the higher-level modules is devoid of scientific interest. In fact, we have shown that metrical constituent structure is most naturally described by means of sets of predicates and logical formulae of the kind found in certain types of declarative programming languages. This formalization has allowed us to bring to light the underspecified character of the metrical representations that are subjected to the various rules of deletion or insertion. For example, consider the structure in (2).

(2) . . . *
   (* * * *)
    1 2 3 4

In this structure position 4 is assigned the property of "headship," but positions 1, 2, and 3 are unspecified for that property. This lack of specification permits a formal account of the phenomenon of stress shift under deletion. The particular logical formalism adopted in chapter 5 also gives an account of the notion of "conjugate components," gives rise to a natural description of persistent rules, and reveals that more levels of description must be posited than are usually assumed.

A striking difference between syntax as it has developed since about 1975 and phonology lies in the radically different roles assigned to rules in these two components. In modern syntax, phenomena are characterized in terms of *principles* and *parameters*; and (transformational) rules, once widely employed, have been effectively eliminated. In phonology, by contrast, it does not seem possible to eliminate all recourse to rules, even though numerous phonological phenomena have been shown to be the result of principles rather than of rules. We assume that the essential difference between rules and principles is the very different way that rules and principles interact when several of them apply to a given string. A string to which several principles apply will be well formed only if it satisfies each of the principles. By contrast, if a given string satisfies the structural description of several rules, it does not necessarily undergo the structural changes of each rule. Rather, certain rules take precedence in ways captured by extrinsic ordering. For example, in Chamorro the rule of Lowering may either precede or follow the Alternator rule. If Lowering precedes the Alternator, it does not affect vowels stressed by the Alternator. If, on the other hand, Lowering is ordered after the Alternator, vowels stressed by the Alternator will be lowered. There are, to our knowledge, no comparable phenomena in syntax, and it is for this reason that syntactic rules play no role in the formalization of particular grammars.

One might speculate about the reasons for this difference between phonology and syntax. An obvious difference between these two components of a grammar is that phonology is much more directly involved with the physical actualization of the string than is syntax. We obtain from the syntax the linear order of the words (or morphemes) in a sentence, but to obtain information about the articulatory and acoustical properties of the sentence we must appeal to the phonology, which characterizes words and morphemes in terms of segments and distinctive feature complexes. It is the output of the phonology that determines directly the neural commands to the articulatory and sensory organs. Since these commands must surely be given a temporal sequence, an ordering of the rules is to be expected. At what level of abstraction ordering ceases to play a role is currently unknown.

References

Allen, M. (1978). "Morphological Investigations." Doctoral dissertation, Department of Linguistics, University of Connecticut, Storrs.

Al-Mozainy, H. Q., R. Bley-Vroman, and J. McCarthy (1985). "Stress Shift and Metrical Structure." *Linguistic Inquiry* 16, 135–144.

Anderson, S. R. (1969). "West Scandinavian Vowel Systems and the Ordering of Phonological Rules." Doctoral dissertation, Department of Linguistics, MIT, Cambridge, MA.

Anderson, S. R. (1974). *The Organization of Phonology*. New York: Academic Press.

Archangeli, D. (1984). "Underspecification in Yawelmani Phonology and Morphology." Doctoral dissertation, Department of Linguistics, MIT, Cambridge, MA.

Archangeli, D. (1986). "Extrametricality and the Percolation Convention." Ms., Department of Linguistics, University of Arizona, Tucson.

Aronoff, M., and S. N. Sridhar (1983). "Morphological Levels in English and Kannada, or Atarizing Reagan." In *Papers from the Parasession on the Interplay of Phonology, Morphology, and Syntax*. Chicago Linguistic Society, University of Chicago, IL.

Barker, M. (1963). *Klamath Dictionary*. University of California Publications in Linguistics 31, Berkeley.

Barker, M. (1964). *Klamath Grammar*. University of California Publications in Linguistics 32, Berkeley.

Berwick, R., and A. Weinberg (1984). *The Grammatical Basis of Linguistic Performance*. Cambridge, MA: MIT Press.

Bohas, G., and D. E. Kouloughli (1981). "Processus accentuels en arabe." In *Théorie-Analyses*. Département d'arabe, Université de Paris VIII.

Borowsky, T. (1984). "On Resyllabification in English." Ms., Department of Linguistics, University of Massachusetts, Amherst.

Boxwell, H., and M. Boxwell (1966). "Weri Phonemes." In S. A. Wurm, ed., *Papers in New Guinea Linguistics 5*. Australian National University, Canberra.

Chai, N. (1971). "A Grammar of Aklan." Doctoral dissertation, Department of Linguistics, University of Pennsylvania, Philadelphia.

Chomsky, N. (1965). *Aspects of the Theory of Syntax*. Cambridge, MA: MIT Press.

Chomsky, N. (1970). "Remarks on Nominalizations." In R. Jacobs and P. Rosenbaum, eds., *Readings in English Transformational Grammar*. Waltham, MA: Ginn.

Chomsky, N. (1986). *Knowledge of Language: Its Nature, Origin, and Use*. New York: Praeger.

Chomsky, N., and M. Halle (1968). *The Sound Pattern of English*. New York: Harper and Row.

Chung, S. (1983). "Transderivational Relationships in Chamorro Phonology." *Language* 59, 35–66.

Clocksin, W. F., and C. S. Mellish (1981). *Programming in Prolog*. New York: Springer-Verlag.

Crespi-Reghizzi, S. Guida, and G. Mandrioli (1978). "Non-counting Context-Free Languages." *Journal of the Association for Computing Machinery* 25.4.

Davis, S. (1984). "Syllable Weight in Some Australian Languages." Paper presented at the Parasession on Metrical Phonology, Berkeley Linguistic Society 11.

Davis, S. (1985). "Ternary Feet Reconsidered." Ms., Department of Linguistics, MIT, Cambridge, MA.

de Cornulier, B. (1982/5). "De Gallina: l'air et les paroles d'une comptine." *Le Français Moderne* 53, 231–241.

Dell, F. (1984). "L'accentuation dans les phrases en français." In F. Dell, D. Hirst, and J.-R. Vergnaud, eds., *Forme sonore du langage*. Paris: Hermann.

Dell, F., and M. Elmedlaoui (1985). "On Syllabification in Imdlawn Tashlhiyt Berber." *Journal of African Languages and Linguistics* 7, 105–130.

Dixon, R. M. W. (1977a). "Some Phonological Rules in Yidin[y]." *Linguistic Inquiry* 8, 1–34.

Dixon, R. M. W. (1977b). *A Grammar of Yidin[y]*. Cambridge: Cambridge University Press.

Dudas, K. (1972). "The Accentuation of Lithuanian Derived Nominals." In *Studies in the Linguistic Sciences* 2.2. Department of Linguistics, University of Illinois, Urbana.

Everett, D., and K. Everett (1984). "On the Relevance of Syllable Onsets to Stress Placement." *Linguistic Inquiry* 15, 705–711.

Franks, S. (1983). "Stress in Polish and Macedonian." Ms., Department of Linguistics, Cornell University, Ithaca, NY.

Franks, S. (1985). "Extrametricality and Stress in Polish." *Linguistic Inquiry* 16, 144–151.

Furby, C. (1974). *Garawa Phonology*. (Pacific Linguistics Series A, #37.) Australian National University, Canberra.

Goldsmith, J. (1976). "Autosegmental Phonology." Doctoral dissertation, Department of Linguistics, MIT, Cambridge, MA. (Published by Garland Publishing, New York.)

Haas, M. R. (1977). "The Tonal Accent in Creek." In L. Hyman, ed., *Studies in Stress and Accent.* (Southern California Occasional Papers in Linguistics 4.) Department of Linguistics, University of Southern California, Los Angeles.

Hale, K., and J. White Eagle (1980). "A Preliminary Account of Winnebago Accent." *International Journal of American Linguistics* 46, 117–132.

Halle, M. (1975). "Confessio grammatici." *Language* 51, 525–535.

Halle, M. (1984). "Grids and Trees." Paper to appear in *Phonologica 1985.*

Halle, M. (1985). "Metrical Constituent Structure." Paper presented at the spring 1985 meeting of the Linguistic Association of Great Britain in Salford.

Halle, M., and G. N. Clements (1983). *Problem Book in Phonology.* Cambridge, MA: MIT Press.

Halle, M., and K. P. Mohanan (1985). "Segmental Phonology of Modern English." *Linguistic Inquiry* 16, 57–116.

Halle, M., and J. R. Vergnaud (1978). "Metrical Structures in Phonology." Ms., Department of Linguistics, MIT, Cambrige, MA.

Halle, M., and J.-R. Vergnaud (1980). "Three Dimensional Phonology." *Journal of Linguistic Research* 1, 83–105.

Halle, M., and J.-R. Vergnaud (1987). "Stress and the Cycle." *Linguistic Inquiry* 18, 45–84.

Hammond, M. (1984a). "Metrical Structure in Lenakel and the Directionality-Dominance Hypothesis." In *Papers from the Regional Conference on Language and Linguistics.* Department of Linguistics, University of Minnesota, Minneapolis.

Hammond, M. (1984b). "Constraining Metrical Theory." Doctoral dissertation, Department of Linguistics, University of California, Los Angeles. (Revised version published by Indiana University Linguistics Club, Bloomington.)

Hammond, M. (1985). "Obligatory Branching Revisited." In *Proceedings of the North East Linguistic Society* 15. GLSA, University of Massachusetts, Amherst.

Hammond, M. (1986). "The Obligatory-branching Parameter in Metrical Theory." *Natural Language and Linguistic Theory* 4, 185–228.

Harms, R. (1981). "A Backwards Metrical Approach to Cairo Arabic Stress." *Linguistic Analysis* 7, 429–450.

Harris, J. (1969). *Spanish Phonology.* Cambridge, MA: MIT Press.

Harris, J. (1983). *Syllable Structure and Stress in Spanish: A Nonlinear Analysis.* Cambridge, MA: MIT Press.

Hayes, B. (1980/1). "A Metrical Theory of Stress Rules." Doctoral dissertation, Department of Linguistics, MIT, Cambridge, MA. (All quotations are from the revised version published in 1981 by Indiana University Linguistics Club, Bloomington.)

Hayes, B. (1982). "Extrametricality and English Stress." *Linguistic Inquiry* 13, 227–276.

Hayes, B. (1984). "The Phonology of Rhythm in English." *Linguistic Inquiry* 15, 33–74.

Jackendoff, R. S. (1977). *X̄ Syntax: A Study of Phrase Structure*. Cambridge, MA: MIT Press.

Johnson, C. D. (1972). *Formal Aspects of Phonological Description*. The Hague: Mouton.

Kaye, J. (1973). "Odawa Stress and Related Phenomena." In *Odawa Language Project: Second Report*. (Linguistic Series No. 1.) Centre for Linguistic Studies, University of Toronto.

Kaye, J., and J. Lowenstamm (1985). "Compensatory Lengthening in Tiberian Hebrew." In L. Wetzels and E. Sezer, eds., *Studies in Compensatory Lengthening*. Dordrecht: Foris.

Kenstowicz, M. (1972). "Lithuanian Phonology." In *Studies in the Linguistic Sciences* 2.2. Department of Linguistics, University of Illinois, Urbana.

Kenstowicz, M. (1980). "Notes on Cairene Arabic Syncope." In *Studies in the Linguistic Sciences* 10.2. Department of Linguistics, University of Illinois, Urbana.

Kenstowicz, M. (1983). "Parametric Variation in Accent Assignment." In J. Richardson, M. Marks, and A. Chukerman, eds., *Proceedings of the 19th Regional Meeting of the Chicago Linguistic Society*. Chicago Linguistic Society, University of Chicago, Chicago, IL.

Kenstowicz, M., and J. Rubach (1986). "The Geometry of Syllable Nuclei." Ms., Department of Linguistics, University of Illinois, Urbana.

Kenyon, J., and T. A. Knott (1944). *A Pronouncing Dictionary of American English*. Springfield, MA: G. C. Merriam Co.

Key, H. (1961). "Phonotactics of Cayuvava." *International Journal of American Linguistics* 27, 143–150.

Kiparsky, P. (1973). "'Elsewhere' in Phonology." In S. R. Anderson and P. Kiparsky, eds., *A Festschrift for Morris Halle*. New York: Holt, Rinehart and Winston.

Kiparsky, P. (1979). "Metrical Structure Assignment Is Cyclic." *Linguistic Inquiry* 10, 421–442.

Kiparsky, P. (1982a). "Lexical Morphology and Phonology." In *Linguistics in the Morning Calm*. Seoul: Hanshin.

Kiparsky, P. (1982b). "The Lexical Phonology of Vedic Accent." Ms., Department of Linguistics, MIT, Cambridge, MA.

Kiparsky, P. (1982c). "The Vedic and Pāṇinean Accent System." In *Some Theoretical Problems in Pāṇini's Grammar*. Poona, India: Bhandarkar Oriental Research Institute.

Kiparsky, P. (1983). "Word Formation and the Lexicon." In F. A. Ingeman, ed., *Proceedings of the 1982 Mid-America Linguistics Conference*. University of Kansas, Lawrence.

Kiparsky, P. (1984). "On the Lexical Phonology of Icelandic." In C. C. Elert, I. Johansson, and E. Straugert, eds., *Nordic Prosody III: Papers from a Symposium.* University of Umea, Umea.

Kiparsky, P. (1985). "Some Consequences of Lexical Phonology." In C. Ewen and J. Anderson, eds., *Phonology Yearbook 2.* Cambridge: Cambridge University Press.

Kiparsky, P. (1986). "Systematic Optionality in the Lexical Phonology of Chamorro." Ms., Department of Linguistics, Stanford University, Stanford, CA.

Kiparsky, P., and M. Halle (1977). "Towards a Reconstruction of the Indo-European Accent." In L. Hyman, ed., *Studies in Stress and Accent.* Southern California Occasional Papers in Linguistics 4. Department of Linguistics, University of Southern California, Los Angeles.

Langendoen, D. T. (1968). *The London School of Linguistics.* Cambridge, MA: MIT Press.

Leskien, A. (1919). *Litauisches Lesebuch.* Heidelberg: Carl Winter Universitäts-buchhandlung.

Levin, J. (1985a). "A Metrical Theory of Syllabicity." Doctoral dissertation, Department of Linguistics, MIT, Cambridge, MA.

Levin, J. (1985b). "Evidence for Ternary Feet and Implications for a Metrical Theory of Stress Rules." Ms., University of Texas, Austin.

Liberman, M. (1975). "The Intonational System of English." Doctoral dissertation, Department of Linguistics, MIT, Cambridge, MA.

Liberman, M., and A. Prince (1977). "On Stress and Linguistic Rhythm." *Linguistic Inquiry* 8, 249–336.

Lightner, T. (1972). *Problems in the Theory of Phonology.* Edmonton: Linguistic Research, Inc.

Lunt, H. (1952). *A Grammar of the Macedonian Literary Language.* Skopje.

Lynch, J. (1974). *Lenakel Phonology.* In *University of Hawaii Working Papers in Linguistics* 7. Department of Linguistics, University of Hawaii, Honolulu.

Lynch, J. (1978). *A Grammar of Lenakel.* (Pacific Linguistics Series B, #55.) Australian National University, Canberra.

Lyndon, R. C. (1966). *Notes on Logic.* New York: D. van Nostrand Company.

McArthur, H., and L. McArthur (1956). "Aguacatec (Mayan) Phonemes in the Stress Group." *International Journal of American Linguistics* 22, 72–76.

McCarthy, J. (1979). "Formal Problems in Semitic Phonology and Morphology." Doctoral dissertation, Department of Linguistics, MIT, Cambridge, MA.

McCarthy, J. (1986). "OCP Effects: Gemination and Antigemination." *Linguistic Inquiry* 17, 207–263.

McNaughton, R., and S. Papert (1971). *Counter-Free Automata.* Cambridge, MA: MIT Press.

Martin, P. (1981). "Pour une théorie de l'intonation: l'intonation est-elle une structure congruente à la syntaxe?" In M. Rossi, A. di Cristo, D. Hirst, P. Martin, and Y. Nishinuma, eds., *L'intonation, de l'acoustique à la sémantique*. Paris: Klincksieck.

Mascaró, J. (1978). "Catalan Phonology and the Phonological Cycle." Doctoral dissertation, Department of Linguistics, MIT, Cambridge, MA. (Published by Indiana University Linguistics Club, Bloomington.)

Mendelson, E. (1979). *Introduction to Mathematical Logic*. 2nd ed. New York: D. van Nostrand Company.

Mohanan, K. P. (1982). "Lexical Phonology." Doctoral dissertation, Department of Linguistics, MIT, Cambridge, MA. (Published by Indiana University Linguistics Club, Bloomington.)

Myers, S. (1985). "Vowel Shortening in English." In *Proceedings of the 21st Regional Meeting of the Chicago Linguistic Society*. Chicago Linguistic Society, University of Chicago, Chicago, IL.

Nanni, D. (1977). "Stressing Words in *-Ative*." *Linguistic Inquiry* 8, 752–763.

Osborn, H. (1966). "Warao I: Phonology and Morphophonemics." *International Journal of American Linguistics* 32, 108–123.

Pesetsky, D. (1979). "Russian and Lexical Theory." Ms., Department of Linguistics, MIT, Cambridge, MA.

Pesetsky, D. (1985). "Morphology and Logical Form." *Linguistic Inquiry* 16, 193–246.

Piggott, G. L. (1980). *Aspects of Odawa Morphophonemics*. New York: Garland Publishing.

Piggott, G. L. (1983). "Extrametricality and Ojibwa Stress." Ms., Department of Linguistics, McGill University, Montreal.

Poser, W. (1984). "The Phonetics and Phonology of Tone and Intonation in Japanese." Doctoral dissertation, Department of Linguistics, MIT, Cambridge, MA.

Poser, W. (1986). "Diyari Stress, Metrical Structure Assignment and the Nature of Metrical Representations." Ms., Department of Linguistics, Stanford University, Stanford, CA.

Prince, A. S. (1975)." The Phonology and Morphology of Tiberian Hebrew." Doctoral dissertation, Department of Linguistics, MIT, Cambridge, MA.

Prince, A. S. (1976). "Applying Stress." Ms., Department of Linguistics, University of Massachusetts, Amherst.

Prince, A. S. (1983). "Relating to the Grid." *Linguistic Inquiry* 14, 19–100.

Prince, A. S. (1985). "Improving Tree Theory." Paper presented at the Berkeley Linguistic Society, February 1985.

Principles of the International Phonetic Association (1949). Department of Phonetics, University College, London.

Pulleyblank, D. (1983). "Tone in Lexical Phonology." Doctoral dissertation, Department of Linguistics, MIT, Cambridge, MA. (Revised edition (1986). Dodrecht: Reidel.)

Rappaport, M. (1984). "Issues in the Phonology of Tiberian Hebrew." Doctoral dissertation, MIT, Cambridge, MA.

Riemsdijk, H. van, and E. Williams (1986). *Introduction to the Theory of Grammar.* Cambridge, MA: MIT Press.

Roca, I. M. (1986). "Secondary Stress and Metrical Rhythm." In *Phonology Yearbook 3.* Cambridge: Cambridge University Press.

Ross, J. R. (1972). "A Reanalysis of English Word Stress (Part I)." In M. Brame, ed., *Contributions to Generative Phonology.* Austin, TX: University of Texas Press.

Rubach, J. (1984). "Segmental Rules of English and Segmental Phonology." *Language* 60, 21–54.

Rubach, J., and G. Booij (1985). "A Grid Theory of Stress in Polish." *Lingua* 66, 281–319.

Sagey, E. C. (1986). "The Representation of Features and Relations in Nonlinear Phonology." Doctoral dissertation, Department of Linguistics, MIT, Cambridge, MA.

Sapir, E. (1930). *Southern Paiute: A Shoshonean Language. Proceedings of the American Academy of Arts and Sciences 65.* 1–3. Boston.

Saussure, F. de (1894). "A propos de l'accentuation lituanienne." *Mémoires de la Société Linguistique de Paris* 8, 425–444.

Saussure, F. de (1896). "Accentuation lituanienne." *Indogermanische Forschungen: Anzeiger für indogermanische Sprache und Altertumskunde* 6, 157–166.

Selkirk, E. O. (1984). *Phonology and Syntax.* Cambridge, MA: MIT Press.

Senn, A. (1966). *Handbuch der litauischen Sprache.* Heidelberg: Carl Winter Universitätsverlag.

Shaw, P. (1985). "Modularisation and Substantive Constraints in Dakota Lexical Phonology." In C. Ewen and J. Anderson, eds., *Phonology Yearbook 2.* Cambridge: Cambridge University Press.

Siegel, D. (1974). "Topics in English Morphology." Doctoral dissertation, Department of Linguistics, MIT, Cambridge, MA. (Published by Garland Publishing, New York.)

Skardžius, P. (1935). *Daukšos Akcentologija.* Kaunas.

Sproat, R. (1985). "On Deriving the Lexicon." Doctoral dissertation , Department of Linguistics, MIT, Cambridge, MA.

Stang, C. (1966). "'Métatonie douce' in Baltic." *International Journal of Slavic Linguistics and Poetics* 10, 111–119.

Steriade, D. (1986). "Two Types of Nonunderlying Specifications." Paper presented at Workshop on Distinctive Features, University of Leyden, Leyden, Holland.

Stowell, T. (1979). "Stress Systems of the World, Unite!" In *MIT Working Papers in Linguistics* 1. Department of Linguistics, MIT, Cambridge, MA.

Street, J. C. (1963). *Khalkha Structure.* Bloomington, IN: Indiana University Press.

Thomason, R. H. (1970). *Symbolic Logic: an Introduction.* London: Macmillan.

Tryon, D. T. (1970). *An Introduction to Maranungku.* (Pacific Linguistics Series B, #14.) Australian National University, Canberra.

Tyler, S. A. (1969). *Koya: An Outline Grammar.* University of California Publications in Linguistics 54, Berkeley.

Welden, A. (1980). "Stress in Cairo Arabic." *Studies in the Linguistic Sciences* 10, 99–120.

Williams, E. (1971/6). "Underlying Tone in Margi and Igbo." *Linguistic Inquiry* 7, 463–484.

Williams, E. (1984). "Review of N. Chomsky, *Lectures on Government and Binding* and *Some Concepts and Consequences of the Theory of Government and Binding.*" *Language* 60, 400–408.

Name and Reference Index

Language Index

Subject Index